Elias Colbert

Humanity in its origins and early growth

Elias Colbert

Humanity in its origins and early growth

ISBN/EAN: 9783742897954

Manufactured in Europe, USA, Canada, Australia, Japa

Cover: Foto ©Thomas Meinert / pixelio.de

Manufactured and distributed by brebook publishing software
(www.brebook.com)

Elias Colbert

Humanity in its origins and early growth

HUMANITY

IN ITS

ORIGIN AND EARLY GROWTH.

BY

E. COLBERT, M. A.,

FORMERLY SUPERINTENDENT OF THE DEARBORN OBSERVA-
TORY, AND (EX-OFFICIO) PROFESSOR OF ASTRONOMY
IN THE (OLD) UNIVERSITY OF CHICAGO.

CHICAGO:

THE OPEN COURT PUBLISHING COMPANY.

1892.

SYNOPSIS OF CONTENTS.

(The figures refer to the pages.)

INTRODUCTION.

Value of history. Studying it in a fog. Ordinary mortals looming up as giants. The book and its subject matter.

I. ORIGIN OF MAN.

II. PRIMEVAL LIFE.

III.　SERMONS IN STONES.

IV.　THE PLOWING ERA.

V.　EARLY ORIENTALS.

VI. LIGHT IN ASIA.

VII. THE FIRST GODS.

VIII. TIMES AND SEASONS.

XII. PICTURE READING.

XIII. EARLY PHYSIC.

XIV. DEAD MAN'S DAY.

XV. CROSSING THE LINE.

XVI. STAR GROUPING.

XVII. SCIENCE OF LANGUAGE.

XVIII. ORIGIN OF SPEECH.

XIX. LET THERE BE LIGHT.

XX. NATURE AND FATE.

SUMMARY.

INDEX.

INTRODUCTION.

Less than a century ago it was remarked that there was very little of existent history worthy of the name. What was so called treated rather of the doings of rulers than of peoples; it told the story of war but not of peace. Since then much of real history has been written. The student can now trace the successive stages in the progress achieved by more than one set of people, but the story is still one of action rather than of thought. We know comparatively little of the ideas entertained by ordinary men and women more than a few score years ago, except what is indicated by changes in the use of words and of the meanings attached to them, while even this may be called a closed book to the general reader though not one that is sealed against his examination. But it is evident that as the thought of the man measures the individual, better than do his surroundings or his actions, it is equally so with a people, and if with them then it is true of the whole race. A study of action is of great value, but does not always reveal the motives which prompted it, though a knowledge of the latter is of far the greater importance, standing to the other in the relation of cause to effect. It is interesting to trace out the groovings occasionally met with on the surfaces of hard rocks, but the discovery is of little scientific

9

value till we have connected those markings with other phenomena of the past, and from that read a page in the history of glacial action on the face of our globe. The finding of a stone at some particular spot may be of no consequence by itself, but if we discover that it once belonged to some other place and then investigate till we find the agency that transported it, with perhaps a clue to the time when the action occurred, we have arrived at a fact of real importance as one of the links in a chain of knowledge. So it is with human history. Viewed merely as a panorama of persons and events it may be of interest to the curious, but cannot be said to be instructive. The study of history is of little worth except that it enables us to understand how the people of former times acted under the stimulus of their surroundings. To be of real value it must help us to see how they thought as well as how they acted.

Of course, the further back we can trace these processes the better. It is with human thought as with a material organism in the study of natural history. We may learn much of an animal by studying it in the adult condition, but many bad mistakes thus made have been corrected by the modern process of watching the animal through the successive stages of its growth, from the embryo up to adult age. In fact, the study of embryology has been carried so far that it is almost entitled to rank as a separate department of science. Surely an attempt to understand something of the nascent forms of human thought cannot be less interesting or instructive. It should be transcendently so, since the highest as well as the proper study of mankind is man. We cannot hope by searching to find out God if the comprehension of His attributes lies above the range of our thought

The child's idea that as a baby he was found under a currant bush is fully as philosophical as that of the Jewish historian who made it out that Adam was created fully grown in the Garden of Eden and that Eve was manufactured out of one of his ribs while he slept. But why should we expect anything better? And why feel called upon to believe anything so logically bad? Yet we may just as well and wisely accept that as the Scripture story that "there were giants in those days," while neither is a whit more absurd than the Grecian tales about gods and demi-gods, the latter being the progenitors of the first real mortals. The thought of the adult in the infancy of the race was hardly more logical than that of the individual child of to-day. With both the process of thinking back to a supposable origin ends in a mental fog. The simile is a happy one. Anybody who has been in a dense fog will remember how difficult it was to discern objects at the distance of a few feet, and how those sufficiently near to be visible seemed to be vastly bigger than the normal size. This is because the fact of indistinctness carries with it the idea of distance, and the object seems to be larger on account of that delusion, precisely as in the case of an apparently larger sun and moon when near the horizon. Now, this was exactly the situation of the people of several centuries ago when they tried to peer through the mists of tradition towards the beginning of their race history. Those of their ancestors who were so deeply in the fog as to be just inside the limit of traditional remembrance loomed up as giants, heroes, demi-gods. A smaller edition of the same mental weakness may often be met with to-day. Otherwise well informed people will deplore the supposed fact that all the great men are dead, with no one to take their places, even should necessity arise. No poet, orator, playwright, statesman, soldier or astronomer can hope to compare otherwise than unfavorably with some of those who have gone before. Our fathers and grandfathers (that is, some of them), talked in precisely the same way; and so did *their* ancestors, back through the generations without number. The only difference lies in the fact that the earlier the comparison and the less extensive the information the more was the supposed superiority exaggerated, and that is the reason why we now read of giants and demi-gods descended from the skies to take their places among mortals.

The writer has endeavored to trace out a few of the salient points in the early unfolding of man and his thought, principally in those ages which preceded the writing of history. It is attempted to show some of the steps of development by which man was evolved from merely inanimate matter, and more especially those by which he rose from the level of his immediate predecessor in the scale of progress towards perfection, though like the hyperbolic curve that approaches nearer and nearer to its asymptote he can never meet it. Then is sketched the widening out of the human mentality from the infantile phase to that of the child in knowledge, at which point history takes up the thread of the narrative. The principal object has been to discover primitive ideas about the causation of events and the constitution of things, and show that to a great extent man's religious creeds and ceremonies, with much of his philosophy, grew out of notions which appear to have been first entertained as a result of observing the stars. The writer will not be surprised if some of his readers think his enthusiasm has carried him too far. others censure him for his free criticisms of human claims to infallible inspiration, and a few charge him with having attempted to demolish one set of temples for the purpose of building on their ruins altars to false gods. Such conclusions may be anticipated by the remark that the book was written in all seriousness as a candid exposition of views long held by the writer, and that nothing is advanced which does not to him wear at least an air of probability. Of course a considerable part of the material here presented is to be found in the cyclopedias and other books, some of which are quoted from. But some of it is new, and if not acceptable as eternal verity it may stimulate to valuable thought and perhaps to research by some who read it. In that case the labor will not have been in vain. It will be of great value if it help the Christian world to deal with its creeds on the plan suggested by Hamlet:

> " Throw away the worser part of it,
> And live the purer with the other half."

The first and penultimate chapters were published over the initials of the author in the Chicago *Tribune* of May 17, 1891, and September 13, 1890. The two chapters on the origin of language are re-written from an address delivered by him in June, 1887, before the Chicago Academy of Sciences, but prepared much earlier. The rest of the matter was produced at different times since the last date in the intervals of daily labor on the *Tribune*.

I.

ORIGIN OF MAN.

"I have said to the worm, 'Thou art my mother and my sister.' "—Job.

Life Before and After the Glacial Epoch.—The Primeval Hunter.—The
Most Probable Theory of His Evolution.—Descended From an Ances-
tral Ape.—The First Step.—Wearing a skin.—Then Flint-Flakes.—Afterwards Speech.—Did Life began at the North Pole?

The statement that the first man lived within
about 4,000 years of the Christian era was accepted
without question for many centuries. It was believed alike by Jews, Catholics, Protestants, and
Mohammedans. But when modern investigators
turned the pages in the great book of Nature with
intent to read out if possible something of her
history, they soon found reasons for suspecting
there was some mistake in the previously undisputed
story. Subsequent research has confirmed the doubt
and also furnished good grounds for believing that
the Genesis story of the fall of Adam and Eve from
a state of happy innocence to one of miserable deg-
radation cannot be literally true. Scientific men
now refuse assent to it and also to the commonly
accepted Bible chronology of events from the creation to the deluge.

The doctrine of evolution, which is now generally
admitted by students of the natural sciences to hold

good so far as our observation extends, obliges us to take a different view of the early history of the human race. We cannot doubt that the earth has existed during many millions of years, instead of less than 6,000, that during a large part of that immense span of existence its surface has teemed with animal life, that the lowest forms were first evolved from the inanimate state of matter, that higher and again higher orders of vegetable and animal organism followed in successions which were slow as compared with the length of a human life, and that man himself appeared as the last in the ascending series of evolutions, each step in which was a degree above the one next preceding it. We are obliged to believe also that the human race itself has been from the first subject to the workings of the same law of progression from a lower to a higher plane in the great scale of animated existence. Different peoples and communities may have attained to great power as well as a high state of civilization and relapsed into states of low culture, if not semi-barbarism, but these are to the race only as the individual is to the community. It is reasonable to suppose that a time may come when the race considered as a unit will have reached its maximum of possible development and then enter on a phase of decadence, but the first of these stages has not been reached yet.

The idea that the first men were evolved from some lower form or forms of existence is far from being exclusively a modern one, though the demonstration as a necessary corollary to other knowledge of natural history, in the widest sense of the term, was not possible till within the last few years. It is said Anaximander (B. C. 610 to 547) held that animals were begotten from earth by means of heat and moisture, and that man did not originate in a perfectly developed state, but was engendered from beings of a different form. The Roman poet Horace (65 to 8 B. C.) was a little more definite, and if uncomplimentary to the primeval man was hardly more so than St. Paul to his successors. (See Romans I., 24 to 31.) Horace writes in his third Satire (first book):

> Quum prorepserunt primis animalia terris,
> Mutum et turpe pecus, glandem atque cubilia propter
> Unguibus et pugnis, dein fustibus, atque ita porro,
> Pugnabant armis, quae post fabricaverat usus:
> Donec verba, quibus voces sensusque notarent.
> Nominaque invenere.

That is to say: "When first these creatures crawled out of the ground, dumb and foul brutes, they fought for nuts (acorns) and sheltering places, first with nails and fists, then with sticks, and afterwards with weapons made of metal, until words (speech) came, with which they expressed feelings and designated objects."

How long ago man first appeared on earth, naked and otherwise "on the level of the brute," cannot be told. But his remains are found "in place" by

2

the side of those of animals now extinct in the climate where their bones are discovered, and which
must have been dead many more than 6,000 years.
It is even probable that man existed on the earth
previous to the latest glacial epoch, that some members of his race retreated before the ice cap as it
advanced from the north, and followed its receding
edge as the glaciers left portions of the surface uncovered by successive shrinkages towards the present dimensions of the polar ice shroud. It is
alleged that at first he must have been essentially
carnivorous, as indicated by the structure of the
teeth, and probably a cannibal. Also it might be
supposed that the dawn of reasoning powers was
marked by the use of sticks or stones as weapons
with which to kill the larger animals whose flesh
was taken for food. But this may be wrong. If
the ape, which is that animal most nearly approaching man in anatomical structure, be regarded as his
progenitor it will be more natural to suppose that
man at first fed on fruits and nuts, the ape not being carnivorous except in his old age. Neither will
it be necessary to suppose that the first men were
strictly on the brute level in point of intelligence.
It is well established that the apes stretch themselves on the ground for repose, and some of them
have been known to choose a pillow for the head.
Also they readily betake themselves to the use of
stones and clubs, sometimes hurling the first with
considerable dexterity, and at others using either in

a hand to hand encounter. It has been noted, too, that in confinement the ape is deliberate in its actions, even circumspect, and capable of showing a decided attachment to attendants and companions. Add to this the fact that apes and even gorillas show a rather high degree of natural affection, and live in troops, and that the chimpanzee, which is still lower in the scale, makes a shelter for itself, and it will be seen that we do not need to assume the very lowest plane of intelligence as that from which man took his first step towards the civilization of our own day. The first men, for there may have been many of them, were pretty respectable brutes after all.

It is most probable that the first distinctive step made by man above the level of the ape was in taking the skin of a larger animal for clothing. But he may not have killed that animal with intent to use its flesh as food. On the contrary, it may have been killed strictly as an act of self-defense, or the skin taken from the ground after the flesh of its original wearer had been eaten by some other beast of prey. Perhaps the picture of Hercules with his club, and the skin of the Nemean lion thrown over his shoulders, tells the story quite as accurately as does the writer of the third chapter of Genesis. But as the ape is believed to become carnivorous if spared to old age in his native wilds, so the improvement on the ape may have soon developed into a flesh eater, and that as a direct outgrowth from his use of the skin as a protection against the elements. We may even suppose it as more than possible that this first step in the process of development was taken as a consequence of climatic change, since there is every reason to believe the successive evolutions of all the lower forms of organic life were brought about by the same agency.

It has been ascertained that the latest great glacial visitation from the north extended on this continent as far as 38 degrees of latitude and to about the same distance in Europe and Asia. The ice sheet extended well up towards that limit as late as about 7,000 years ago. But on its approach, long before that epoch, a much greater cold than the normal must have been experienced many degrees further south, and the fall in temperature must have been felt most keenly by the most highly organized members of the animal kingdom. They were forced to retreat from it, or die. This would be true with one possible exception. Suppose that by a happy inspiration, for we are not entitled to call it a thought, one of the beings which had reached the highest phase of development possible without rising out of the pithecoid class seized upon the skin of a large animal that had in some way succumbed to the inevitable, and wrapped himself in it. As the ape is an imitative creature the example would probably be followed by many others in that vicinity. Can any of us doubt that the skins would be found so comfortable that they were retained and became permanent protection against the cold? But see the difference between that supposed act and the story of the first clothing just before the expulsion from Paradise as told in Genesis! According to the Bible account it was the sequel to a fall so severe that, in the estimation of many people to-day, the race has not yet recovered from the blunder of its first parents. In our version it was the first step in the ascent from the condition of the ape towards that of our modern civilization.

We shall pursue the subject a little further before considering the probability that the evolution did not occur on the edge of an advancing glacier. The process could be substantially the same, though the scene were several thousand miles away and the time removed further back through some thousands of centuries.

The flesh adhering to the first worn skin would soon become offensive from decomposition, and it would require but a single gleam of intelligence to rise further to the idea of removing it by rubbing with the sticks or stones already used in combat. The flesh fragments would then be removed from the other skins immediately after slaughter, and from this to eating the savory smelling morsels was but another step. It was taken all the more readily as the advancing cold wave had stunted the growth of the fruits and nuts upon which the being had up to that time fed, and perhaps killed them off completely. The new fledged man was then not necessarily entirely carnivorous as a speedy result of the discovery. He would eat either fruit or animal food, whichever was more easily procured, but another step was taken, and that an important one, though purely physical. The man was no longer obliged to keep within the shade and warmth of the forest. He could leave his Eden voluntarily. He was willing to go outside in pursuit of his game, because he had found out how to keep himself warm in situations where he must otherwise have perished. The apes had to go further south, and he thus parted company from them forever till the time arrived when by successive stages of development his progeny could capture the ape as a being so far inferior that there was no thought of such a thing as equality having existed in the long-forgotten past.

Hence the primitive men soon became hunters, and it depended upon their location as to whether or not they were migratory. There would at first be no tie to prevent the individual from roaming as far as it seemed safe and desirable to go in quest of his food. Doubtless the one who found and could retain possession of a natural shelter as against all comers did so, but the beings whom we now designate as the "cave dwellers" belong to a much higher order of development, which was not attained till after the lapse of long ages of geologic change. Of the primeval men, properly speaking, a few would remain in one location, because they found animal food in satisfactory quantity on the ground or easily caught fish in the adjacent shallow waters, and the rest would resemble Cain in the respect of being wanderers and vagabonds upon the face of the earth. But it is not improbable that at a very early stage two or more would hunt or fish in company, for the sake of the advantage thus obtained in coping with the larger game, and here would be established the social compact long before they knew they possessed the ability to give verbal assurances of friendship. Also the feeling of individual attachment between two persons of opposite sexes appears to be so deeply ingrained in human nature that it is easy to suppose the family tie was soon recognized instinctively, though in exceedingly savage fashion.

The same dawn of reason that led to the systematic use of the rough stone as a weapon and a cleaning tool would ere long incite to the selection of the most easily-handled shapes, and then to the search for them; resulting in the employment of the sharp-edged flint where it could be obtained, and then to its splitting into flakes by the aid of larger stones. It would not take long to rise from this to the idea of shaping and sharpening by rubbing and even by chipping. With this would begin the use of tools with which fragments of flesh were more neatly dressed from the skins worn as clothing, and perhaps the first essay made at cutting meat instead of tearing it asunder, this being fol-

lowed by a scooping out of earth and removal of
stones for the providing of artificial shelter where
natural recesses were not within reach. With this
would gradually grow up the idea of a "home,"
and perhaps ages after that the first dawning
recognition of a proprietary right thereto by the
one who had fashioned it, this being fostered by
the knowledge that another could proceed in the
same way and thus obviate the necessity of fighting
for what up to that time could not have been
secured without a conflict. But the tenant would
still have to dispute possession with the savage
animals that roamed in his vicinity, and perhaps
even routed them from their dens, or took the caves
as "homes" after killing off the brutes.

We can be equally exact with some of the writers
of scripture in saying "And it came to pass in
those days" that the thinking process had been
carried sufficiently far to make men and women feel
the need of some other mode of communication
than by signs. But no full fledged speech fell
from the lips of those who first essayed to make
vocal utterance. On the contrary, the first sounds
would be those of exclamation, and a series of
grunts is suggested by the preponderance of guttural sounds in the earliest of the languages known
to us. But the discovery that speech was possible,
and could be understood, must have led in comparatively short time to the formation of a considerable vocabulary, that is perhaps as many as a few

dozen words, understood by those who were near each other, but each set incomprehensible to the world outside. It may be assumed almost without question that these earlier utterances all belonged to what we now call the Turanian forms of speech. That is, they were not only without system in the sense of having a common origin, but unsystematic among themselves, each vocabulary being a law unto itself, in the sense that it was utterly without law in the absence of a motive for choosing any particular combination of sounds to express a specified desire or name a given object. The recognition of any sort of system in arrangement, grammatical or otherwise, such as marks members of the Shemitic or Aryan families of languages, must have been a matter of much later mental development. It would seem most probable that communication by means of spoken words must have preceded the effort to depict the forms of animals, and perhaps other objects, some of which was done by the cave dwellers, whose best graving tools must have been flints, and who still gained their living exclusively by hunting, as their remains have not been found in company with those of now domesticated animals, nor with any signs of cereal food or the use of fire.

But these tools, works, or remains of early man are found scattered over a large part of the surface of the globe, and it is hard to suppose it possible that all these proceeded from a single individual or

troop originating in those areas. The flint flake,
bearing unmistakable evidence of having been used
as a tool, is found in the late Pleistocene strata
attesting the great antiquity of man, and is abundant in later formations, showing that he roamed
over a vast extent of earth area. It is found in
Japan, India, Europe, Africa, and on the American
continent, while its discovery in two separate places
in the lower valley of the Thames has led to the
inference that it was used there before the arctic
mammalia had taken possession. It may be mentioned that the rhinoceros, elephant, hippopota-
mus, lion, and hyena all had a habitat there when
man was a mere hunter in that region. Also the
remains of apes have been found in the mid-eocene
forests of France, Switzerland, Germany, and Italy,
and identified as belonging to the most highly
developed quadrumana.

Boyd Dawkins, in his work on " Early Man in
Britain," says in summing up the results of investigation : " When the living species (of mammalia)
became abundant (in Europe) man appears just in
the Pleistocene stage in the evolution of mamma-
lian life in which he might be expected to appear.
The river-drift man first comes before us, endowed
with all human attributes and without any signs of
a closer alliance with the lower animals than is
presented by the savages of to-day ; as a hunter
armed with rude stone implements, living not
merely in Britain, but throughout Western and

Southern Europe, Northern Africa, Asia Minor and India. Next follows the cave-man, possessed of better implements, and endowed with the faculty of representing animal forms with extraordinary fidelity, living in Europe north of the Alps and Pyrenees as far as Derbyshire."

Therefore it is necessary to look much further back than the last glacial visitation for the origin of human life upon the earth, and we can hardly resist the conclusion that the whole race came into existence when the entire globe was much hotter than it is now. In the language of Dawkins: Three phases of life may be traced over the whole earth, and their succession is invariable, whence it may be inferred that they are due to causes acting universally and not sporadically in one or more centers. "They prove that the earth as a whole has passed through a series of biological changes analogous to those which are to be seen in the animal world in the passage from birth to old age." In the first phase the fishes and amphibians dominated, and a few reptiles are found in the upper rock formation. Vegetation was principally represented by the coal seams. In the second phase the reptiles were the lords of creation, some walking, some flying, and some swimming in the seas; and the "testimony of the rocks" is to the effect that the birds were emerging from the reptile class as the reptiles had formerly from the fishes and amphibians. The forests of that time were dense, but trees with deciduous leaves did not appear till near the close of the period. In the third the higher placental mammals appear first in the series, taking the place of the reptiles as the dominant class, and flying like bats, while the true birds had graduated away from the reptiles. The mammalia belonged to this period, and the angiosperms rose to great prominence in the world of vegetable life.

We have the best of reasons to believe that this order of things was first established at or near the north pole, and spread thence to the equator and beyond it. But this carries us back in thought to a time when the earth was intensely hot, having recently formed a comparatively thin crust over the seething interior. Naturally the cooling process was most rapid at the pole, the radiation of heat into space being there little compensated by the solar ray. Hence the first forms, not only of life, but of all classes of organic existence, first appear in the region of the pole, and the habitable area gradually extended southward with the successive cooling of one belt after another down to the temperature at which life was possible. On this hypothesis one may explain the finding in the far north of the remains of some animals belonging to species which are now confined to the torrid zone, and thrive best under the burning heats of the equatorial regions. But it has far wider application than this. It furnishes a solution to the otherwise vexed problem of general diffusion of the differ-

ent forms of life through a wide range of latitude
on each of the continents which were practically out
of reach of each other at moderate distances from
the pole. The fact that this Gordian knot of distribution of species can only be cut by supposing
them all to be of polar origin has been recognized
by Quatrefages, the Marquis de Saporta, and Dr.
W. F. Warren, of Boston.

It may be concluded, therefore, that the first
primeval man or men came into existence in the
neighborhood of the north pole, rising there above
the plane of ape life by reason of decreasing temperature, and following in the rear of the vast pro-
cession that marched southward, being able to lag
behind in the movement because he early learned
how to obtain artificial protection from greater
degrees of cold than he could have endured if naked.
That he did follow the other forms of animal life to
the equator and beyond it, passing along each of
the continental routes, admits of little doubt; and
it is therefore reasonable to suppose that he followed from the equatorial regions the edge of the
ice-cap in its retreat towards the pole thousands of
centuries afterwards, moving in the reverse direction to that traversed originally. And all this
before man had risen above the dignity of a mere
hunter, with perhaps not one of his race possessing
an idea superior to that entertained by the veriest
savages of the Christian era.

II

PRIMEVAL LIFE.

" Let the waters bring forth abundantly."—Genesis.

Great Antiquity of the Human Race.—Animal Life on the Earth Twenty
Millions of Years Ago.—The Eozoon.—Paleozoic, Mesozoic, and Ter-
tiary Developments.—Glacial Epochs.—The Quaternary.—Paleolithic
Man and the Ice Sheet.—Contemporary Animals.—The Neolithic Age.—
Survival of the Fittest.—Subsequent Distribution.—Polar versus
Equatorial Origin of Man.

The results of archæological investigation, briefly
alluded to in the first chapter, furnish abundant
proof that human beings must have existed on the
earth a great many centuries ago. It is difficult to
make that statement much more definite than by
saying that the number of centuries may have been
somewhat less than a thousand, and perhaps very
much greater; but it may be of interest to take a
glance at the possibilities of the case. A study of
the rate of changes now in progress in geological
strata indicates that at least a hundred millions of
years have elapsed since the formation of a comparatively stable crust over the molten mass furnished
a habitat for organic life. But it may be inferred
that the development of vegetable and animal forms
proceeded far more rapidly in the earlier part of the
period than now, because of the greater abundance

of carbonic acid gas in the atmosphere, and the greater warmth of the crust in the days "when time was young." Also the quantity of heat received from the sun must have been larger, as the central mass of our system has since parted with a portion of his heat by continuous radiation into space. In addition to that the mathematics of the solar system furnish indubitable evidence that many millions of years ago the moon was much nearer to the earth than at present, causing far higher tides in our oceans and corresponding activity in the displacement of material in tearing up older strata and constructing newer ones. But a recognition of the comparative rapidity of change due to these facts in the long ago does not warrant us in reducing the estimate to less than a tenth, and perhaps not to less than a quarter of the immense term stated above. Probably some twenty million years ago the little Eozoön began its work of reef building at the bottom of a vast ocean which covered most, if not all, of the thin crust of solidified matter that divided the water from the interior molten sea. His limestone product appears to have been the first departure from the crystalline form of matter. The Eozoic age lasted probably several millions of years. It was marked by the upheaval of continental masses, chiefly because of wrinklings in the crust due to cooling of its mass, with here and there ejections of molten matter from the interior, coming through the fissures and overflowing areas so great

that the work of Vesuvius compares with it as a
molehill to a mountain.

The Paleozoic age succeeded. The change was
marked by a subsidence of some elevations, and a
rising of others, while the ocean soon swarmed with
corals and invertebrates. The Cambrian, Silurian,
Devonian, and Carboniferous stages followed in
succession, the latter marking the period during
which the coal making plants grew, and in such pro-
fusion as to clear the atmosphere to the condition
in which vertebrate animals could exist. This was
also the great cooling time, not so much by lessening of heat received at the surface from the interior
as because the clearing of the air permitted more
rapid radiation into space. Previously the aerial
envelope had acted pretty much as a blanket of
clouds occasionally does in our day, allowing the
heat to come in from without, but denying egress.
Of course the cooling would proceed most rapidly
at the poles, and by the end of the Paleozoic age the
general climatic conditions must have settled down
to nearly those of our own period. It has been
proved by Sir William Thompson, to the satisfaction
of everybody who has followed him in the reasoning, that the present influence of internal heat on
the temperature at the surface only amounts to
about one seventy-fifth part of a degree. But since
then many important changes of temperature have
occurred, not merely in small areas but over large
portions of the surface. It is yet open to question

whether these were due to variations in the supply of solar heat to the globe as a whole, to changes in the eccentricity of the earth's orbit combined with the relative motions of the perihelion point and the line of equinoxes, or to changes in the elevation of land masses with variations in the direction and volume of ocean currents due to alterations in shape of the continents.

The Mesozoic age which followed was emphatically the age of reptiles. They dominated land, air and sea. Also it marked the unification of the American continent by lifting up the bed of a great sea that had covered the whole plains and plateau region from the gulf of Mexico to the Arctic ocean, lifting the Rocky Mountains to a higher range, and bringing up from the level the Wahsatch ridge and the Colorado and Uintah Mountains, while adding a fringe of land fifty to a hundred miles wide to the Atlantic coast. In this age the fishes, birds and mammalia began to appear, the latter only as marsupials, or pouch bearers; a form which, except our opossum, is now met with only in Australia and its neighboring islands.

The Cenozoic or Tertiary age followed, with a general break in the rock system and a great change in life forms. It brought in the true mammals and many of the types of other animals and plants which exist to-day, while the reptile class retired to a subordinate place both in regard to number and size. Even the monkeys came into existence, but only as

3

a generalized type, and the animals which represented the carnivora and herbivora of our own times
were all omnivorous. The coast range of California and Oregon was lifted up, and the general temperature of Europe and the United States was
twenty to thirty degrees higher than now. The
interior of this continent experienced a general
depression that was filled with water, above which
the summits of the Rocky Mountains peered as so
many islands, and about this time the extreme
Northwest was desolated by a great flood of lava.
Towards the end of the Tertiary age the northern
lands became elevated, both in the old world and the
new, and there was a genuine glacial visitation in
the northern hemisphere. This may be placed
about 850,000 years ago, for which time Croll has
calculated that the midwinter intensity of the sun's
heat in the north temperate zone was one-sixth less
than now, causing a lowering of about 45 degrees
from the normal range of the thermometer. This
is the first glacial visitation that has been distinctly
traced by the marks it left behind, but Croll's computations point to the existence of similar astronomical conditions 2,500,000 years ago; and, for
aught we know, even that may have been far from
the beginning of a rather long series.

The Quaternary age came next, with great
changes in the elevation of different portions of the
land surface from the sea level, and corresponding
changes in the character of climate and species of

both plants and animals. It is divided into three periods, namely, the Glacial, Champlain and Terrace. The first was marked by a rise in the land in high latitudes, the elevation being from one to two thousand feet from the present level. The ground was covered with a sheet of ice, forming a glacial cap and causing extreme cold. In the second stage this land was depressed to perhaps a thousand feet below the level of to-day, possibly as a consequence of the weight of ice, which would account for the subsequent rising after the pressure had been removed. The downward movement of the Champlain epoch was accompanied by a melting of the ice, and a submerging of the higher land by floods while the lower portions were covered by the sea, and in these waters icebergs floated southward till melted by the heat of a more southerly sun. In the third epoch the lands rose to about their present level, and the receding waters left behind them the boulders and smaller drift which the ice had brought from higher latitudes. The change of climate in the Quaternary age is strikingly shown by the fact that while the plants and invertebrate animals of that time were mostly identical with existing species their remains are found further north than the range of those now living. The mammals attained in this age their full development, elephants roamed in herds over a large part of Europe, the lion, tiger and hyena inhabited England, and the mastodon had a home in America.

Of course it will be understood that while all the great changes mentioned, other than local, have occurred all over the earth's surface they have not necessarily been strictly contemporaneous. Also it may be mentioned that at not a few places the great glacial sheet has left signs of advance and recession, perhaps several times during a single ice period. This was the case in England. The great south polar ice cap is believed to have a present diameter of some 2,800 miles, with a maximum thickness of about twelve miles.

It has been claimed that primeval man lived in the Tertiary age. While this may be doubted, there is no disputing the assertion that he lived in the Quaternary, which is sometimes called the Pleistocene. His flint flakes have been found in the earlier strata of that period along with the cave bear, the mammoth, and other now extinct animals. And these animals are in place where they must have been previous to the advent of glaciers, whence it is inferred that man was pre-glacial. There is not the shadow of a doubt as to his being inter-glacial and as such simply a nomad hunter. From the fact that his flint flakes were roughly chipped to an edge, and some of them pointed as if for boring, this period in his existence has been called the Paleolithic (old stone) age. We cannot trace him further back than this. He has no known antecedents. But it is not difficult to follow him along the stream of geologic history. In the course of the next few

centuries the mammoth became extinct and the rein-
deer abundant in the southern half of Europe, and
during that time the law of evolution wrought a
vast improvement in the man. He was still a
hunter, but with much better weapons. The flints
found in association with the remains of the rein-
deer are carefully chipped, and some other stones
are ground down by rubbing. But up to that time
man had not learned how to procure or use fire, had
no domestic animals, and was a stranger to agriculture. The extent of his progress was little or great
according to the position from which it was viewed.
As a man, he was "low down," probably inferior
in intelligence and moral sense to the most degraded
savages that have been found within the last few
centuries, and did not know how to talk. But
regarded as a development from the ape he had
made a wonderful advance. He was no longer
restricted to the use of hands, nails and teeth for
weapons, as suggested in the fifth book of Lucretius:
"*De Rerum Nat.*" He was truly a man, with a
good sized, well formed brain, and not a "missing
link" between the human being and any other kind
of animal. As such he roamed over a vast area. His
relics are found in England, France, Spain, Italy,
Greece, Africa, Palestine, India, in California and
on our Atlantic coast. In most of these places his
bones have been found in company with the flints
and with the remains of animals which were inter-
glacial if not pre-glacial.

Several paleolithic implements have been found
in the last fifteen years in the valley of the Delaware near Trenton, New Jersey, in a formation
which is declared to have been a direct result of the
melting of glaciers as they receded Northward.
Chipped implements have been found in the same
formation in Ohio and at Little Falls, Minnesota.
These and other discoveries are believed by Dr.
Putnam to prove that man has occupied a portion
of North America from the Mississippi river to the
Atlantic ocean at a time when the northern part of
the United States was covered with ice, and that he
was then contemporary with the mammoth and
mastodon. The same authority says that on the
western side of this continent human remains have
been found in geological beds which, unquestiona-
bly, are older than the gravels of the Mississippi,
Ohio and Delaware valleys. He has also arrived at
the remarkable conclusion that these early denizens
of the Pacific slope had reached a degree of development equal to that of the inhabitants of California
at the time of European contact, so far as can be
inferred from the character of the stone mortars,
chipped and polished stone implements, and shell
beads found in the auriferous gravels. Thus we
may regard it as exceedingly probable that in both
hemispheres human beings lived comparatively near
to the edge of the ice sheet in the glacial period
north of the equator. We may infer that they
retreated southward when the temperature became

relatively low, and returned northward when it grew warmer — acting with a kindred instinct to that which governs the migration of birds. They follow their food.

The latter half of the Stone age is called the Neolithic (new stone), and is the one that first brings out man as a being at once ingenious, industrious, provident and sociable. It was the era of the so-called cave men whose bones and implements have been found rather numerously distributed in the area extending from the Alps and Pyrenees as far north as Belgium and the middle of England, but not further east than Poland and Styria. This, and the fact that in some places the remains have been found in geological strata above that containing relics of the river drift men, has led to the suspicion that there was not only a wide gap of time between the two, but that they belonged to entirely distinct races and could hardly be referred to the same origin. And it has been hinted as logical to infer that the one disappeared before the other came on the scene. Indeed, the interval must have been a tremendous one if it were measured at all points on the earth by the British standard laid down by Boyd Dawkins. He says that between the earliest date we can assign for the Neolithic period and the close of the Paleolithic, as indicated by the low level gravels, there was such a vast stretch of time that out of forty-eight well ascertained species living in the earlier, only thirty-one were able to live on into

the surface stone period. It is not necessary to suppose, under these conditions, that the river drift
men were exterminated by the Neolithics. It is
more natural to think that the older race succumbed
to the unhealthy climatic influences incident to the
glacial visitation over a large part of the north
temperate zone, and that there was literally a "survival of the fittest," who were either mentally or
physically far superior to their fellows. May not
that chosen few have made their way out of Europe
into Asia across the neck of land that formerly
united those two land masses at the place where the
Bosporus now divides them? The latitude of that
passage is little more than forty degrees, or not far
from the greatest reach of the ice cap, as there are
said to be few if any traces of the visitation on the
shores of the Mediterranean. If they did thus
escape the threatened destruction in Europe by
migrating to Asia, and there moving southward
some ten degrees or more in search of a warmer
clime, they landed in the very region from which we
get our earliest written history except what came
from Egypt, which country lies but a short distance
to the west of it. Their new found home was in
the region from which both history and tradition
tell us went out the bands of men who formed the
original *nuclei* of many nations, the tract of country
assigned by the Mosaic account as the first home
of those who escaped the deluge. Furthermore, if
a very few of the fugitives instead of crossing into

Asia slowly followed the receding ice cap northward, crossing either the Balkans west of the Black
Sea or the Caucasus to the east of it, they reached
the tract of country which Huxley tells us is indicated by the latest scientific researches into the
subject to be the original home of the progenitors
of the Aryan race.

Some such migration of a few from Europe, or
even the total extinction of man on that continent
by the ice king, leaving it to be peopled anew, must
have occurred, or the researches of modern times
would surely have brought to light some tokens of
human existence in the immense stretch of ages
that separates the latest of the drift period from the
earliest known cave men west of the Mediterranean.
The idea of utter extinction there is just as tenable
as is that of migration. In any event we may think
it probable that those who remained in Europe,
even in the south of Spain and Italy, must have
succumbed to the bitter cold or, perhaps, rather to
the terrors of starvation from an absence of food.
It is true that men and women clothed in skins and
living in snow houses, with little of what is known
as the refinement of aristocratic circles, are found
dwelling in rigorous climates of the far North
within the last few centuries. But they have been
more or less closely identified with the cave men of
the Neolithic age in the important matter of cranial
development, and must have reached the ability to
provide against intense cold by the exercise of an

intelligence far above that possessed by the drift men. Undoubtedly the Lapps and the Esquimaux belong to the earliest of the Neolithic peoples, but do not date back of that origin except through a long migration from climes much further South. We may even suppose that during the maximum of the glacial invasion such existence was barely possible at any great distance north from the tropic of Cancer, which would limit it to India, the southern portion of China, and the area between them and the terminus of the Malay Peninsula. In that case the only other habitable portions of the Old World on this side of the equator would be a strip on each shore of the Red Sea and one in Africa bordering the Mediterranean. These areas lie on the east and north of the great Desert of Sahara, which was once a vast inland sea. From these comparatively small tracts of land surface the descendants of the men who lived on through the ice age had to spread north and west after its close to re-people the whole of Europe and a great part of Asia. But a widely different condition existed on the American continent. What has since been called the New World could be invaded by primeval man from within the Arctic circle, if he originated at or near the north pole; and for aught we know he may have been the ancestor of a long line of generations on this continent stretching down to the Indians and Aztecs of the nineteenth century. There might necessarily be a vacation of every part of what is now the United States, except perhaps a small tract in Southern Texas, and no return to it till after the lapse of many centuries. But the retreating tide of humanity could escape into Mexico and over the isthmus to Central America. If this hypothesis be correct there is room for hope that comparatively consecutive deposits of human remains will yet be found in the region south of the United States, though north of the Gulf of Mexico we may never discover any relic that will enable the investigator to bridge the abyss of time that in the Old World separates the remains of the river drift man from those of the cave period. Possibly the missing links may be unearthed in land formerly occupied by the Toltecs and Nahuatlecas.

It should be stated that some have assigned a comparatively recent origin to primeval man. The remains of apes of the highest class have been found in Alpine regions near what are believed to be unmistakable signs of the former presence of the river drift man. Here is a suggestion of a possible derivation of the second from the first without having to seek it near the pole. And the human relics discovered in Spain and Portugal are thought to be among the earliest of all those that have been unearthed from their long rest under accumulated strata. From this it may be argued that the evolution of man from the mere animal occurred long after the region around the pole had cooled down to uninhabitability, and that in the most southerly

portion of the European continent. On this
hypothesis his descendants may be inferred to have
spread eastward across the narrow gut of nine
miles which now separates Spain from the coast of
Africa, and thence round the Mediterranean into
Egypt, from which they subsequently threw out
branches to Mesopotamia and thence to India and
China; that another stream went northeast to the
western side of the Ural Mountains, where afterwards originated the waves of Aryan migration that
spread over a large part of both Europe and Asia;
and that still another offshoot went northwest to
the Atlantic shores of Europe, from which they and
their successors found a way to the Hudson Bay
region, where perhaps the earliest human remains
on this continent have been discovered. The latter
may have crossed by way of the Shetland and Faroe
Islands to Iceland, and thence to the Western continent by way of Greenland, or possibly traveled
over a ridge of now submerged land which is known
to have connected northern Europe with Greenland
in the Tertiary age, if not much later. Also it is
thought that men may have crossed either eastward
or westward between Asia and North America, by
way of the Aleutian Islands or by Bering Strait,
which at its narrowest point is only thirty-eight
miles wide and intersected by three islands, while
it is frozen over in winter.

This hypothesis would place in the Alpine regions
and perhaps south of the Pyrenees the distinction

of being the home of the first man, and in support
of it has been adduced the discovery that a race of
small statured humans had a wide range on the
continent of Europe in the early Neolithic age, who
left traces of their presence in numerous chambered
tombs and caverns in Belgium, France, Spain and
Gibraltar. Also there is good reason to believe
that at one time in the Neolithic period the population of France, Germany, Denmark, England and
Ireland were uniform in physique. But all this
proves nothing in regard to men of the river drift
age, and it may be remarked that the evolution of
man from the ape was not necessarily limited to one
small area, nor to one little span of time. The
change may have occurred in the south of Europe as
only one of several areas, and even later than in the
rest by many centuries. The greatest objection to
the hypothesis of first appearance at the North pole
is perhaps found in the deduction by Sir William
Thompson, that not more than about fifteen thous-
and years could have elapsed from the first cooling
of a moderately thin crust to the time when radia-
tions from the molten interior would exert little
perceptible effect upon the surface temperature.

The improperly-called dog faced men in the Bay
of Bengal, and the more recently discovered dwarfs
in the interior of Africa, are perhaps the least
removed from the original type of any human
beings now existing. Both are near the equator.
From these and other facts many ethnologists have

argued that human life first appeared in the vicinity of the equator, and some have fancied there is reason for assigning the location of "Paradise" to a land now submerged in the Indian Ocean, or perhaps in its northern extension, the Arabian Sea. This would allow of easy migration to Africa, Arabia and Hindostan. It is remarkable that the Mohammedans believe the first man to have lived in or near Ceylon after his expulsion from Paradise, and a conical mountain in the southern part of that island is still called "Adam's Peak." At the top of this there is the impression of a gigantic human foot in the rock, which the "true believers" say was made by our first parent, while the natives assert it was made by Buddha when he stepped from this peak to the adjacent land of Siam.

III

SERMONS IN STONES.

" If these should hold their peace the stones would immediately cry out."—
Luke.

The Neolithic age was that in which man used
only stone weapons and tools, but displayed some
ingenuity in selecting and shaping them, while perhaps for the first time regarding them as desirable
to keep, the river drift man having thrown his
implements away after the occasion for their temporary use had passed. Also we find that with the
incoming of this age man had set out on the ascent
towards the civilization which comes from associating together for the attainment of a common object.
To use a simile attributed to Solomon, the association
brought improvement through a process analogous
to that by which " iron sharpeneth iron." As previously intimated, it is probable this age did not
begin till after the rigorous character of the glacial
epoch had rendered it necessary to invent in order
to live. Something more than the single unshapen
skin was needed to keep out the cold, and methods

47

for fastening two or more together had to be
resorted to. Inclement weather led to a systematic
resort to the shelter afforded by caves, and this
would bring men near each other, especially with
diminishing area of occupancy. From this would
naturally follow at least an occasional working in
harmony for protection from wild beasts and then
in the catching of the animals used for food. And
then would develop the need for oral communication, which we cannot doubt was at first restricted
to the few sounds necessary to represent the limited
range of needs. It may now be well to glance at
the evidence left behind them by the human beings
who had advanced thus far and those who followed
them in fighting the battle of life, introducing new
features and rising still higher in the scale.

The men and women of the Neolithic age used
caves and rock shelters, and undoubtedly occupied
them in company. But they did not confine themselves to these, sometimes camping outside. It
seems probable that the caves in which human
remains are found were mostly places of periodic
resort, perhaps during the inclement season, and
that at least in some instances wild beasts tenanted
them while the human beings were absent. Around
them, and at places on the sea shore where fish are
abundant only for a short time in each year, are
found refuse heaps, some of those near the water
being shell mounds. In the refuse heaps, or
"middens," are found for the first time the remains

of domestic animals, as the dog, cow and sheep,
and occasionally evidences of agriculture. The
weapons are more skilfully made, and some of the
implements have risen to the dignity of tools, while
in more than one were the supposed fragments of
utensils made of sun baked clay.

At some time during the Neolithic age man
learned how to obtain fire and use it for cooking.
In his "Ancient stone implements of Great Britain,"
Evans has collected a mass of evidence tending to
show that fire was first procured by the striking of
flint against iron pyrites (*Pyr* is the Greek word for
fire), and there need be no doubt that this "followed
hard upon" the effort to improve the weapons of the
chase and the tools used for scraping flesh from the
skins before using them for clothing. Evans shows
how flint can be separated into flakes by blows with
a boulder, and then shaped into cutting tools, lance
heads. etc., by rubbing and chipping. He also
shows that the sharpening of those early days was
not performed on a turning grindstone, a discovery
which has led to the detection of some spurious
material offered as alleged relics of the stone age.
Yet it seems more reasonable to suppose, in the
absence of any indications to the contrary, that the
first fire witnessed by mortals was caused by the fall
of a meteorite, a volcanic eruption, or a lightning
flash; and that it was from experience of what this
fire would do they hit upon the idea of letting the
sparks fall upon highly combustible material. If

4

the first fire thus produced without their agency
caused the destruction of animal life, the odor of the
burning flesh would lead up to the earliest taste of
cooked meat, and the desire to repeat the feast
would incite to the procuring of artificial fire long.
before they were aware it could be made available
for the fusing of metal from the ore or even the
baking of clay. It may be inferred that these uses
were not stumbled upon till long after man had
learned how to roast his food, to keep himself
warmer than he could do with skins alone, and to
frighten beasts of prey away from his resting place.
And this discovery of fire, marking the fourth of the
great steps in human advancement, was not less
important than any that preceded it. Perhaps we
may say it was the most important of them all, and
it was certainly the most distinctive. We have
seen that the apes can use sticks and stones for
weapons, and there is good reason to believe that
the sounds emitted by many of the animals, though
meaningless to us, are understood by their fellows
as truly as spoken words are comprehended by men
and women. But the animals below man have never
learned how to cook, the nearest approach thereto
being referred to in the story of the monkey which
used the cat's paw to pull certain chestnuts out of
the fire.

The later Neolithic peoples buried their dead. It
has been suggested that they did this by families,
but this is not proven by the fact of many skele-

tons being found together. The people of that time were often at war with each other, in small bands, and after one of these conflicts the dead would naturally be buried together. Some chambered tombs have been discovered which were evidently family receptacles, but it may be they belong to a comparatively late date. And in this early resort to burial, which for aught we know might have been performed rather from sanitary than religious motives, we have an element of uncertainty as to the age of the deposit by the hand of man compared with that made in the same place by mother Nature. It is quite possible that a human corpus should be interred close to the bones of an animal that passed out of existence centuries previously. But these are only minor considerations when gauged against differences of several hundred feet in the depth of some such deposits as separate the remains of the river drift men from those of some who lived in the Neolithic age. Besides, it is a point that has been carefully taken into the account by those who have instituted archæological comparisons, and is mentioned here only for the purpose of indicating the existence of a difficulty in the way of drawing summary conclusions in regard to the antiquity of human remains found in any particular spot.

We find indubitable evidences of commerce, at least in the latter portion of the Neolithic age. Axes made of nephrite, or jade, have been discovered in Western Europe, but that material is never found there in its native state. So far as known it is exclusively a product of China and Turkestan. Undoubtedly it was worked there in the early times, and the product passed from one hand to another through Asia into the western countries of the European continent and the British Isles. Also we have reason to believe that intercourse between Europe and the other continents of the old world was facilitated by the use of the canoe, probably without the aid of sails. The canoe was made of the trunk of a tree, like the "alnus cavatus" of the men who are said to have journeyed under the command of Jason in search of the golden fleece. The smaller animals and even cattle were transported in these frail vessels from the continent to England and Ireland.

Some of the Neolithic men (or women) were artists. They did not know how to write, in our sense of the term, but they could draw, or engrave; and undoubtedly this was the first step taken in the art of communicating by signs or tokens which could be understood in the absence of the person who made them. The pictures of animals were cut on pieces of bone, previously rubbed to a polish, and probably these pictures were first etched for the purpose of informing others that such an animal had been in that place, or perhaps that it might be expected to come there. Later Neolithics used the spindle, the distaff, and the comb in spinning and weaving flax, and probably wool. Also they made

pottery, by hand, the material being clay; while
the uniformly rounded bottoms of the vessels indicate that the people had not learned to use tables,
but placed their utensils on the ground. The
improvements here alluded to form such a great
advance over the work of the cave men of the early
Neolithic period as to indicate that a vast stretch of
years must have been occupied in the evolution of
the spinning, weaving, and pottery making phase
of human development; — a period perhaps measured by more than a hundred centuries, though we
cannot say that the time was not short when we
look at what has been done in the invention and use
of machinery in the last few years.

The age of copper followed that of stone. It is
considered most probable that the earliest use of the
metal was in the form known as "native," the lumps
found being beaten into shape by stone hammers
and afterwards brought to a smooth edge by rubbing. But with his mastery over fire, man learned
how to cast copper into desirable shapes. The copper used by the Romans was mostly obtained from
the Island of Cyprus, as indicated by its Latin
name, *Cuprum.* Then tin was got from Cornwall by the commercial means already in use in the
Neolithic age, and the fusion of the two metals in-
augurated the age of bronze. The iron age followed
with the application of that metal to numerous uses,
but especially to those of war. This brings us into
the historic period, which may be read about in the

books. In reality when we reach this point we have passed a considerable distance beyond the limit of the pre-historic ; as the development from the use of stone to that of copper, then bronze, and afterwards iron is so recent that we can watch the process among some of the peoples of the last few centuries. Doubtless the changes in the anterior progress of humanity would be found equally lacking in the synchronous element if we could trace them as clearly as is possible with the metallic phases. There are people to-day who have not progressed far beyond the use of stone, and others to whom iron is almost unknown; while the civilized nations have long since learned the wisdom of the remark said to have been made by an "ancient" sage: He who possesses iron will soon be master of all the gold.

It is not difficult to trace, at least tentatively, the progress of this development, in its most prominent features. A few of the steps in it are rather plainly indicated, and there is no point on which we may feel more sure than that a distinct pastoral era separated the purely hunting stage from that which was partly agricultural. Man may have continued to eat fruits and nuts more or less sparingly from the time when he first rose above the ape level till now, but till a comparatively recent date he was to all intents and purposes a carnivorous animal, and in many places exclusively so. The pastoral age must have dawned upon the domestically inclined

man with the discovery that certain animals were
disposed to be friendly to him on invitations of the
practical kind. The dog would first accompany the
hunter and aid him in the chase, his own flesh
furnishing sustenance to the master after the animal
had yielded up its life in struggles with those hunted
for food. Dog flesh has been accounted a delicacy
on this continent long since the visit by Columbus.
Then would follow the domestication of the sheep,
the cow and the goat, an order of subjugation which
is possibly crystallized into the picture story told
by the first three signs of the Zodiac. Afterwards
would come the ass, and lastly the horse and camel
under the direct dominion of man, all three being
used exclusively for bearing human or other burdens
till long after the ox had been harnessed to the plow.
In the course of a few generations at most the property right in all these animals would be acknowledged, at least as between neighbors; not because of
promptings by conscience, but from a conviction
that such mutual respect was for the advantage of
all concerned in the tacit compact. Yet we may
well suppose that the idea of property right was
widely different from that now obtaining in Europe
and the United States. Doubtless the notions of
hospitality still existing among the nomadic tribes
of the Orient are remnants of the old time usages
which originated solely from prudential motives.
The proprietary right to flocks and herds was conceded only on the understanding that the stranger

should be fed, and even allowed to remain with the pastoral community for weeks and months under certain conditions which did not essentially include slavery. And the indifference to human suffering displayed by the Asiatics of all ages may be accepted as proof that the hospitality of those early days was far less a matter of charity than of self preservation.

The recently added power of verbal intercourse would tend to consolidation. Already the family tie had fostered the formation of communities for the sake of companionship as well as mutual protection. The family would hold together through perhaps several generations, and the accessions by "marriage" more or less compensate for defections from the same cause. This would permit and promote the first division of labor, some guarding the flocks while others attended to the preparation of the family supply of food and clothing of skins, and still others to the maintenance of the shelter provided. This again would lead up to the arts of felting wool, and ultimately spinning and weaving it for tent covering as well as clothing, as also to the improvement of weapons for the chase of predatory animals and perhaps defence against human marauders. By and by, as the greater accumulation of pastoral wealth incited covetousness, would come the pitched battle between numbers on both sides, the one anxious to defend its possessions and the other wanting to take what it had not earned — the right of the strongest being the only one known as between strangers. The adult males who were beaten in the contest were put to death, and the women and little ones absorbed into the victorious party. In these and accompaning conditions we see the elements which resulted in the formation of the clan or tribe and the necessity of adopting some kind of (arbitrary) government, the patriarchal being so much the most natural that it seems to have almost universally prevailed. The senior male member of the family was acknowledged ruler or chief, and his word was law as between the rest. The numerical strength of some of the largest of these aggregations may be inferred from the fourteenth chapter of Genesis, which professedly treats of events belonging to a comparatively recent date. With a force of only three hundred and eighteen men Abraham utterly routed four "kings" who had come all the way from the countries north of the Persian Gulf, the list being headed by the redoubtable Chedorlaomer, who shines in history as the "mighty conqueror." With the resulting increase in the flocks and herds of the community would come the necessity of moving from one place to another in search of fresh pastures, and even to a dividing up into smaller parties, as in the case of Abraham and Lot. And in this condition we have the nomadic pastoral life established as an apparent retrogradation towards the prevalent features of a much earlier age.

The progress sketched in the last preceding paragraph is told in few words, but its development into fact must have occupied a course of several centuries. It embraced the discovery that thorns and fish bones could be used for fastening together the skins for tent coverings, that strips of the same, cut by the use of stones sharpened to an edge by rubbing, could be made into effective ligatures which were strongest when twisted, and from this would follow the use of the sling as a weapon, the halter, by the use of which the ox, ass, and horse were reduced to servitude, and the harness by which those animals were made to draw as well as to carry. Then the tied skin was made to hold water and milk, vessels made of clay dried in the sun found to be much stronger when grass or other vegetable stalks formed a part of the composition, from which would follow the idea of making baskets by the interlacing of twigs, and thence that of obtaining a fabric of wool, all of this being accomplished without the aid of metal tools or the use of fire. In all these operations the patriarchal voice would be the director and ruler, and would necessarily become stronger as they multiplied, with the accompanying necessity for care taking of the property of the family or tribe, and directing their disposition on occasions of moving from one place to another in search of fresh pasturage.

These pastoral conditions imposed a limit to the number of persons composing a family or tribe, that limit varying with the natural fertility of the area occupied for the grazing of the animals. The story told in Genesis xiii, about the separation of Abraham and Lot, may not be true as to particular individuals named but is undoubtedly historical as to fact, and for that reason is the history of thousands of dividings instead of only one. This favored the scattering of a comparatively small number over a very wide area within the limits of abundant vegetation combined with the greatest freedom from depredations by ferocious beasts. With these points in mind it will be easy to explain the peculiarly rich development of the pastoral mode of life in that region which has furnished about all that purports to be history of the very earliest times that can be reached by modern enquiry. In the tropical portions of Africa and Asia beasts of prey were so numerous as to forbid the pasturage of domesticated animals, and the northern edge of the torrid zone is marked by the presence of an arid belt which stretches entirely across Africa and the greater portion of Asia. On the latter continent, it includes most of Arabia, then skipping a fertile tract it begins a little east from Persia, though a part of that country is little better than desert, and thence runs northeast by east nearly to Okhotsk, on the Pacific coast, taking in the Desert of Gobi. The area immediately north of this desert belt was precisely the one that could support the greatest population, and, other things being equal, the best portion was that lying nearest the Tropic of Cancer. The cold in winter was less severe there than further to the north, rendering the climate more enjoyable for man and less fatal to his beasts. Even to-day low winter temperatures are met with in the mountain ranges that are near and beyond the thirty-eighth parallel of latitude; but in the ages now under consideration the pastoral limit must have been much nearer the equator because of the then recent glacial retreat from the vicinity of those mountains. And succeeding the glacial epoch there was a submergence of a vast tract of country under what has been termed the Ponto-Aralian Sea, the southern limit of which was about 36 degrees and 30 minutes, stretching far east and west of the Caspian. Accordingly we find that a belt of land only two or three hundred miles wide on the northern side of the latitude of 30 degrees was that along which were distributed the greater number of the people of antiquity of whom we have any historic traces down to the close of the pastoral age. That belt extended from the Mediterranean eastward to the other side of Persia. The earlier concentration seems to have been greatest in the western half of this belt, and in the region since known as Turkey in Asia. It lies between the Mediterranean, Euxine (Black Sea), Caspian, and Persian Gulf. The prevailing religious creed of the people inhabiting that region is the Mohammedan, and has been so for more than a thousand years past.

The purely pastoral life was the full extent of the development attained by the most progressive portion of the human race down to perhaps a little more than six thousand years ago, or fully two thousand years before the time assigned to Abraham. The rest were still savage, or struggling along upward at a lesser remove from the original slough of brutality, and some of the peoples have not got far away from it to-day. The toil up that ascent could not have occupied less than about eight thousand years, and may have taken as much as a thousand centuries to accomplish. To the casual observer it may seem almost insignificant by comparison with what has been achieved since then, but it is not less wonderful. It is a small thing for the savage in this generation to have his eyes opened to the flood of sunlight when the clouds have been dispersed by other agencies. He can learn with the aid of a teacher, but hardly more without him than does the tiger in his native jungle. During the long course of ages we have glanced at, the uneducated man had to be his own instructor. A few of the more intelligent, who, like Socrates, were of an enquiring turn of mind, picked up shreds of knowledge here and there as a result of bitter experience, and what the individual got to know could be communicated to few others. It is probable that in the latter part of the period the more peaceful conditions obtaining from a recognition of the right to property powerfully tended to check the spread of knowledge from one small community to another. They were separate and distinct entities, holding no communication except when it was necessary to call upon neighbors for protection against some one of the number which had turned marauder. In such cases they rallied promptly for its suppression, instinctively feeling that their common safety lay in preserving the balance of power, by preventing any one from lording it over the rest.

All this was changed by the advent of the agricultural era. Strange as it may seem now, that phase of development was the signal for an armed strife such as had not been witnessed since thousands of years previously when the pastoral plan was adopted. It was the beginning of what most people think is entitled to be called "history:" that is the gathering of the people into large aggregations, the consolidation of power and its employment in directing the operation of invading armies. It brought about a series of fierce struggles for the possession of *place*, the capturing of food stores and the localities where they could be most readily accumulated for use in the future. Also it led up directly to the establishment of priestcraft as a means of controlling the multitudes.

It is easy to deceive ourselves in regard to the amount of progress achieved by the whole race as a result of its toilsome march through later centuries. The sum total of that progress is vastly less than might be supposed by one sufficiently intelligent to

observe it at all.   It is estimated that about one-
sixth of the human beings on the face of the earth
to-day habitually go naked, one-half clothe portions
of the body, and only the remaining third part wear
clothes in the civilized acceptation of the term,
though that include rags as well as silks and broad-
cloth.   One-sixth have virtually no shelter from
the elements, one-half live in huts and caves, and
one-third in houses.   Only one-third part is entitled to be called civilized, and of that minority by
far the greater number are steeped in ignorance and
superstition.   Many of them have learned to read
more or less fluently, but comparatively few are
able to think for themselves as to what is right or
wrong, or to form anything like a correct idea of
what is meant by the expression, ''A law of
Nature.''   The great majority believe just what they
are told by a few leaders in religion and politics,
and only a sprinkling among those few leaders are
well informed.   The number of real thinkers in any
community that is not a very large one may usually
be told on the fingers of one hand, and probably it
is a liberal estimate to place the proportion at one
in ten thousand of the race.   But this ''little
leaven leaveneth the whole lump,'' not only preserving the race from mental decay but ensuring its
further progress and the ultimate spread of real
intelligence over the whole earth ''as the waters
cover the sea.''

IV

THE PLOWING ERA.

" If ye had not plowed with my heifer ye had not found out my riddle."—Judges.

The Agricultural Era.—Cultivating the Cereals.—Spontaneous Growth of Dates and Wheat in Chaldea.—Migrations of 4,400 Years Ago.—Confusion of Tongues.—Increase in Skill.—Tools and Metals.—Organization and Law.—Property and Commerce.—War and Slavery.—Writing and Thought.

The first use of cereals and other vegetables for human food must have been in a place where they grew naturally, and the yield must also have been abundant in order to lead to a steady consumption so as to constitute them permanent articles of diet. Man was not likely to begin to cultivate the soil except where he could do so with little trouble and moderate assurance of a quick return. The first named condition was hardly supplied in the valley of the Nile, and the second certainly not so well near Nineveh as around the site of the Babylon of the then future. Hence it may be inferred that though Nineveh is by some supposed to have been built before Babylon, the country around the latter was first settled. In fact this agrees with Genesis x. 10, though we cannot accept the generally received Bible date of about 2,348 B. C. Probably it was

64

at some distance below the most southerly of those two cities that agriculture on a formal scale began. The ancient historians tell us that on the alluvial plains of Chaldea the soil is so fertile and the climate so favorable that several abundant crops of a considerable number of vegetables were gathered in a single year. These conditions were subsequently appreciated so much that numerous irrigating canals were constructed for the purpose of obtaining the best possible results from the culture of the soil.

A line drawn east and west through Hit, on the Euphrates, in latitude about 33 degrees, 50 minutes, divides the upper and lower valleys of that river and the Tigris. Hit is now some 430 miles from the nearest point on the Persian Gulf, but at the time under consideration the distance was only about 300 miles, the alluvium brought down by the river having made considerably more than a hundred miles of ground in the last forty centuries. On that parallel from Hit to the Mediterranean is scarcely 400 miles, the line passing close to the city of Damascus. The land in the lower valley, between the rivers and to a short distance west from the Euphrates, where it meets the Arabian desert, composed the ancient Chaldea, a district little more than half the area of Illinois and somewhat less than that of Indiana. It was bounded on the East by the Elamite country, back of which are the hills of Elam, or "Mountains of the East," which extend

5

into Media, where the mountain of Nizir, now "Elwend," is still pointed out as the spot where the ark is supposed by some to have rested after the subsidence of the Deluge. According to Herodotus the soil of the region was so fertile that grain commonly returned two hundred fold to the sower, and sometimes as much as three hundred fold. Pliny said that wheat was cut twice, and afterwards was good for sheep grazing. Berosus wrote that wheat, barley, sesame, palms, apples and many kinds of shelled fruit grew wild, as wheat still does in the neighborhood of Ana. The climate is very hot in summer, particularly in the marshes near the gulf, but the higher areas are cool in the hottest months, and only a suspicion of ice forms in winter in the low region.

The soil of the Chaldean country is pronounced to be not less fertile now than that on the banks of the Nile, and it is less productive simply because the water courses are neglected. The pre-eminent products of the region were then as now the wheat plant and the date palm, and there can be little doubt that the latter formed the first attraction, feeding many thousands, perhaps through a course of some centuries, before the wheat grains were tried for food. It is not impossible that "Elam" is a slight change from a word which originally signified "land of the palm." Rawlinson says:

"It is certain that dates formed the main food of the inhabitants. The dried fruit being to them the

staff of life was regarded by the Greeks as their
bread. It was perhaps pressed into cakes, as now
common, and on this and goat's milk, which we
know to have been in use, the poorer classes probably almost entirely subsisted. Palm wine was
made from the fermented sap of the tree. Gourds,
melons, and cucumbers must have been cheap. The
richer classes ate wheaten bread, meats of various
kinds, luscious fruits, fish and game, with imported
wine. The date palm was spread widely, and for
its cultivation nothing was needed but a proper
water supply and a little attention at the time of
fructification."

It can hardly be doubted that the date formed
the first important variant from the use of animal
food, owing to the fact that it grows without cultivation and needs not to be prepared by cooking or
otherwise for use by man. Also it may be stored
so as to carry over a supply from one time to
another. It is noteworthy that while the date palm
will grow and furnish valuable wood (lumber),
further north than about 35 degrees, that latitude
is near the limit of its fruit producing capacity,
and this consideration renders it probable that the
early migrants to Mesopotamia did not go so far
north as Assyria. The date grows indigenously in
Egypt, but only where that country is overflowed
annually by the waters of the Nile, a condition which
would seem to be fatal to the supposition that Egypt
was the first country peopled by a settled race. Men

must have learned the art of agriculture elsewhere, and then settled in the valley of the Nile on finding they could cultivate on the plan used in other lands. Still, it is most consistent with what we know of the history of the two countries to suppose that the peculiar conditions in which the Egyptians were placed by the annual overflow stimulated them to the study of Geometry for the purposes of determining boundaries after each flood, to the erection of the pyramids as surveying stations, and to observation of the rising and setting of the stars, particularly of Sirius as a monitor of the approach of floods. Also that they then carried or sent back to the Mesopotamian country the first knowledge there possessed in regard to the movements of the heavenly bodies and of some other arts. Hence we infer that Chaldea was the first area in which man made a serious departure from the exclusive use of animal food, which belonged to the purely pastoral life, that the date was the vegetable food first used in the transition, that the ease of gathering it attracted to the spot people from the surrounding regions, and that the population ultimately became so dense in proportion to the supply that the inhabitants were forced to look around for other food to save themselves from starvation. Then would come recourse to the indigenous wheat, and subsequently other plants. When the dwellers had learned to crush the kernels of grain between stones, make the resulting meal into dough, and bake it,

the value of the newly discovered addition to the
food supply would soon lead to its regular cultivation, and that would furnish still greater attraction
to come in and possess the land which afforded such
a welcome change from hitherto imperative modes
of existence.

No date can be assigned for this important
change in the habits and modes of life of a portion
of the race, which involves a partial return to first
principles, namely the use of vegetable food after
the race had relinquished it perhaps hundreds of
centuries earlier in leaving the condition of ape life
to become human hunters. We might infer from
previous considerations that it would be about the
beginning of recorded history, the change being the
occasion of the first gathering into peoples, tribes,
or clans numerous enough to assert a right to
occupy and till the soil of a particular district.
Then we might cite the fact that three apparently
separate chronologies point to practically the same
date. There is a Hindoo chronology which according to Gentil stretches to 6174 B. C., a Babylonian
to 6158 B. C., and a Chinese one to 6157 B. C.
But there is room for grave suspicion that these are
all but slightly different versions of one story of
planetary cycle as computed by astronomers, and
do not correspond to any events on the surface of
the earth. Neither one has even the shadow of a
known fact to authenticate it, and we are not sure
that the Hindoos have a right to begin their alleged

histories 3,000 years later.   The Hindoo claim to a historical beginning of the Kali-Yuga or Iron age, 3102 B. C. is clouded by finding that it was reckoned back from about the year 572 A. D., when their fundamental star for that age, Zeta Piscium, was in the vernal equinox.   The latter date corresponds nearly, however, with the 3124 B. C. which Professor Lepsius thinks is the most probable time of closing for the third Egyptian dynasty, that marking the construction of the great pyramids long thought to be the most antique monuments on the banks of the Nile.   But Mariette assigns to them a probable origin of about 4235 B.C. so that here again we are metaphorically at sea. Neither do we obtain any assistance from a close study of the Bible account of the creation.   The accepted Hebrew chronology places it at 3761 years B. C., the commonly accepted 4004 of the Catholic and Protestant churches was computed by Archbishop Usher, the Russian Greek church " swears by " the 5508 given by the Septuagint translation of the Hebrew Scriptures, and Regiomontanus made it out that no less than 6984 years elapsed between the creation of the world and the christian era. Evidently there is nothing to be depended upon, in a scientific sense, when equally respectable authorities differ so widely.

The earliest historical date we have, that is entitled to be regarded as trustworthy, is that given by Berosus for Assyria—2458 B. C., since we are not

sure as to the age of the pyramids. The Bible
account of the Deluge places that alleged event at
2348 B. C. and the cuneiform inscription gives 2280
B. C. as the year in which, according to the data
furnished by Asshur-banipal, the Elamite king
Kudur-nankundi, carried away the image of the
goddess Nana from Babylon to Shusan, the latter
being identical with Susa, some 250 miles southeast from Babylon. But it ought not to be inferred
from this that previous to these dates there was no
history. In a recently discovered inscription a
Babylonian prince mentions that (at a time which
must have been) as early as 3000 B. C. he had
imported blocks of stone for statues, and gold and
fine wood, from Magan and Melu-ah—understood
to be districts in Northern Arabia, just south from
the Syrian desert. This was practically coincident
with the building of the pyramids, and both indicate the existence of a state of decided civilization
which could hardly have been attained in less than
a century or two of settled conditions such as we
suppose to have been favored by the development
of the art of agriculture. But we have a trace of
history much farther back than that. The cylinder
of Nabonidus, unearthed about ten years ago from
the ruins of the temple at Sippara, some eighty
miles above Babylon, gives for the date of the older
Sargon about 3800 B. C.; and the most eminent
archæologists accept this as probably correct, the
historical statements on other parts of the same cyl-

inder having been verified. At that early date there was a record, though it has not been preserved to us. We simply have a reference to it, and for aught we know it may have belonged to the pastoral era. It seems to the writer fairly probable that the Kali-Yug epoch of 3102 B. C. was about the date of some most important movement in Western Asia or Northern Africa, or both, which was intended to be commemorated by the construction of the pyramid of Cheops, and that the reckoning was carried to India much later, being preserved there after it was forgotten in the lands further west. We may infer that then, if not earlier, the agricultural era began in Chaldea and Egypt, that being probably the time of commencement for the whole world. It is not logical to think there was no history worthy of the name during the next few centuries, but not strange if little of it has been preserved to us. Along about 2500 B. C. there must have been a wave of migration, at another great epoch. Long before as well as after that time there would be pretty general fighting at intervals wherever it was supposed there was anything worth fighting for.

At whatever time the agricultural discovery was made in Chaldea it must have been pretty well developed as early as about 2200 B. C. Some of the Sippara cylinders record the restoration of the great canal, Nahr Malka, by Khammurabi, who reigned near that date. The canal had to be made

to connect the city with the Euphrates, the course
of which had shifted westward since the city stood
on the banks of the river in the time of the older
Sargon; and the Babylonian records tell us that it
was cut for the purposes of agriculture. The canal
had to be further extended about 550 B. C. because of
the continued shifting of the channel. And according to our theory the settlement of Sippara must
have followed the rush of migration to the plains,
which set in soon after the first cultivation of the
cereals there. We still have traces of some of the
circumstances of that mingling. The Sumir, or
people who spoke the home tongue of the Chaldean
plains, found themselves reinforced by the Accads,
who came some 300 miles from the mountains on
what is now the eastern border of Persia, which
they are said to have regarded as the cradle of the
race. Then came from the head of the Persian Gulf
Oannes, described by Berosus as "half man and
half fish," and a lot of strange looking companions,
which strangeness we may suppose to have been
mostly a matter of dress, or undress, as the case
may be. Probably the so-called Aryan wave did not
flow across that part of the world until some centuries later.

These three sets of people may have got along
passably well together after the shock of the mutual
and probably unceremonious introduction. They
may have found "room enough for all" in cultivating
the soil, and there is little reason to doubt that the

attrition and amalgamation of their several kinds of rude speech was the starting point from which sprang the Shemitic family of languages! And let it be here noted, that for the time at least, while they were becoming accustomed to one another and before they had settled down to a common form of verbal expression, there would be a genuine "confusion of tongues," such as might well have been remembered by the people, spoken of by them to their children, and handed down as a tradition to those of many a succeeding generation.

It must not, however, be supposed that this fusing people became exclusively agricultural. On the contrary, the cultivation of the cereals was a direct aid to the raising of what in these degenerate days is called live stock. The cattle and sheep would secure better and more regular feeding all the year round, and improve in character as a consequence. Now, see what an immense amount of invention the rapidly arising necessities of the new order of things had to be the mother of. The animals must be prevented from browsing in the grain fields at will; therefore tethering or fencing had to be resorted to, the latter being the first formal enclosure of the soil. Then storage room had to be provided for the crops, and out of this need arose the first buildings, with perhaps the primary making of clay into sun dried bricks and the cutting and shaping of boughs from the trees to make roofs over the walls, unless the long reeds which grew profusely in that region were used

for the latter purpose. Then arose a demand for
better tools. The bough of a tree was for a long
time the only thing used as a plow for stirring up
the soil, but it needed to be shaped by the aid of
sharp stones, and perhaps these were the first implements with which the stalks were cut after the grain
had ripened, as we know that the flat stone was long
after that the only mill used for grinding the grain
into meal. The use of fire may have been discovered much earlier, but it can readily be conceived as
probable that it was not kept steadily burning till
after men had settled down into more permanent
dwellings than the movable tents of the mere nomad.
Men would then find that this fire could be kept
alive with the minimum of waste by enclosing it with
stones. Some of these stones contained ore, which
melted with the heat, and lo, they had copper in
more convenient shape than the native lump, as they
could run it into sheets or cakes that were easily
sharpened by rubbing. And then;—But we have
now reached a point which is treated of in the books,
and need not pursue this part of the subject further,
except to remark that this stage of civilization was
not reached in many other lands till a much later
date. It is said that as far down the stream of
time as A. D. 80 the Roman invaders of the north
ern portion of Britain found the people there had
not progressed out of the pastoral era, and were
scarcely better than hunters. In that country which
for a long time led the world in the manufacture

and use of machinery, as well as the culture of the
cereals, the latter was unknown over a large part of
its area till about 1800 years ago.

Out of all this arose the necessity for regulations
of industry and care, if not formal laws. It was
seen to be for the best interest of all that they should
act intelligently, and do so in concert. A single
person could not survey the whole area, and so several had to be appointed to supervise, one of them
being chief. The appropriate times for seeding and
harvesting had to be determined by some one of
superior knowledge, and it was soon observed that
there was some connection between these times and
the movements of the heavenly bodies, while it
would be natural to regard the fire as a direct gift
from heaven, and here came in the work of the
priests, as will be more fully considered hereafter.
It was found that houses constructed of brick (which
by this time could be kiln burnt) were more comfortable to sleep in than the old fashioned tent,
besides permitting more of family privacy: and this
point reached it would not be long before the residents began to accumulate private stores of food,
clothing and utensils, constituting personal property. This public and private heaping up of material, with a vast superiority in wealth and comfort
over the nomads, incited many of them to "go and
do likewise," and thus there would in the course of
a few years be a number of these settlements called
cities but in reality agricultural communities, scat-

tered over the length and breadth of that part of
Mesopotamia which was adapted to land culture, and
on the outer banks of the rivers forming its boundaries.   Others of the nomad people would prefer to
adhere to the pastoral life, but to exchange a portion
of their animal wealth for the cereals and perhaps
other desirable things made by the trinity of human
elements who first learned to use the plow and are,
therefore, best entitled to be called "Aryans."
Here was the beginning of commerce, conducted
strictly on the basis of an equitable exchange of
commodities before gold and silver had been found
or thought of.   But the art of handling fire once
mastered, and the discovery made that other things
besides copper could be extracted from stones by
its aid, a little more time sufficed to extract silver
from its ore and to fuse together the grains of gold
that were gathered from the mountain streams.   The
fact of the indestructibility of these metals by fire,
and their attractiveness for ornamentation, was sufficient to cause their wide recognition as having an
exchangeable value.

Out of this condition of things arose war, the
incitements thereto being plentiful.   Prosperity is
apt to breed strife in more ways than one.   First,
there was jealousy, perhaps not so much among the
working members of different communities as between their chiefs who wished to extend their power
by increasing the area of their dominion, and perhaps by taking captives who could be made to labor

in the construction of public works testifying to the
greatness of their conquerors.   Then there was the
even more dangerous element of envious rapacity
on the part of poorer peoples.   One has but to
look at the invasion of Rome by the Goths in later
times, and still nearer to our own day at the gathering of all sorts of desperadoes at the summons of
William of Normandy for the invasion of England,
to know what this would mean.   It was a deliberate
betting of their own lives against the comparative
riches of others.   One needs but to think back to
the senseless ambition of Alexander, Julius Cæsar,
and some others, to understand the motives that
animated the great men of earlier days in Mesopotamia and its vicinity in deluging the land with
human blood, viciously razing buildings to the
ground that they might erect others upon their
ruins, and destroying records, apparently in the
vain hope of obliterating from the recollection of
the race that such and such cities had ever existed.
It is to those miserable ambitions that we must
ascribe the paucity of information we possess in
regard to the doings of the old time rulers, if not
the condition of those ruled by them.

It must be so, for the people of those early days
knew how to write, and some among them were
anxious to make permanent record of their laws
and deeds.   The pictorial mode of writing, or
rather recording, had undoubtedly come into use as
early as 3000 B. C., and the ideographic form

within a few centuries after that date, while the
alphabetic would seem to date from at least 1500 B. C.
Observations of the stars were made at the temple
of Jupiter Belus (Babylon), the results, undoubtedly
placed on record for comparison, as early as 2300
B. C., and writing of the oldest kind was performed
in Egypt fully 700 years earlier. But it is exceedingly probable that the arts of agriculture were
carried to that land over the wide stretch of about
800 miles which separates it from Babylon, and it
is most natural to suppose there was not much of
either settlement or culture in the valley of the Nile
previous to that event. Of course this transporta-
tion was not performed directly, as a courier would
do it now-a-days. It was the work of many years,
during which wanderers from the Mesopotamia
region moved slowly to the westward in search of
favorable sites on which to settle down and live.
The finding of the cuneiform inscriptions at Babylon and Nineveh, and what has been read from
them, are described in the cyclopedias, which may
be referred to by those anxious to obtain general
information on the subject. In the present enquiry
a considerable part of their value consists in
the light they throw on so-called Old Testament
history.

The earliest of the inscriptions mark the dividing line between the known and the unknown of
written history. Not every account of things
alleged to have happened since then is to be credited,

but all previous to that is in fog, and we cannot hope to do much more in relation to it than to guess broadly at its most salient features, as man now infers certain facts about the last glacial epoch from examination of a few scattered fragments and the markings left on some of them. It is in that sense we have endeavored to sketch the probable development of the most progressive portion of the race up to the point at which agriculture and commerce were well recognized essential features of existence. Accompanying this was a progress of thought from material things to supposably higher entities, to a conception of the possibility of a higher form of existence than that seen by the ordinary mortal, to a sense of responsibility to some superior power through his or its earthly representatives. This also was development, but opinions as to its value may be far more diverse than those entertained in regard to the transition from a state little higher than that of the mere brute to one in which he was practically the lord of all the rest of the animate creation, and if not able to make the winds and waves do his bidding could at least take advantage of them to some extent by a study of times and seasons. It may be well to look back for a moment at the mental status of the most highly cultivated human being at this stage in his career.

The mature man was then an adult in experience, but in reason a mere child. He appears to have had no conception of such a thing as a law of nature,

but supposed all the affairs of human life to be regulated or ordered by some fate, that word here
being used in its broadest sense as the result of a fiat
either uttered long ago or expressed at the moment.
Human government was of the most despotic kind,
the will of the ruler being law, irrespective of right,
and subject to change by mere flattery or the more
substantial present with which the suitor for "justice" always approached the potentate unless
reduced to the very lowest extreme of poverty by
exactions of tax gatherer or usurer; for he could be
sold as a slave because of the non-payment of debt as
for the misfortune of being taken captive in war.
As the ruler acknowledged the superior power of
some being or beings whom the priests were reputed
to have in their confidence, it is no wonder that the
poor wretches of the common sort bowed abjectly
before priestly power and influence, believed it could
do or procure to be done whatever it willed, were
only too glad to propitiate it by offerings of their
money or other possessions, and knew nothing of
what folks now call conscience, as they held everything to be right that was allowed by the priests,
and found the decision to depend pretty much on
the value of their votive offerings. It is no wonder
if they ascribed every reverse, disease included, to
the outraged feeling of an offended god, that they
thought there was no right except the might of the
strongest, and accepted without question the most
absurd explanations of natural phenomena.

6

So these poor children of nature found no difficulty in believing that the world was an extended
plane, that the sun, moon and planets were only a
few thousand stadia distant, that the motions of
these bodies were controlled by intelligent deities
who were sufficiently near to earth to take an interest in the every day affairs of mortals and so little
removed from them in nature that they could be
mixed up in their intrigues and even play fast and
loose with them sexually as well as in war. To
them it was a matter of living faith that these gods
could be propitiated by putting under their noses a
sweet smelling morsel in the shape of a sacrifice, and
the destinies of nations as well as individuals be
altered in consequence. They saw nothing unbelievable in the story of a man coming into the
world without a mortal father, or the first one entering it full grown without either father or mother, or
any one of their number being taken up to the skies
in defiance of the then unknown law of gravitation
to dwell among the gods. Of course the subsequently alleged resurrection of Jesus was a miracle
of the minor sort, and no more of a stumbling block
to faith than a small pebble would be in the path of
an athlete. We may smile at these things now, but
are we quite sure that in doing so we are not laugh-
ing at our age by implication, and proving ourselves
much the worst fools by sinning against reason in
the light of vastly greater knowledge than was possessed by the men of twenty-five centuries ago ?

V

EARLY ORIENTALS.

" The greatest of all the men of the East."—Job.

Ancient Conditions in Egypt, Mesopotamia, Arabia, China and India.—
Accounts Which are Partly Historical.—The Records of Those Early
Days are Chiefly in Regard to Fighting.

The points adduced in the last preceding chapter
will enable us to understand why we have so little
history of events in the progress of the human race
down to a comparatively recent period. There was
little that was worth placing on record till the
advent of the agricultural era, and this did not
begin at the same time in widely separated countries: Perhaps the cereals were cultivated in Chaldea more than a thousand years before the turning
of the first sod by the plow in Greece or Rome.
Then a large proportion of the written material was
destroyed amid the wild rush of war which characterized the surging back and forth of different tribes
or hordes during many centuries over the sub-trop-
ical and south temperate regions of Asia and Europe.
It may be of interest to note some of the more prominent statements of the earlier histories which have
been preserved, and views thereof by recent writers.
The facts stated may not all of them bear directly

upon the more theoretical conclusions previously presented, but it is none the less desirable to gather the scattered fragments where they can be surveyed as in a bird's eye view.

Rawlinson thinks that civilization in the valley of the Nile preceded by many centuries that of primitive Chaldea, and that this comparative Egyptian antiquity is an argument in favor of the migration having been from west to east;—he notes that the monuments and traditions of the Chaldeans themselves have been thought to present some curious indications of an East African origin. This is far from being impossible. There may have been a pastoral migration northwards from Nubia to Egypt and thence eastward to the head of the Persian Gulf. There was an early belief among the Greeks in the existence of an Asiatic Ethiopia between India and Arabia, on the shores of the Erythrean Sea, and Eusebius has preserved a tradition that in the reign of Amenophis III. (perhaps 1600 B. C.), a body of Ethiopians migrated from the country about the Indus and settled in the valley of the Nile. (Is it possible this can be a twisting of the Jewish story about the descent of Jacob and his family into Egypt?) But this migration was too recent to have had anything to do with the original settlement of the country.

The history of Egypt begins with King Menes, whose time before the Christian Era was 3643 according to Bunsen, 3893 according to Lepsius,

4455 according to Brugsch, and 5004 according to Mariette. No monuments of his remain. The second king, Teta, is reported to have built a palace and written a work on surgery. The fifth, Hespu, was the author of a sacred (hieroglyphic) writing. A tablet now in the Ashmolean museum at Oxford, England, is believed to have been made about his time, and it is thought the first use of papyrus for writing could not date more than a couple of centuries later. About 300 years after Menes came King Kekeu, who built the pyramid at Sakkarah, which is the oldest monument in Egypt. Also he established the worship of sacred animals. A few remains of sculpture, assigned to two or three hundred years later than Kekeu, indicate the rude beginning of the Art phase of Egyptian civilization. About 550 years after the Menes era Saker-Nefer-Ke founded the third dynasty, establishing his seat of power at Memphis, and conquered the Lybians. His dynasty lasted 214 years, and near its close king Snefru, or Senefru, conquered some of the nomadic tribes of Arabia. He built the pyramid at Meydoum, the entrance to which was discovered little more than ten years ago. This is considered to be nearly a century older than the great pyramid at Ghizeh, its date being about 3766 according to the chronology of Brugsch, and 4200 B. C. according to that of Mariette. The pictures found in the tombs of this epoch show that nearly all the animals which are now domesticated had then been brought under subjection, and the Egyptian language seems by that time to have been fully formed. In the next dynasty the three great pyramids and the Sphinx were built by kings Khufu, Shafra, and Menkara. The first two of these were named by Herodotus Cheops and Cephren, and these are the names usually applied to them as the builders of the two great pyramids. The time of Cheops is fixed according to Lepsius at from 3095 to 3032 B. C. and Herodotus says he was the first bad king of Egypt. His brother Cephren reigned about 3032 to 2966 B. C. Both of them were so much hated by the people over whom they ruled that even in the time of the Grecian historian the Egyptians would not mention the names of the two monarchs. Khufu, or Cheops, was victorious over Anu, a tribe of northern Arabia. His dynasty ended in a rebellion about 2840 B. C. according to the chronology of Lepsius. It was succeeded by a peaceful dynasty of nine kings, under whom a high state of civilization was developed, as evidenced by sculptures and paintings, as also by writings on papyrus recently found in the tombs. One of these, written in the eighth reign, and probably the oldest book in the world, is described as a handbook of manners for young people, and a treatise on practical morality. Pepi Merira, the second king of the fifth dynasty, conquered a tribe of negro invaders named Wa-Wa, and left numerous monuments: and about 100 years afterwards another period of internal strife set in which was ended by

Nitocris, celebrated for her beauty and wisdom. She invited the chief revolutionary conspirators to a subterranean banquet, and then drowned them all by letting in the waters of the Nile through a secret channel. Her reign lasted twelve years, and with it ended the sixth dynasty. This was succeeded by four others of which little is known except that they existed through about 400 years and that the country was probably at the mercy of foreign invaders, in whose presence art declined. In 2423 B. C. according to Lepsius' reckoning, the eleventh dynasty was founded, with Thebes as the seat of government. Its six kings reigned for about two centuries, and during most of that time were at war with the inhabitants of the Delta, who finally yielded. The next dynasty was peaceful and prosperous. It included Osortasen I, who extended his domain to Nubia and Arabia, leaving a record of the latter on the rocks of Sinai, Osortasen III who conquered Ethiopia, and Amenemhe III who constructed Lake Moeris. One of the number built the labyrinth, and under this dynasty the art of sculpture attained its highest perfection. The next consisted of sixteen kings of whom little is known except that they lived in very troublous times. They were succeeded by a dynasty which established itself at Xois, on the Delta, and under it the country was divided into two kingdoms. About 2100 B. C. it was invaded by the Hyksos or Shepherd Kings, who seem to have been a combination of

nomads from Arabia and Syria. They established
their capital at Avaris on the northeastern frontier,
and ruled for about four centuries. At first they treated the natives with great cruelty, and defaced or destroyed the temples, but the later ones were more
mild, and adopted Egyptian names and manners.
The last of the line was Apepi who is supposed by
some to have been the king that made Joseph governor. Finally the shepherds were besieged in their
fortress at Avaris, and compelled to surrender.
Under treaty most of them departed into Palestine,
and the rest were allowed to settle in a district in
the eastern part of Lower Egypt. According to
Mariette this occurred about 1703 B. C. but other
reckonings make it much later, Rawlinson placing
the date at about 1525 B. C.. This is pretty closely
in accord with the 1491 B. C. which is usually
named for the departure of the children of Israel
from the land of Egypt, that being strictly assigned
(I Kings vi. 1.) as 480 years previous to the building of the temple by Solomon, whose reign is computed to have begun about 1015 B. C. The suggestion is not original in this place, and has been
sneered at by some who stoutly defend the accuracy
of the Bible narrative; but it will be seen subsequently that there is good ground for rejecting that
story. It may also be noted that the region assigned
to those of the Hyksos who remained corresponds
closely to the account which places the Hebrews in
the land of Goshen. The remains of king Rasek-

enen Taaken and queen Ansera of this dynasty, with twenty-seven mummies of kings, queens, and other persons of distinction in three following dynasties, were recently found in a rock chamber behind an ancient temple among the hills west of Thebes. It was evident that they had not been originally deposited there, though on the breasts of some of them still rested the floral wreaths used at the time of burial. With them were about 3,700 mortuary statues.

After the departure of the Hyksos King Ahmes established the eighteenth dynasty, at Thebes, and rebuilt the temples and palaces they had destroyed. Rich jewels have been found on the mummy of Queen Aah Hotep, his mother, and other discoveries made in the present century show his reign to have been one of great prosperity. He conquered Canaan and Upper Egypt (perhaps Nubia), and his successor, Amenophis, subdued a large part of Arabia. The next king, Thothmes I, defeated the Syrians near Damascus, and then crossed into Mesopotamia, which he conquered. There his people first learned the use of horses, which were soon found to thrive in the valley of the Nile, and became important aids to subsequent Egyptian warfare.

Thothmes III, succeeding his brother, was a son of the last named. His elder sister, Hatasu or Amen-set, was the actual governor of his kingdom during many years. She built the temple of Deir-el-Bahri, and the two great obelisks of Karnak to the memory of her father. One of these was removed a few years ago to the Place de la Concorde in Paris. The so-called Cleopatra's Needle, recently placed in Central Park, New York, is also believed to have been built in that reign; and according to Plutarch the god Thoth (King Thothmes), taught the Egyptians the true length of the year, which probably means that he instituted the reform in the calendar, held to date 1321 B. C. On a tablet removed to the Louvre in Paris this king is represented as making offerings before the images of sixty-one of his predecessors. He extended his power by conquest over Nubia, Abyssinia, Arabia (Felix), Syria, Mesopotamia, Kurdistan, Armenia, all Northern Africa as far west as Algeria, the southern coasts of Greece and Italy, also Cyprus and Crete. For the subjugation of the latter named countries he created a powerful fleet, which is thought to have been manned mostly by Phenecian sailors. Two short reigns followed and then came Amen-hotep III, who held the throne twenty-six years and was a great builder; the temple at Luxor and the colossal statue at Thebes, called Memnon by the Greeks and Romans, being among the works credited to him. His son Amen-hotep IV abandoned Thebes and erected monuments at a new capital, now called Tel-el-Amarna. On them he caused to be inscribed figures representing the ceremonies of a new worship, which seem to strongly resemble those said to have been observed by the Israelites in the wilderness. This religion was monotheistic, and those who believe in a Hebrew exodus as related in the Pentateuch, think it marked the close of a period of slavery brought about by a reaction from this attempt to replace the old polytheistic worship by a new one. A large number of clay tablets inscribed with cuneiform characters have recently been found among the ruins of Tel-el-Amarna. They consist of letters and reports sent by the rulers of Palestine, Syria and Mesopotamia, to Amenophis III and IV (Amen-Hotep); and a note in hieratic on one of the tablets tells that a large proportion of them had been transferred from Thebes to the new capital. At that time Palestine was held by Egyptian garrisons. The writer of the Book of Joshua seems not to have been aware of such occupancy, though (iii, 10) he carefully specifies the Canaanites, Hittites, Hivites, Perrizites, Girgashites, Amorites and Jebusites, as possessors of the land.

The reign of Her-em Hebi, son of Amen-Hotep, closed the eighteenth dynasty about 1462 B. C. Rameses I followed, succeeded by Seti I, the Sethos of the Greeks, who is said to have been of the Shepherd race and a great builder as well as a conqueror. So was his son Rameses II, who reigned about sixty-six years, suppressed an extensive rebellion, and seems to have been a tyrant. He employed many thousands of captives at forced labor on public works, including great monuments. The inscriptions at Abydos represent Seti I and his son Rameses, then heir apparent, offering incense to seventy-six kings, their predecessors. By doing a seeming violence to chronology it has been inferred that this Rameses was the Pharaoh who most oppressed the Israelites, and that they left the country under the reign of his son Menoptah. There is little room to doubt that under these two kings the nation lost much of its power and territory, first by a Pelasgian invasion and then by the Khitas, the latter rallying to the help of some 60,000 foreigners who had revolted from forced labor on the public granaries of Egypt. These Khitas are believed to have been the Hittites of Scripture, and recent discoveries show that from the seventeenth to the twelfth century B. C. they were the leading nation in Western Asia, holding the balance of power between Egypt and Assyria. A treaty between their king and Rameses II is described as "containing provisions worthy of the highest civilization of modern times." Yet in the Old Testament they are mentioned briefly as if of no more account than the Perrizites and the Jebusites, which probably were no better than roving bands, though the latter for some time occupied the site of the future Jerusalem.

Rameses III, the second king of the twentieth dynasty, which was founded about 1288 B. C., was a great soldier, acting chiefly on the defensive. From him to the beginning of the twenty-second dynasty there appears to have been little worth recording except that one of the kings is reported to have given his daughter as a wife to Solomon,

the son of David. About 970 B. C. Shishonk
(Shishak), the first of his line, invaded Judea
and plundered Jerusalem. From that time the
country was again in almost continuous trouble,
being subdued by Ethiopians and negroes about
716 B. C., but rose once more to prominence
under the twenty-sixth dynasty, which began about
685 B. C. and raised Egypt to a prosperity greater
than any it had previously experienced. The
capital was now at Sais, and a vast number of
papyri of this period have recently been discovered,
giving in demotic characters a great mass of information in regard to the business methods and social
life of the people. During this time of prosperity
corruption crept in, and decline followed. The
military class emigrated in a body to Ethiopia, and
about 525 B. C. Egypt became a Persian province.
In 332 B. C. it was subdued by Alexander the Great.

The historic chronology of Assyria, as given by
Berosus, begins with 2458 B. C.; and the records
left by Tiglath Pileser I, about 1130 B. C., show
that it had become a compact kingdom at least a
century before the latter date. As an empire it had
ceased to exist by the time Rome had gained a
place on the pages of history, or Greece laid a
foundation for dates by establishing the reckoning
by Olympiads. The Assyrian monuments tell of a
conquest of Babylon by a Susanian monarch 1,635
years before Susa was captured by Ashur-banipal;
and the date of the latter event is fixed at about 651

B. C., which would place the former at 2286 B. C. Copies of the records and literary works of many hundreds of years preceding the reign of Ashurbanipal have been recovered at Nineveh, where they formed part of his library. Still older records were unearthed in 1881 at Sippara, which is situated about sixteen miles southwest of Bagdad and eighty above Babylon, some distance east from the Euphrates. It is in latitude 33° 36′ north and longitude 43° 50′ east from Greenwich. One of the inscriptions indicates the ancient existence of another extensive city called Sippara Anat, the two being supposed to have formed the Hebrew Sepharvaim. Mr. Hormuzd Rassam found at Sippara the temple of the sun-god, and within it a tablet dated in the reign of Nabupaliddina, who lived in the ninth century B. C. It tells of the destruction of the original temple by invaders named the Sutu, and that its restoration was begun by Simas Sugu—who is the fortieth on the list of about two hundred of the earliest kings of Babylonia, which begins with the first kings after the flood. The tablet first referred to tells that the work of restoring the temple was carried on by another monarch, and completed by Nabupaliddina who also finally destroyed the Sutu. The temple was subsequently repaired by Nabonidus, about 550 B. C., who placed in it clay cylinders recording the event. One of these contains a statement to the effect that when burrowing beneath the temple, forty-five years after Nebuchad-

nezzar had sought in vain for the ancient records,
he had revealed to him " the cylinder of Naram-Sin,
son of Sargon, which for 3200 years no king going
before me had seen." That carries us back about
1000 years further than the earliest date previously
known to have been specified in the cuneiform inscriptions. In company with M. de Sarzec Mr.
Rassam has also unearthed at Tel-loh, the *Zirgul*
of the ancients, documents treating of events between 1400 and 891 B. C., one of which gives a synchronous history of Assyria and Babylonia. These
inscriptions also show that in the time of Gudea,
one of the earliest kings in the series, there was an
active intercourse between Chaldea and Egypt.

Rawlinson thought that Chaldean history may be
regarded as opening at least a century before the
2286 B. C. previously named; Nimrod, a descendant of Cush, then setting up a kingdom in Lower
Mesopotamia. We have seen in the last preceding
chapter that it is probable the country was agri-
culturally settled long anterior to 2450 B. C., but
personal records are lacking. It would seem that
the people led by Nimrod came up from the sea (Persian Gulf), which then extended some 125 miles
further inland than now. At least their early settlements were on the coast, and Ur, or Hur, on the eastern bank of the Euphrates, was their primitive capital.
His dominion extended northwards, certainly as far
as Babylon, which was founded by him as well as
Erech or Huruk, and some other cities. We may

infer that he came there as a hunter, and developed
the beginning of civilization. He was worshiped
under the title of Bilu-Nipru or Bel Nimrod, which
is translated to mean " Lord of the chase;" and it
is considered probable that the constellation Orion
was named after him as the Giant;—in Arabic, El
Jabbar or El Giausar. An early successor was
named Urukh, who was the first great builder, and
probably Ur and Erech were named after him. The
interval between him and Nimrod may be conject-
ured to have been one of war, as a result of which
the earlier Shemites emigrated, the Assyrians going
to the north and northwest. (Query, is this referred to in the story of the separation of Abram
and Lot?)

Urukh or Urkham was the first Chaldean monarch whose works have been identified. His bricks
are found at the very foundations of buildings, are
rude and coarse, and the inscriptions are in very old
form. Also his bricks are irregular in size and
shape, mostly sun-dried and joined together with
mud or bitumen. He erected many great buildings,
one of them being estimated to have required more
than 30,000,000 bricks, and all of them seem to
have been intended for temples. He must have had
an immense army of workers at his command, and
it is fair to infer they were captives taken in
war. But it is significant that the writings on his
bricks had passed out of the earliest or hieroglyphic
stage and entered on the second or transitional,

" when pictures are no longer attempted but the lines or wedges follow roughly the old outlines of the objects." He left a son who completed some of his buildings at Ur, and on his signet ring is called King of Ur. The science of astronomy must have been studied during these reigns if the series of observations sent by Calisthenes to Aristotle, dating from B. C. 2234, was a real record and not a mere dating back, such as has been detected in the alleged astronomical records of India. About 2300 B. C. a king of Elam, whose court was at Susa, ravaged Chaldea and took away the images of the deities. His name was Kudur-Nakhunta (or Nankundi) which is thought to be identical with Zoroaster, who, according to Berosus and Polyhistor, was the first of eight Medean kings who composed the second dynasty. Probably next to him was Kudur-Lagamer (Chedor-laomer) who conquered the upper valley of the Euphrates and invaded Palestine, a great battle being fought on a plain which is believed to be now submerged by the Dead Sea. About 1600 B. C. Zur-Sin erected some buildings near Babylon, which exhibit some improvements on the architecture of the earlier times; but their debris contain proofs that the simple arts had not advanced much, from which we may infer that the people had been for several centuries almost continually at war. Flint knives and stone hatchets are abundant in these ruins. A few specimens of gold and bronze are found, but no other metal ex-

cept iron, which appears to have been used altogether for personal ornament.

It must have been about 2200 B. C., instead of
the 1546 to 1520 given by Rawlinson, that Khammurabi rebuilt the temple of the sun at Senkerah,
or Sippara, and gave an important stimulus to the
artificial cultivation of the cereals.   He constructed
"a canal for carrying the water of one of the great
rivers to the fields," which may have been the one
elsewhere referred to as connecting Sippara with the
river, or may possibly have been one additional
to that.   An inscription says this agricultural canal
was a blessing to the people; "it changed desert
plains into well watered fields, it spread around fertility and abundance."

Probably if Rawlinson had known of the existence of the date for the older Sargon, derivable
from the inscription on the cylinder of Nabonidus,
he would hardly have claimed that the Babylonian
monarchy was less ancient than the Egyptian.   Yet
he concedes to it priority over all that have grown
up on the soil of Asia. He says the Aryan, Turanian,
and even the Shemitic tribes appear to have been in
the nomadic condition when the Cushite settlers in
Lower Babylonia betook themselves to agriculture,
built cities and established a strong and settled government.   He refers to three of the kings as having each
achieved greatness in his own particular field of action.
Nimrod is distinguished as the invader, Uruch as the
builder, and Kudur-Lagamer as the conqueror.

Down to about 1300, when Tiglathi-Nin subdued Babylon, the different rulers seem to have been of kindred race. Then a strong Shemitic influence came in, the monarchs ceased to have Turanian or Cushite names, and the inscriptions became Assyrian. After about 650 years the Chaldeans renewed the struggle, and in 625 established a second kingdom, the Babylonian monarchy which was extinguished by Cyrus, though the nationality of the people remained for ages after, being recognized as distinct by the Persians and Parthians. They cultivated astronomy and astrology from the time of Nimrod to that of Alexander, a space of nearly 2200 years.

As far back as can be traced Arabia has been a land of commerce; but mostly as a traveling route between other countries. It was then as now the home of the camel, and the glories of its caravans only began to fade after the advent of steamship navigation, to be further dimmed by the cutting of the Suez Canal in the latter part of this century. The caravans transported merchandise back and forth between Egypt and Chaldea possibly before the times for which we have any record, and then extended their commercial intercourse to Palestine and Phenecia. This business was conducted by merchants and not by common carriers. The rest of the people of Arabia were nomads down to a late period, except that a few agriculturists might have been found in the southwestern portion, since called Yemen. The first government formed in the peninsula is believed to have been in that section, which is the home of the Mocha coffee berry. The recent researches of Edouard Glaser show that some 1500 years B. C. the empire of Ma'in, or of the Mineans, existed there, and that it must have lasted fully 500 years. The inscriptions left by that people are described as being sharply distinct from those of the Sabaeans who conquered the first named as a result of many battles. The ancient capital, Ma'in, was in a place which bears the same name to-day.

The Chinese seem to have cultivated the science of astronomy at a very early date. A book written in the reign of Yao, about 2332 B. C., tells the oft related story about the two astronomers Hi and Ho who observed the places of the sun, moon and stars, and instructed the people in regard to the seasons for the regulation of husbandry. It tells that the stars Niao, Ho, Hiu and Mao marked the places of the spring equinox, the summer solstice, the autumnal equinox and the winter solstice. If these stars were Alpha Tauri, Delta Leonis, Alpha Scorpii and Delta Aquarii, which are nearly equidistant and not far from the ecliptic circle, and be supposed to have been in conjunction with the sun at the beginning of the four quarters of the year at the epoch, the count would have been made from just about 3000 B. C.; and it is stated that in 2952 reigned Fohi, the first emperor of China, who appears to have been the first to compose astronomical tables and describe the figures of some of the heavenly bodies (constellations). The same book alludes to a year consisting of 366 days and three of 365 days each, also to a lunar intercalary, from which it must be inferred that the Chinese had a luni-solar year. In the reign of Hoang-ti, about 2697 B. C., they had constructed a sphere with the various circles thereto belonging, and Yu-Chi observed the pole star with the constellations near it. Hoang-ti, or his astronomer, constructed instruments with which to observe the stars, and also one to find the cardinal points without observing the heavens. This must have been the compass, which is referred to in Chinese literature about 1400 years later. In this reign a society of mathematicians and historians is said to have been instituted. In 2513 B. C. the emperor Chuen-I composed an ephemeris, showing the motions of the five planets, and it is said he was raised to the governorship of the empire because of his astronomical attainments. In 2169, or perhaps 2137, B. C. under the reign of Chou-Kang, occurred the most ancient eclipse known to have been recorded, and their history makes no mention of any eclipse between that and 776 B. C. China seems to have suffered in much the same way as more western countries during the last few centuries before the Christian era. From 480 to 206 B. C. astronomy was almost entirely neglected, the society of mathematicians was destroyed, and the empire cut up into small states. These were reunited in the third century B. C. by

Tsin-Chi-Hoang, but in the year 246 he collected all the historical and mathematical works and burned them, setting a pitiful example which was followed nine hundred years later in the destruction of the Alexandrian library by order of the Caliph Omar. The ancestors of the Chinese of to-day invaded the country from the northwest, probably not much earlier than 1500 B. C. The aborigines were killed off or retreated before them into the extreme south, where a few of their descendants are yet to be found. During that long blank in the astronomical record noted above the land was completely revolutionized. The invaders appropriated the knowledge as well as the lands of their predecessors, and appear to have added little to the original stock till forced to do so by contact with Europeans in the present century. The Khitas were Mongols.

It has previously been stated that there is grave reason to doubt the claim of a high antiquity for astronomical knowledge in India. Yet it should be said that the epoch of the Tirvalore tables, 3102 B. C. corresponds very well with several facts deduced for that date by modern astronomers. They give 24° for the obliquity of the ecliptic, the equation of the center for Saturn 7° 39' 44", his annual mean motion as 12° 13' 13", and the annual mean motion of Jupiter as 30° 20' 42". These and some other quantities are almost identical with those which would now be calculated for that date, but none of them were necessarily deduced from obser-

vations made in India. The knowledge may have
been carried there, for aught that we know to the
contrary. The aboriginal inhabitants appear to
have been a very degraded race when the country
was invaded by the great Aryan wave of migration
that swept into it from the direction of Persia about
1500 B. C. The new comers brought with them the
Sanscrit language, in which the oldest of their works,
the Vedas, were compiled perhaps in the fourteenth
century B. C. It has been thought that the Sudras,
or servile caste, are descendants of the aborigines,
but this is by no means certain. From the Vedic
era to the invasion by Darius the Persian, about 520
B. C. little is known except that the country appears
to have been the theatre of numerous wars between
native chiefs and the men whom they could induce
to fight for them. The historians who accompanied
Alexander when he invaded the land about 327 B. C.
described the manners and customs of the people in
a way that shows they had changed little between
that time and a few years ago when under English
rule the civilizing progress began. The religious
literature of India is remarkable as having formed
the basis for the modern science of philology. A
study of the language in which it was written, in
comparison with the Latin and Greek, showed that
the three belong to one linguistic family, and
caused the abandonment of the previously prevalent
notion that all the languages of the earth had sprung
from the Hebrew tongue.

VI.

LIGHT IN ASIA.

" Who commanded the light to shine out of darkness."—II. Corinthians.

The Great Aryan Migration.— Beginning of History.— Invention of Alphabetic Writing.—The Shemites as Wandering Tribes.—Jewish Fables about Divine Rule Through Prophets and Judges.—Missing Property.— The Mythical Ten Tribes.— The History of the Jews as a People Began with David, and was first written after the Return from Babylon.

Of other countries it may be said that nothing is known previous to about 1500 B. C., and little for the first half of that fifteen century interval. The year 1493 B. C. is assigned in some of the chronological tables as that in which Cadmus enacted the role of the first letter carrier by taking with him an alphabet of sixteen letters to Greece, and the next two or three centuries include the heroic age, the supposed prominent events in which became a part of the Greek mythology. It is more than probable that about this time the great Aryan wave passed from Europe across Asia. The home of that race is now believed, for linguistic reasons, to have been in European Russia, west of the Ural mountains and probably not far north of the Caucasus. Migrants from that region spread out over the southern half of Europe, as far west as the British Islands. Oth-

ers passed into Asia, and if we suppose that they
took the comparatively easy route around the northern shore of the Caspian Sea it will not be difficult
to understand how they would leave the Shemites in
unmolested possession of the Mesopotamian country
in passing further to the east. The Asiatic stream
appears to have passed up the valley of the Oxus
and rested for some time in Bactria, where probably
before 1200 B. C. Zoroaster flourished and taught
at a place called after him Zariaspe, and now known
as Balkh, near the Upper Oxus. Thence a swarm
was thrown off into Persia, while the main body
moved in the direction of India. The Aryans
moved slowly in this migration, taking their flocks
with them, staying in one place long enough to raise
a crop of some cereal, then going further and halt-
ing again when the season came round for cultivating roughly a patch of soil. They were thus a
semi-agricultural people, and probably their movements had no object in the shape of a particular
place. They were in search of some favorable location, and every now and then struck out afresh in
hopes of finding a better one than had yet been
occupied by them. In these migrations we have a
series of supposed events grouped within about a
century each way from 1400 B. C. which constitute
that a most important epoch in the history of the
race. And it appears to have been a period of wide
spread development, which without much of a stretch
of fancy may be referred to a common origin.

Within these limits we have the alleged writing of the Tables of the Law by the finger of God on Mount Sinai, the penning of the earliest portions of the Avesta in Bactria, and the carrying of the Phenecian letters to Greece by Cadmus. These were followed a century or two later by the writing of probably the most ancient of the Vedic hymns, which sing the invasion of India as the Iliad does the Siege of Troy; and the clay cylinders at Ashur, containing the records of King Tiglath Pileser I. of Assyria. All of this points to a most important change in the art of writing, by which it became a representative of words instead of ideas to be expressed in language. Doubtless it was about this time that the most progressive nations began to use an alphabet consisting of characters each of which represented a single sound, while a few, including those in the Mesopotamian region, had perhaps previously adopted the syllabic method; and there is some reason to think it probable that the letters of the Shemitic alphabets had syllabic values at the outset if not for a long time after their introduction. We may add that the art of working iron from the ore and using it for tools and weapons, may be dated back to about this period or a little earlier, to fully 1500 B. C. It has recently been claimed for the Chinese that they used wrought iron as early as about 2000 B. C.

The middle of the eighth century before Christ was a memorable time. Several remarkable events occurred about then; and if they do not mark the beginning of all that we are really entitled to call history, little that preceded them could be stated methodically previous to a few years ago. We have no precision of dates for any chain of events earlier than that period except in Egypt and Mesopotamia. The foundation of Rome is alleged to date from about 753 B. C. In 748 the first money was coined in Greece, and five years later witnessed the beginning of its first historic war;—that between the Spartans and the Messenians. In 747 we have the celebrated historic record of the Babylonians in the shape of a date for the accession of Nabonassar and the introduction of the Egyptian solar year among the dwellers on the banks of the Euphrates. Between 770 and 720 B. C. a number of Israelites were taken into captivity by the kings of Assyria. Most of them were deported from Samaria to the country around the southern end of the Caspian Sea, and their places in the Holy Land are said to have been taken by men carried thither from the cities of Babylonia. In the latter part of that century the Medeans successfully revolted from Assyrian bondage; their first judge, Dioces, being made general ruler in 708 B. C. according to Herodotus, and afterwards founding the fortified capital Ecbatana. It is fair to state that Rawlinson thinks it probable the Medean Kingdom was not established till about 633 B. C. by Cyaxares, the third king named by Herodotus. This, however, is not inconsistent with a throwing off the foreign yoke a century earlier. Bactria became a Persian province in the time of Cyrus, who took it shortly before he conquered Babylon in 538 B. C.

During the greater part of the interval between these two epochs the lands since considered to have been then most specifically peopled by Shemites were in little better than the nomadic stage of civilization. In Arabia a few small tribes roamed almost at will. Occasionally one or more of them would make a dash into Egyptian territory and be forced to retire with loss, the event being celebrated as a victory over the Arabs. We are obliged to conclude that the same is true in regard to Palestine, the inhabitants of that country being mostly of the shepherd class and not deemed worth conquering in the same sense as we use the word to-day. Then, as in much more recent times, it was "all right" to make slaves of those taken captive in a fight, and there can be no doubt that numbers of these people were every now and then forced into the service of the Egyptian kings, who made them build dykes, excavate lakes, construct pyramids and temples, and do other servile work with the minimum of food needed to sustain life. The same remark may be made of the relation of the dwellers in Palestine to the more settled inhabitants of Mesopotamia. Bands of men went out from time to time in search of what they could find, and anything worth taking was legitimate prey, whether person or property. But there is no evidence that any of these bands, since dignified by the name of armies, ever engaged in the work of deporting a whole people. If they wanted workers they would take the able bodied, and kill or leave the rest; while if they wanted women they did not capture them for the sake of providing wives for their slaves. There is absolutely no evidence that any breeding of such slaves, and keeping them in bondage one generation after another, was ever resorted to in these olden times.

It may be boldly assumed that all there is of real history in the Old Testament claiming to apply to any time previous to about 1050 B. C. was taken from the Babylonian records. The book is explicit in its statements about many things that may be presumed to have happened in the Mesopotamian region and in relation to it before the return from the great Babylonish captivity, but tells nothing otherwise that commends itself to a sensible man as worthy of belief in a literal sense. The Bible narrations of happenings to the people alleged to have descended from Abraham and the other patriarchs are no worse than those told of the early beings of Greece, who are treated as demi-gods; but they must be held to stand on the same plane in regard to credibility. It may even be considered probable that if the Jews knew how to write previous to the seventh century they either did not make records of their own history or else that such records were destroyed by the conquerors in obedience to the then universal rule of taking everything of apparent value and burning all the rest or in some other way wiping it out of all recognizable existence. Probably more because of the defilement supposed to result from contact with a corpse than from motives of economy, the Jews were not in the habit of burying with their dead material of value to future generations, and many of the corpses appear not to have been buried at all, while according to their own accounts their temples were systematically looted of every portable thing they contained. They had no other depositing places for records, and a dreary dearth of inscriptions in the land of Judea attests either that they were not made or that they suffered complete obliteration at the hands of the invader. Only two pre-Herodic inscriptions have been found in that region. One of them marked the boundaries of a Levitical "city," the name of which is given by it as "Gezer." The other was found in 1868 at Dibon in the land of Moab. Its thirty-four lines of inscription contained an account of the wars of king Mesha, or Mesa, with Omri of Israel and his successors. The account may be supposed to have been written about 850 B. C. and to relate events some of which occurred more than half a century earlier. It does not agree closely with the story as told at the opening of the Second Book of Kings and in the third chapter of that history; and we are obliged to conclude

that in regard to some important particulars if one
account is the product of infallible inspiration the
other is not true. The characters are those of a
Hebræo-Phenecian alphabet, and the language of
the Moabite stone closely resembled ancient Hebrew.
This is proof that the art of writing Hebrew alpha-
betically was known in that region about the middle of the ninth century B. C. Also we may infer
from the Book of Ruth that less than five centuries
earlier this art was unknown there, since the transfer of a shoe was the only "testimony" to a change
of ownership in a piece of real estate about 1312
B. C. A boundary stone recently discovered in
Babylonia shows that about 1200 B. C. the title to
a piece of real estate was passed by means of the
said stone; the inscription on which tells the boundaries of the land and the names of witnesses.

It is most natural to suppose that the Jews as a
people were densely ignorant down to the middle of
the seventh century B. C.; and that they were so
rated by the men who then expected them to believe that their God had hundreds of times come
down from the clouds to interfere in their own
especial behalf, like the *deus ex machina* of the
Roman plays who always came out from the flies
to disentangle things when they had got badly
mixed up. The Jews may have had traditions,
such as were handed down through successive generations of Indians on this continent previous to
the visit of the white man, and some of them had

assumed a formal shape early in the history of the people. Such were embodied in some of the Psalms ascribed to David, the so-called Proverbs of Solomon, the songs of Miriam and Deborah, the first few chapters of Isaiah, and the stories said to have been written in the Book of Jasher. But there is no proof that a single one of these had been reduced to writing previous to the great Babylonish captivity, and good reason to believe that if written at all it had been in the merest fragmentary form. It is thought by some Bible critics that a portion of Deuteronomy was written in the time of Josiah, about 620 B. C.

Near the beginning of the sixth century Nebuchadnezzar invaded Judea, plundering the temple and the king's residence, and sent the royal family with many other captives to Babylon. In 588 Nebuchadnezzar invaded it a second time, burned the temple, destroyed the walls of the city and its palaces, and carried away "all important or wealthy citizens," among whom was the blinded Zedekiah in chains. But it is not true, as generally supposed, that the country was depopulated; or if so it had been far from so thickly settled as indicated by the historians. The number carried away was but about 200,000, and of these or their descendants only 42,360 embraced the opportunity to return when they got permission to leave after Cyrus had brought the kingdom of Babylon to an end in the year 538 B. C.

Rawlinson assigns as a reason for this permission to return that Cyrus evidently identified the Jehovah of the Israelites with the Persian Ormuzd, "and accepting as a divine command the prophecy of Isaiah, he undertook to rebuild the temple for a people who, like his own, allowed no image of God to defile the sanctuary." Darius similarly encouraged the completion of the work after it had been interrupted by the troubles which followed the death of Cambyses, and "the foundation was thus laid for that friendly intimacy between the two peoples which caused the Jews to continue faithful to Persia to the last." But it should be remarked that the last twenty-seven chapters of the book of that prophet, being those which treat of the victories of Cyrus, the fall of Babylon, and the return to Palestine, are considered by good critics to have been written many years after the death of Isaiah, which is believed to have occurred about 700 years B. C. If not written in Chaldea as a song of gladness after the issuance of the order of release they were probably added by a still later hand. We shall subsequently see reasons for concluding that it was not a Jewish prophecy at all, but one uttered by the Magi of another religion, which made the Persian conqueror eager to release the captives and assist them in preparing for the coming of a promised Messiah of whom the Jews themselves knew nothing till they heard of it in Chaldea.

S

When the exiles got back they found the country well occupied. There had been some mingling, the Samaritans having amalgamated with the older Jewish population, none of whom seem to have been aware that there was such a thing as a Book of the Law in existence, or that it was their duty to keep a Sabbath. They welcomed the exiles home, and met with but a chilly response to their greetings. The new arrivals formed themselves into a holy brotherhood, and finally refused to recognize as brethren any who could not trace their descent from some one of the 200,000 that had been carried away to Babylon. They were wiser than the rest, having learned the wisdom of the Babylonians, and perhaps perused their historical records. They were richer because bearing the treasures of which the country had been despoiled by the army of Nebuchadnezzar. They were holier, in their own estimation at least, because charged by God as well as Cyrus with a mission to rebuild the temple and re-institute the worship of Jehovah, which strangely enough none of those who were left behind seem to have thought it worth while to keep up or revive. Strange that none of the multitude who were permitted to remain in the land should have been grateful for preservation from the evils of slavery, and at least have remembered something about the Law, if too poor to keep up the morning or evening sacrifice. Curious, too, that in all the record which tells minutely of the vessels of gold and silver that were returned after having been carried off, there is no mention of that mysterious ark of the covenant that had been such a priceless treasure up to a few years previously, and for the well intentioned touching of which Uzzah had lost his life so lately as in the reign of King David. Passing strange that the contained tables of the Law, (the pot of Manna, and " Aaron's rod that budded " were said to have been lost earlier), and the gold plated cherubim that rested above the Mercy Seat, should all have vanished like the baseless fabric of a vision, leaving not a wreck behind, if they had ever existed save in the heated imagination of a " prophet " who was equal to reading the past as well as the future. A thousand times more strange is it that no one ever thought of preserving those two broken tables of the Law on which God himself had written his commandments. (Exodus xxxii.) They would be worth millions of dollars to-day if properly authenticated.

These exiles went from home to learn the news about themselves and the rest of mankind. A few of those who " returned," to a land they had never before seen, probably after having been employed about the royal libraries in Babylon, carried with them the recollection of what they had read there and interwove it with stories of their own intended to make it out that the Hebrews were one of the oldest races on the face of the earth instead of being a mere agglomeration of Arabian or Chaldean roving bands. Of course there is nothing impossible in the statement that the first of their people came from the head of the Persian Gulf, though it may well be questioned if the statement would ever have been written but for the fact of the scribes having learned in that vicinity nearly all they knew. But there is absolutely no ground for the story that as a race they were at any time in Egypt, as slaves or otherwise, unless it may be that the Hyksos or Shepherd Kings were of Chaldean origin. Certainly we have no satisfactory proof that there were twelve tribes of Israel in Palestine or elsewhere previous to the time of David, if then; or that there was any such wholesale carrying away in the eighth century as is claimed by the Jews. The deportation previously alluded to seems to have been limited to people who occupied the little tract called Samaria, and it is important to note that neither of the writers of the four Gospels appears to have been aware of any such dispossession north of that area. One of them says that the parents of Jesus lived in Nazareth before he was born, and another that they went there after the return from Egypt because Joseph was warned in a dream (not to go home); but they agree that nearly all the miracles performed by Christ were done in Galilee, most of his life passed there, and the people of that country preached to by him as if they were Jews of the old stock. It may be admitted that according to their story when Christ sent out his disciples he instructed them not to preach to the people of Samaria, but John wrote that He talked to one of them himself and did not dispute her claim to be a descendant of Jacob. There is no occasion for hunting the world over in search of the "Lost Ten." It would be as easy to find the site of the mythical Paradise as to discover the descendants of tribes that never existed save in the imagination of a priestly scribe who wanted to fasten the power of his class upon a people by flattering their vanity.

The better informed among the Jews of the present day are gradually coming round to the conviction that it is not wise to accept as literally true the so-called historical narrations found in the books of Moses, Joshua and Judges. They differ from the "orthodox" in doubting the truth of the story about a veritable *passing over* by their forefathers in the land of Egypt or out of it; and when they are willing to abandon the story as false why should others hesitate to pronounce it untrue? One of their papers, the *Occident*, said in the leading editorial of its issue for April 24, 1891: "Present Egyptologists have deciphered the writings and inscriptions of nearly all Egyptian dynasties, yet none profess to have discovered any edicts, laws or enactments relating to the Jews as serfs or slaves under the reputed Rameses II. Maspero totally ignores the entire account of the slavery of the Jews, as such." And then in the same connection, the writer of the above admits what has been claimed on a preceding page of this work, that the Bible cannot

be dated further back than the return from the Babylonian captivity in the sixth century B. C. He says:
" It is stated by the ablest critics and exegetics that
the Exodus, and in fact the whole five books of
Moses, were written or edited by Ezra, an exile in
Babylonia; who no doubt collected all the legends,
stories and fables of our people many centuries after
the supposed Exodus."

It is true that the last few years have witnessed
a probable identification of Pithom and Rameses,
the two treasure cities claimed to have been built by
the Hebrew slaves, and that a Jewish burying
ground was recently discovered in Egypt.   But the
reference in the book of Exodus to these two cities
may have been a direct consequence of several Jews
being carried from Palestine to Egypt a few score
years before the great Babylonish captivity, and
the cemetery formed the last resting place of Jews
who lived there two or three centuries B. C.

If it be conceded that the Jews of twenty-four
hundred years ago invented the whole story about
passing over the Red Sea dry shod it goes without
saying that there is no necessity for trying to believe that other part of the tale about the destroying
angel " passing over " the whole land of Egypt in
one night and carefully " passing " by every house
which had the blood of the Paschal Lamb sprinkled on
its door posts.   The accounts of the miraculous supply of manna, the brazen serpent in the wilderness,
and the swallowing up of Korah, Dathan and

Abiram with their entire households by an earthquake which spared all the rest, may go for what
they are worth, which is not much. The drinking
of the golden calf in powder (which, according to a
recent idea, would have made the Israelites proof
against the drinking habit had the gold been administered in the form of its chloride), and the
tumbling of the walls of Jericho at the sound of
rams' horns, may equally be relegated to the domain of the fabulous. Of course the poetically
alleged standing still of the sun and moon at the
command of Joshua need no longer be a stumbling
block in the way of the devoutly disposed student
of astronomy. With this vanishes the Garden of
Eden story, and that of the flood; while the Christian will no longer feel obliged to believe that the
God he worships is such a demon as represented
by the writers of the so-called " historical " books
of the Old Testament, who had been partly brutal-
ized by a long captivity in a strange land. One is
not compelled to think that the Jews of the olden
time were such infernal brutes as their own "sacred"
books made them out to be, nor to blaspheme by
ascribing to the Almighty attributes and acts of
which any other being than the devil himself might
well be ashamed.

It is highly probable that everything related of
the history of the Jews previous to the time of
David is purely traditional, and most of it not entitled to a shadow of credence. He seems to have

acted about B. C. 1055 much as the founders of Rome are said to have done some three centuries later. He gathered from different parts of a comparatively peaceful land about four hundred men. In I Sam. xxii. 2, it is expressly said that this band was mostly composed of fellows who were in debt or otherwise discontented. Three or four years later the number had increased to only about six hundred, and Chap. xxv of the same Book shows that they lived by plunder, though assuming credit for having protected the property of Nabal from the depredations of other marauders. Becoming stronger by fresh accessions from the vagabond class he established himself in Hebron, from which place he lorded it over the surrounding country. At that time there was no Jerusalem, in the later sense of the word, though the site was said to have been previously occupied by the Jebusites (not claimed to have been one of the Twelve Tribes), and doubtless its " Rock Zion " had often formed a rallying place for defense by small bands of armed men under the little kings of those days when they suddenly found themselves in the presence of a superior force in its neighborhood. The story about David being anointed by Samuel may be true; but it proves nothing except that a medicine man in one of the parties or "tribes" had an ax to grind and pulled the wool over the eyes of a few dozen people, leaving David to do the rest after having given him a good start. Succeeding in being recognized as the biggest man within

an area of a few score square miles David removed
his headquarters eighteen miles further north, to
Zion, and there gradually built around him and his
companion land pirates the city of Jerusalem as he
was able to pay for its construction by levying contributions upon the people whom he brought under
subjection still further to the northward.   His followers may have been divided off into ten or a dozen
bands, more or less, under subordinate captains;
and these may have had assigned to them as many
different portions of the land when they concluded
it was time to settle down after having made themselves masters of it.   And there would be the
origin of the tribes, bound together simply by a
rope of sand, and ready to fight among one another
when no longer held in check by the strong hand of
David.   The story of Solomon is probably one of
those pleasant fibs with which many of the writers
of past ages were wont to fill in gaps that it was not
seemly to leave blank, and it is by no means certain
that his magnificent temple was anything more substantial than " the baseless fabric of a vision," unless indeed the description is that of the temple at
Sippara which was unearthed in 1881.   It corresponds to that with a startling degree of fidelity.
It has been pointed out by Mr. St. Chad Boscawen
that the internal arrangement and even the names
of the different portions of the Sippara temple were
identical with those claimed for the alleged Solomon structure, even to the veil which separated the

Holy Place from the Holy of Holies. As for all that is alleged to have preceded the time of David it may be dismissed in short order as unworthy of credence. We may admire the ingenuity of the narrator who was not hampered by the regard for scientific possibility that limits the efforts of writers now-a-days, but we cannot believe him. The wandering for forty years in the wilderness, supported by a daily miraculous fall of manna, is too tough a story to be swallowed in our day; also those of the passages of the Red Sea and the Jordan as direct results of divine interposition in behalf of a self-confessed band of plunderers. The tales of Joshua and his ram's horns, Gideon and his fleece, and Shimshon, with his locks, may not shock the intelligence so much as the narration of the feat of the first named in causing the sun and moon to stand still ever so long while he and the hailstones mowed down his enemies, but are no more worthy of credence. Does any sane man of to-day believe that the earth opened and swallowed up Korah, Dathan and Abiram, with their families at a signal from Moses, that Aaron ever made the children of Israel drink the golden calf after it had been ground to powder and strewn in water, that the theft by Achan was actually discovered by lot, or that Samuel chose out first Saul and then David at the express command of God, to rule over the people? If he does he must be sane on all subjects save that one, and on that in a state of mental darkness unworthy of any being above the intellectual condition of the veriest savage ever discovered in modern times.

No. All that belongs to the domain of the unbelievable; and is of no more value, considered as historical narrative, than are the stories of Aladdin and his wonderful lamp. But when we come to the rule of David we strike different ground. He established order and built cities. He instituted government in place of the condition so often described in the book of Judges: "There was then no king in Israel, but every man did that which was right in the sight of his own eyes." David numbered the people (and for that act incurred the displeasure of his God, though if the stories be true the same thing had been done with Divine approval many times previously). David found out how many fighting men he had got, and was then able to calculate the chances of victory in future wars, not by reference to heavenly aid but on the Napoleonic theory of most power to the strongest battalions. Here is the first cropping up of common sense in the alleged history of the Jews, and, therefore, about the first thing that can be accepted as historical. The idea that it made any difference to the people whether Balaam cursed them or not, or that the strength of Samson resided altogether in his locks, belongs to the same order of thought with that which could accept as literal the story of Achilles and his vulnerable heel.

The Mosaic story is equally incredible in regard to its laws and customs, alleged to have been estab-

lished by direct command of God. There is absolutely no trace of any such thing as a year of
Jubilee ever having been observed by the Jews,
and it is admitted by Ezra that they had never
dwelt in booths during the whole time they had
lived in Judea, though the law of Moses required
them to do so once in every year. It has previously
been intimated we do not know that there was ever
such a man as Solomon, King of Israel, or that he
built a wonderful temple ascribed to him. It may
be added that it is pretty certain the books with the
writing of which he is credited did not exist till several centuries after the time he is said to have lived.
Dr. Cox is confident he has furnished satisfactory
proof that the book of Ecclesiastes was addressed to
the Jews who acknowledged Persian supremacy.
That is, it was written after the second Isaiah instead
of antedating the first Isaiah by some centuries.
This section may appropriately be closed by recom-
mending the reader to a patient perusal of II Esdras,
Chap. xiv, with the remark that the book in question long rated as the fourth book of Ezra, Nehe-
miah being the second of the series. There is
scarcely the shadow of a doubt as to that chapter
telling the story of the writing of the books in the
Old Testament, the "seventy" including several
that were suppressed because they would have taxed
too severely the credulity of the reader.

VII

THE FIRST GODS.

The Most Ancient Religions.—The Stars Were the First Objects Worshipped.—Tzabaism.—Egyptian, Chaldean and Bactrian Theologies.—Evolution in Creed.—Planetary Dominion.—It was Superior even to that of the Luminaries.—Plurality of the Elohim.—Fights Between Worshippers of Different Gods.—Jewish Allegiance to Jupiter; then to the Sun.

It is generally admitted that astronomy, the science which is essentially a knowledge of the laws of celestial motion, originated in a study of the stars for purposes of astrological prediction. A belief in the influences of the planets over human beings and their surroundings not only preceded but directly led up to that close watch on the movements of the planets as they seemed to change place among the stars which has resulted in the brilliant astronomical discoveries made during the last four centuries. That belief was the legitimate ancestor, the first parent, of the large family of facts and principles a knowledge of which has been given to the world by the labors of Copernicus, Tycho. Kepler, Galileo, Newton, and the host of others who followed those illustrious men in the field of stellar research. The formulating and applying of the law of attraction,

and the art of spectrum analysis, have sprung from
it as really as the branches of a tree from its root.

This truth has been practically admitted from
thousands of pulpits, the occupants of which were
equally ready to denounce the study of astrology as
an egregious folly and its practice as a heinous sin,
without being aware that this early study of the
stars was in like manner the parent of religion.
There is a purely devotional feeling which, apart
from any fear of punishment, leads the individual
to think of a higher power that is worthy of reverence; and this seems to be an integral part of the
human mentality, equally engrained in the breast of
the most highly cultured philosopher and the most
ignorant savage, though the mode of expressing it
may exhibit a vast range of diversity in form and
character. But the worship of a visible object or a
supposed unseen entity with reference to consequences, the theory of influence on the affairs of
men, the idea of superior interposition to be obtained
or averted by prayer or the self-denial of sacrifice,
the definiteness of creed binding which is the essential part of theology, and the terrors of future punishment by which the priests of all ages and climes
have striven to enslave the multitude, had their
primary inception in watching the apparent movements of the stars, fixed, wandering or falling. Of
course it is not here intended to intimate a suspicion
that the churches of our day teach and believe nothing but what has been tortuously derived from the

star lore which was delved out in the comparative childhood of the race. This would be no more justifiable than the claim that the alchemists of a few centuries ago believed in substance all that is now known by the chemists, or that the geometry of Euclid included all the reasoning of the calculus. But it is undeniable that astrology was for many ages practiced and cultivated only by the priests for the express purpose of enabling them to dominate the people, and that the star lore of the remote past forms the root and trunk of the great religious tree of our own day, the original stem having been grafted upon again and again by many a pseudo revelation, and perhaps by one that is true.

These remarks should not be construed as attacking the Christian religion, either Catholic or Protestant. The writer is neither assailing nor defending it, as a whole; though some of its features may be shown to be inconsistent with both reason and fact. But for the sake of perspicuity he avows here his conviction, arrived at after a long and painstaking study of the Old Testament, partly in the original Hebrew, that the book is not an inspired production as a whole, and is not in any sense of the word a revelation from the God whom Christians profess to worship. Originality of idea, high order of thought, and great beauty of expression are found there; but these are not infallible marks of divine inspiration, especially not when found to be lacking as guarantees for accuracy of statement.

And the Jehovah of that volume is most emphatically the God of the Jews only.   They have a tradition that the law was first offered to the whole world;
but that when rejected by the race it was then given
only to a peculiar people, who alone are bound by
its requirements and promised reward for obedience
to it.   None others have a right to expect from him
anything but wrath and punishment.   The Jews
were his children, and all the rest aliens, incapable
of becoming members of the royal family; nor could
they enter the kingdom in early times except as
slaves.   In this respect, and in the character of the
motives and acts ascribed to him by his worshippers,
he occupies a position no higher than that claimed
by other nations of antiquity for their deities.

We have indubitable proof that the worship of the
heavenly bodies' as gods prevailed in very early
times in Western Asia.   Arabian historians refer to
it as the oldest religion in the world, and it can be
traced to the foundation of religious belief among
all the nations which have a sufficiently long history;
those of more recently formed peoples being plainly
derivative from the earlier ones.   According to one
tradition this star worship was handed down by
Enoch, and another refers it to Sabai, son of Seth,
who was a son of Adam, while an oft quoted Jewish
writer tells that Seth caused the principles of the
science to be engraved on two pillars, one of which
was still standing in the lifetime of the historian.
The name Sabai, variously written as Tzaba and

Tzeba in Arabic and Hebrew, means "to rise in splendor," as a star; whence the Hebrew *Tzabaoth*, "the heavenly host." The very earliest religion in Mesopotamia was astral, though Rawlinson thinks it is doubtful whether some of the gods are of astronomical origin and not rather primitive deities, whose characters and attributes were to a great extent fixed and determined before the notion arose of connecting them with "certain parts of nature." But he admits that the heaven itself, the sun, the moon and the five planets, have each their representative in the Chaldean Pantheon among the chief objects of worship. Also he calls particular attention to the striking resemblance of the classical mythology of Greece and Rome to the Chaldean system as too general and too close to allow of the supposition that the coincidence is a mere accident. He says there must have been a communication of beliefs, a passage of mythological notions and ideas, in very early times from the shores of the Persian Gulf to the lands washed by the Mediterranean. He notes it as a probable conjecture that among the primitive tribes who dwelt on the banks of the Tigris and Euphrates, when the cuneiform alphabet was invented and when such a writing was first applied to the purposes of religion, there existed a Scythic or Scytho-Aryan race, These people subsequently migrated to Europe, and took with them those mythical traditions which as objects of popular belief had been mixed up in the nascent literature of their

9

native country; and these traditions were passed on to the classical nations who were in part descended from this Scythic or Scytho-Aryan stock.

It will be interesting to glance briefly at the three oldest among the now accessible forms of religious thought and belief, namely the Egyptian, Chaldean and Bactrian. All the rest are modern in comparison with these, Confucius in China dating only from 551 B. C. and the Cingalese count places Buddha eight years later than the great Chinaman, while the oldest of the Vedas are not entitled to be dated further back than some of the Psalms " of David," and like them are mere hymns of a more or less descriptive character.

In the earliest ages of which there is a theological trace, the Egyptians appear to have recognized only one God. This Being was believed to have had no beginning and to have no end. He made all things, without having been himself brought into existence by any agency. The oldest temples, some of which were discovered by Mariette near the pyramids, contained no idols or sculptures. In the course of time the people began to worship the symbols under which the attributes of the Deity were represented, and out of this grew idolatry and polytheism, though some of the priests retained to the last a belief in one God, and taught that doctrine to a select few. The principal gods were Osiris and Isis his wife, who with their daughter Horus formed the most popular triad or trinity in the Egyptian mythology. Osiris was the son of Seb, (time, the equivalent of the Greek Chronos,) and the originator of human civilization, while Isis was adored as the great benefactress who had instructed the people in the art of cultivating wheat and barley. Her worship was subsequently introduced into Greece and Rome. Osiris was slain by Set or Sutekh, the Evil one; and descended to the infernal regions, where he took the name of Serapis, and sits in the hall of double judgment to determine the eternal fate of the souls of the dead. The Egyptians thus believed in a future state of existence, which is not distinctly taught in any part of the Old Testament. They held that the spirits of the good would dwell with the gods, and the wicked in fiery torment amid perpetual darkness. Also they believed that after the lapse of many ages the soul would return to the body, for which reason they embalmed the corpse. The mummies of his ancestors could be pledged by a borrower as security for the payment of a debt, and if he failed to redeem them he was cut off from the privilege of burial.

While Osiris and Isis were worshipped throughout Egypt, Amen or Ammon, called "The King of Gods," was the especial tutelary deity of Thebes. Num, or Knuphis, was the god of the cataracts and oases. In later times he was called Ammon by the Romans, who considered him to be the same as Jupiter. His wife Salé corresponded to Juno. Ptah, worshipped at Memphis, symbolized the creative power, Khem, the generative principle, and Maut the maternal principle. Other goddesses were Nepté, the sky wife of Seb, Neith, corresponding to Minerva, and Pasht, the probable original of the Artemis and Diana of the Greeks and Romans. Seb was also supposed to represent the earth, and was called the father of the gods, while Ra or Phrah was the sun, or sun-god.

Ra, or Il, stood at the head of the Chaldean Pantheon. Little is known of him, but it is remarkable that his second name may be identified with the Hebrew El, and its plural derivative Elohim. Next to him in the ancient theology of lower Mesopotamia was a triad, Anu, Bil, (or Belus,) and Hea, (or Hoa,) each accompanied by a female principle, or wife. The male trinity corresponds rather closely to the classical Pluto, Jupiter, and Neptune. Then follows another triad consisting of Sin, (or Hurki,) San, (or Sansi,) and Vul; these being gods of the moon, sun and atmosphere, and each having a wife. Next in order to these Rawlinson places the representatives of the five planets, namely, Nin, (or Ninip,) Merodach, Nergal, Ishtar, and Nebo; corresponding respectively to Saturn, Jupiter, Mars, Venus and Mercury. He claims these as minor deities, though constituting with those previously named a first or principal class, which is followed by a rather large number of gods of the second and third order. He says Bil or Bilu is "Lord" in the Assyrian and Shemitic Babylonian, while Enu is the corresponding Cushite or Hamitic term. Then the

Il-Enu of Damascius means "The Lord Enu," and this is usually followed by a qualificative adjunct which may be read as "Nipru," or in the feminine "Niprut," which recalls the scriptural Nimrod, he being termed "Nebroth" in the Septuagint. If this is formed from the Syriac Napar, meaning "to pursue," it may be aptly translated as "The hunter lord," or he who presides over the chase; from which it may be concluded that there was in the Chaldean religion an admixture of hero worship. Rawlinson also hints at a possible identification of Hea or Hoa with the Greek On, (the O is long,) of Helladius, the name given to the mystic animal, half man and half fish, which came up from the Persian Gulf to teach astronomy and letters to the first settlers on the banks of the Euphrates and Tigris. The name Oannes, given to this creature by Berosus, may be explained as "Hoa-Ana," or the God Hoa. As this sea god was one of the principal objects of veneration in Chaldea it may be inferred that Berosus preserved an authentic tradition where he makes the primitive people of that country to have derived their arts and civilization (as well as their religion) from the "Red Sea." It has been thought possible to connect the word Hea with the Arabic Hiya, which means both "life" and a "serpent:" since "according to the best authority there are very strong grounds for connecting Hea or Hoa with the serpent of Scripture and the tradition of the trees of knowledge and of life in Paradise."

The Bactrian Zoroaster, (properly Zarathustra,) taught previous to 1200 B. C. His country was conquered by the Assyrians about that date, and his writings contain no intimation of the existence of Assyrians, Medes, Persians or any other nation dwelling in or near the western parts of Iran. The Assyrians conquered Bactria without appropriating the religion of Zarathustra, but it seems to have been adopted by the Medes and from them by the Persians. He taught the worship of one god, Ormuzd, who sprang from eternal light, which in turn was evolved from an incomprehensible being Zeruane Akerene, or Zyrvan Akarana (time without limit, or eternity). It is said the Bactrian teacher held that from the primeval light sprang twins named Ormuzd and Ahriman, that the latter became jealous of his elder brother, and was condemned by the eternal one to pass 3,000 years in a region of utter darkness. But there is some reason to think that Ahriman was a later importation into the creed, he being identified with the Turanian Afrusiab. It is considered probable that as the Turanians formed a large part of the population of Media the Magi, (great ones,) or priests, combined the two in order to render the worship more acceptable to the aborigines, and in this shape the religion was introduced into Persia. It was there called the Mazdean, from Ahura Mazda, the Persian name for Ormuzd. It is not difficult to trace a strong similarity between the story of the origin of Ormuzd and the Genesis account of the creation, to see that he and Ahriman were before the mental eyes of the man who wrote the book of Job, or to understand that the Ahriman story contributed no small amount of the material embodied in Milton's Paradise Lost.

It may be remarked that the fragmentary knowledge obtainable from two out of these three sources points to a very early conception of one great Being, to whom was opposed another of nearly equal power, and perhaps equally entitled to be called "Eternal." But these statements do not necessarily contain anything antagonistic to the theory that the celestial wanderers now called planets were the first objects of worship. All that we have gleaned in regard to these three ancient religions is formulated into system, and there is room back of it in the order of time for a much more primitive kind of thought. There is a tendency in the evolution of theology to level up as well as down, even among the most degraded races; to develop ideas of both heaven and hell; of a greater God and a worse devil than those previously defined by the priests. The Trinity of Egypt and Chaldea may at first have been but a mere symbolization of the fact that the movements of the moon and sun with reference to the earth seemed to govern the march of the seasons for work as well as worship, and the conception of one Being supreme over all the rest would naturally follow from the concentration of earthly power in the hands of one king or chief whose word was law to all the rest of the tribe. But this is evidently a derivative thought, and its acceptance in a formal system of theology simply points us back to an anterior conception by human beings who had yet to learn what it was for thousands to be subject to the will of one earth despot. Such a concentration of power would hardly be possible till after the arts had so far progressed as to permit the accumulation of wealth, (food reserves in the first place,) to be guarded by one party or sought to be forcibly taken by another; and that phase of human existence involves the attainment of a rather high degree of civilization as counted upward from the primeval mud. The later Jewish idea that there is one God above all the rest — a God of gods — may seem a simple thing to one who sees the type of such a being in the central body of the solar system. But it was a most important advance in religious logic, and the parallel a difficult one to draw when the earth was supposed to be incomparably the greatest object in the universe, with the sun but a few yards in diameter and separated from us by less than four hundred miles. Indeed, that conception of one God is so high that the orthodox Christian churches of this century cannot accept it in its simple grandeur. They cling fast to the old Egyptian and Chaldean notion of a Triune Deity.

In the infancy of purely human thought the stars were regarded as intelligences; and the planets, (wanderers), moving among them apparently subject to no law but that of their own will, were gods. The shooting stars were the messengers of the gods, carrying their orders from one part of heaven to another, and occasionally bringing them to earth. A stone believed to have fallen from the skies was regarded with the greatest reverence even at a comparatively late date, and we find it preserved as a hallowed object in one of the Grecian temples. The stars we now call fixed were supposed to surround and perhaps form the thrones of the gods, and to take little interest in the affairs of mortals except when detailed as messengers. Some of them were thought to be at times hurled as thunder-bolts by the hand of Jove, but the idea that a host of them fell from heaven into a bottomless pit, there to become eternal enemies of the human race, is comparatively a modern one. It forms the basis of the story exquisitely re-written by Milton from the pagan classics, with a smaller draft on the Hebrew Scriptures.

The sun and moon were not at first looked upon as deities, since it was easily ascertained that to a crude observer their apparent motions were regular. The two luminaries always seemed to move in one direction among the stars, while the other (five) planets were sometimes retrograding and at others moving direct, with no discovered reason for their changes of direction or place. And in consonance with this idea we find the most ancient of the astrological aphorisms noting the sun and moon as " sig-

nificators " representing the individual or thing under consideration, which was supposed to be "ad-
fected " according to the different ways in which
the luminaries were aspected by the planets as
"promittors." Strong traces of this are preserved
in so much of the Grecian mythology as has come
down through the ages to us, though its accounts
belong to what we may call the Pleistocene era of
astrological thought, in which the earlier inorganic
strata had been built up to form personal organisms. Thus, Apollo (of the sun) ranked among the
gods, but he was far inferior in power to the pon-
derous Jupiter, (Zeus Pater, the father god), and
to Saturn before the latter was deposed from the
throne by his Jov-ial offspring; while Diana, the
goddess. of the moon, did not compare in importance
with Venus, or even with Juno except at a disad-
vantage.

" *B'reshith bara Elohim* " are the three first words
of the Hebrew Bible. The third is in the plural
form. It is translated " God," but incorrectly, as
every Hebrew scholar well knows. He may not
feel quite sure as to what would be the proper equivalent, but he knows it is not *that*. It is impossible
to deny that the word should be understood to mean
more than one, though no number is stated. It may
mean a trinity for aught the word tells to the contrary. But it does not. It simply means a company of Gods, who made the heavens for their own
abiding place, and the earth for man to dwell on.

They made the sun and moon, and "the stars also," the latter forming the asterisms from one to the other of which the planets move as the Elohim Tzabaoth, or lords of the host of heaven. That is what the planets were, to the early Shemitic fancy, and their supposed work is told in the first chapter of Genesis and the first three verses of the second. Then begins a coupling of Jehovah with Elohim. The compound is absurdly translated "Lord God," when it should really be read as designating a Being who is the chief of those planetary gods. This change is all the more significant as constituting the first paragraph in an extended history; as the first few books of the Old Testament are little more than a recount of the struggle by Jovè or Jahveh for pre-eminence, and the sufferings of those poor mortals who did not recognize his claims to superiority. They are largely narrations of the fights made by his worshippers to force others to acknowledge him to be a greater personage than Ashtoreth, Moloch and Baal, which were but other names for Venus, Saturn and the sun. The arrangement was not strictly a fair one, if the alleged record is to be trusted; since when the soldiers of Jahveh were beaten, which was not seldom, it was said to be their own fault, and when victorious they were required to give him all the glory. Occasionally we meet with a concealed hint of an alliance between the gods as well as their peoples. For instance: a conflict between Jupiter (who according to the astrolo-

gers rules tin, and therefore bronze), and Mars, the
god of iron, is alluded to in Judges i. 19; and it
would seem that Jahveh or Yahevah sided with one
of the parties.   It is stated that he was with Ya-
hoodah, and he drave out the inhabitants of the
mountains, but could not dislodge the inhabitants of
the valleys because the latter had chariots (and
weapons), made of iron.   There is, however, some
reason to think that for a long course of ages this
Jupiter, or Yupiter, the largest of all the planets,
was himself the Yahveh of the Jews;—that he was
their acknowledged leader because chief of the Elohim of planets, as indicated in the opening of the
"Phenomena" of the Greek poet Aratus, the fifth
line in which poem was very unfairly quoted from
by St. Paul in his sermon on Mars' Hill.   The
passage is in Acts xvii. 28, and reads in the Greek
Tou gar kai genos esmen, which in the English Bible
is translated to read "For we also are his offspring."
This with its context may be literally rendered:

> All of us everywhere have need of Jupiter,
> For we spring from him.   He kindly towards men
> Points out the things which are for their good, and makes the
>   people to work,
> Putting them in mind of the need of subsistence.

It may be remarked that this language of Aratus,
thus appropriated by Paul to the God whom *he*
wished the Athenians to worship, embodies a noble
conception of the value of labor which contrasts
forcibly with the Mosaic account of the Fall, where

it is treated as a curse, not a blessing. But we can readily understand the reason for the latter view when we remember that whether written by Moses after an escape from Egyptian bondage or by Ezra after the return from Babylon it was addressed to people who were still smarting from the lash of the taskmaster.

There is no reasonable doubt that the early Jews, as well as the Greeks who lived in the time of Aratus (about 270 B. C.), were worshippers of Jupiter; and the Hebrew transition from his worship to that of the greater God of whom Elijah, (Eli-Yah, the sun god) was the distinctive prophet though preceded by Samson (Shimshon, son of the sun), was a later movement. And it marked as we have already stated a most important advance in the history of philosophic thought, which was in keeping with the concentration of a few scattered Ishmael-itish tribes into one Israelitish people. Almost coincidently with that change the Eberim (Hebrews, sons of Eber, and Eberahim), took a leading place among the nations of Western Asia. They held it till in the mental degeneration of prosperity they became again Yah-vees, Yehoodim, Yahoos or Yoos, (the *V* and *Oo* sounds are interchangeable in Hebrew), and sank back to a subordinate position with only the hope of a *Messi-Yah* in the shape of a sunbeam to elevate them again to the first rank.

VIII

TIMES AND SEASONS.

" Wherefore wilt thou go to him to-day? It is neither new moon nor Sabbath."—II. Kings.

The Week and the Planets.—Ancient Day Namings.—Babylonian Week and Lunar Month.—Irregular Sabbath Intervals.—The Creation; As Told in Genesis it was the Work of Planetary Gods.—The Sabbath a Comparatively Modern Institution, and not Exclusively Jewish in Origin.—It was named after Saturn.—The Sunday Question.—Babylonian Legend of the Creation. ·

There can be no doubt that at a very early time, as measured by the short rod of written history, the week of seven days was formed by reference to the seven moving objects in the heavens. The days of the week are named after them, not only in the Saxon, and thence in English, but in the Latin and other tongues derived from it, still further back in the oldest written Sanscrit, with others of the most ancient languages that have been preserved to us in fragmentary fashion by word elements distributed through more modern vocabularies. The Hindoo, Egyptian and Hebrew week would appear to have originated by independent authority in each case and yet to have been formed on the same basic idea, since their weeks began with Friday, Saturday and Sunday respectively. The week was not adopted

by the Greeks and Romans till after the introduction of Christianity. Then they accepted it easily
enough, as it commended itself to them by being
nearly an aliquot part both of the lunar month and
the year. It is now in use among all the Christian
nations and Mohammedans. It was in use in an
irregular way among the Babylonians some 2,500
years ago. They observed as Sabbaths the seventh,
fourteenth, nineteenth, twenty-first and twenty-
eighth days of each lunar month — the "week"
connecting two consecutive months thus consisting
of eight or nine days, according as the first month
of the pair was a short or a long one, while the
third period of seven days in each month had a
Sabbath near its middle. The regular count of fifty-
two weeks of seven days each in three hundred and
sixty-four days appears to have been an after
thought. The ancient Egyptians had a week of
ten days. The Chinese are the only important
people who now employ a week of other than seven
days. They use a five day group, seventy-three of
which groups are contained in one day less than a
common year, and this mode of reckoning was introduced among them long before the Christian era.
Josephus, Philo, Clement of Alexandria, and others
refer to the week of seven days as not of Hebrew
origin, but common to all the oriental (Shemitic)
nations. This is directly opposed to the statement
in Deut. v. 15, that the Jews were commanded to
observe the Sabbath Day because they had been

brought out of the bondage of Egypt; but it harmonizes with the reason given in Exodus xx. 11, that the seventh day was hallowed because on that day God rested from the work of creation.

Yet no discovered antiquity of naming, nor the fact that the Genesis story of creation, when properly read, is found to be a statement of the work done in the first week by the planets or their lords, warrants us in assigning the formation of the week of seven days to a time that is early in the real history of the race. On the contrary, it must be of comparatively recent origin. It required a long period of observation to discover and identify the most fugitive one of the lot. Man could not have attentively watched the movements of the planets from the valley of the Nile or the Plains of Shinar, the pyramid of Ghizeh or the temple of Jupiter Belus, or elsewhere without recognizing before the lapse of many years that Venus was one and the same planet, alternately appearing as a morning and evening star. Yet that she was at one time regarded as two distinct bodies, at least by the common people and the poets or prophets, may be inferred from the fact that she was called by two different names, as the Phosphor and Hesperia of the Greek. Possibly the then recent discovery that it was one and the same planet which alternately rose before the sun and set after him at intervals of a few months, was alluded to by the first writer of the sentence (Isaiah xiv. 12), "How art

thou fallen from Heaven, O Lucifer (phosphor or
light bearer), Son of the morning." But we have
good reason to believe that this knowledge must
have long preceded the identification of Mercury as
the body which is alternately visible for a few minutes at once after sunset and before sunrise, and at
much more irregular intervals than Venus; which
fact we now know to be due to the great eccentricity of his orbit. We may regard it as very probable that some centuries must have elapsed after the
identification of Venus in her two stations ere the
appearances of Mercury on either side of the sun
were supposed to be in any sense periodical. Till
then he could not have been in the estimation of
mortal observers a regular member of the planetary
god group; and it is no wonder that after having
been ranked among the planets he was described by
words signifying the dodger, the nimble one, the
furtive one or thief, and from his sudden dartings
in and out of obscurity in the solar beams have
been thought to be the occasional messenger of the
bigger gods.

Previous to that identification of Mercury the
number of bodies alluded to as planets, including
the luminaries, could not have been more than six,
the week of seven days was unthought of, and the
story of a creation in seven days or one complete
week may well be supposed to have been impossible.
But how much of a reflection of the later planetary
theory is contained in that statement! The five

10

bodies known previous to the discovery of Uranus in 1781, and which are now called planets, were the great powers that summoned into being all else. They created light the first day, without the aid of a sun or a moon. The second day they caused the waters to collect from the previously chaotic mass; and the moon (ruling Moon-day) is well known to have been anciently considered the patroness of water and those who navigate the ocean. On the third day the dry land appeared, being evolved by the retiring or shrinking of the waters, and Tuesday is named after Mars (*Tuisco*) which is the planet described by the astrologers as hot and dry in his nature and influence. On the fourth day the sun, moon and (fixed) stars were created, according to the Mosaic account; which we may conceive to be only a hieratic way of telling that those objects were then for the first time rendered visible from the earth (had any one been here to observe them), because of the clearing atmosphere. This was the especial work of Mercury (who rules Woden's day), as he is visible only when the sky is clear well down towards the horizon. On the fifth (Thor's Day), Jupiter made the fishes and the birds. The sixth was under the especial rule of Venus (it is Friga Day), who then made reptiles and the mammalia, including man. The seventh was the resting day, or *Sh'bo'th*, and Saturn was called in the Hebrew *Sh'b'th;* the inverted commas in these words indicating the places of vowels, which is all that is now really known about it, as the written vocalization of Hebrew words was not perfected till many years after the ancient tongue had ceased to be a spoken one. Here again we are confronted by a comparatively modern fact. The arrangement of the planets in this seemingly arbitrary fashion, neither according to actual distance nor ocular prominence, was consequent on a division of day and night into twelve planetary hours each; and the seven times twenty-four of such hours in the week were named after the seven "planets" taken in their natural order, in much the same manner as the Dominical letters in the alphabet are applied to the days of the month now. This brought the first hour after sunrise under the dominion of the planet named as ruling the whole of that day. But this distribution was not possible till after considerable progress had been made in the study of the celestial motions; and, not to dwell too long on what may seem a comparatively unimportant point, we must conclude that the week of seven days, and the story of a seven days creation, were not adopted till after the invention of the sun dial and the clepsydra or water clock.

Just how far back the use of those things dates we do not know. But the earliest mention of either is the sun dial of Ahaz, at about 700 B. C. And the writer of II Kings xx. 11, could not have understood very well the use of the instrument, or he would never have committed the Lord to that impossible retrogradation of the shadow through ten degrees in response to the prayer of Isaiah. The Melancholy Jacques might have laughed an hour by such a dial for about a hundred minutes if the scripture scribe told the truth; which he did not; though the same story is told later on in the volume, and the Good Book says that out of the mouths of two witnesses shall every word be established. No recognizable vestige of a sun dial has been found among the ruins of Egypt or Mesopotamia, but it has been suggested as possible that the numerous obelisks in the valley of the Nile were used as time pieces, the direction of the shadow showing the hour. The balance of negative testimony is in favor of the supposition that up to within a very few centuries of the Christian era the most observant people did not care to note the divisions of time other than sunrise, noon (when the shadow was due north), and sunset: except as the night was divided into watches by the crowing of the rooster. About 400 B. C. the water clock came into use in Egypt, and was afterwards introduced into Greece and Rome, where it was employed to measure the flights of oratory in the courts and for other purposes. It seems probable that the week of seven days was not known till after the middle of the eighth century B. C. Previous to that time the month was divided into halves or thirds.

And why was Saturn called the resting planet? For the simple yet sufficient reason that he was the laggard of the skies, as he still is to naked eye observers except the very few who know how to "pick up" Uranus when he is not far from opposition to the sun. Chatterton alludes to this fact in his well known lines:

> But farther still the tardy Saturn lags.
> And six attendant luminaries drags.

(We now know he has eight satellites.) The most slow moving of all those with which the ancients were acquainted, he shifts his position among the fixed stars so very slowly as to require close watching in order to be sure that he changes place at all during many nights in succession. Another prominent fact about this planet is suggested by one of the names given him by the Greeks. They called him Chronos, or "Time," doubtless for the reason that he was found to occupy twenty-nine and a half years in making a single circuit of the heavens, and that is the exact number of days in an average synodical lunation. Can it now be deemed strange that the idea has found a place in the Bible, in the shape of an allowance of a year for each day in the computation of prophetic time? There is absolutely no discoverable reason for the analogy other than the coincidence of that count with the relation of the earth's period of revolution to that of rotation on her axis, though the ancients did not know enough to be able to state the latter ratio in the terms here employed. And it is the very rule used by the astrologers in the "casting of nativities" from time immemorial down to the present day. It was familiar to the writer of the Book of Daniel, as to Ptolemy who lays it down at sufficient length in his Tetrabiblos.

Comparatively few people are aware that the observance of Sunday was not obligatory in the Christian churches till the early part of the fourth century, being one of the changes introduced by Constantine the Great in pursuance of his design to effect a wider separation between the church and the Jewish and pagan usages than had existed up to his time. Every reference in the New Testament to a Sabbath is to the Jewish one, which was kept on Saturday; and there is in no part of the book a commandment to observe any other day as the Sabbath. But fewer still know that there is absolutely no trace of that or any other Sabbath having been observed by the Jews as an occasion for special worship previous to the exile, and it may well be suspected from what has been adduced in our sixth chapter that the people of Palestine took no sort of cognizance of such a day till it was impressed upon their attention by the returned Babylonian captives. It is fair to presume that even the most orthodox Jew would not dare to claim it was observed before the exodus; so that the idea of its having been continuously handed down without error in the count from the time of the creation may well be dismissed as an idle one, apart from the planetary facts previously noted, which render it impossible.

It necessarily follows that there is nothing either in Nature or Revelation to make any given day in the week more sacred than another, except as some man may have chosen to so order it, and as others may attach undue importance to the selection. There is the best of reason for believing that the setting apart of one day in seven for rest, recreation and worship by those who are devotionally inclined is a highly beneficial arrangement, tending to prolong life as well as to render it more enjoyable. And the Jews as a people are entitled to the credit of introducing this desirable feature. But the stickling for Saturday by the more orthodox of their number and a few so-called Christian sects, while all others around them are observing Sunday, is an indefensible absurdity. It has not a single valid argument in its favor.

The writer of Genesis and Exodus tells us that the world on which we live, and the universe of which our earth is but a part, were all created in six days, each limited by a morning and an evening. He may have been "inspired" in some way, for aught we know to the contrary, but not in a manner or to a sufficient extent to enable him to describe the process correctly. We may be sure of that. He was ignorant of the revelation by geological science that the work of creation has occupied many millions of years in the past, is not yet ended, and has not been arrested for a moment. He was totally unaware that every one of the shining objects we see

in the sky, with many millions more that we can
never hope to discern even with the aid of the telescope, is a world of itself, having a separate history
of its own not only in space but in time.   He did
not know that while some of those worlds are in
process of formation and being fitted for the residence of living beings others are dying out, some
losing their identity by falling into others, and all
parts of a grand system which has no such dating
point of beginning as stated in the Pentateuch.   He
did not know that in this universe of worlds the individual member has its own phases of formation,
growth, maturity and decay, which with the larger
ones occupies a period of many millions of years,
and for the smaller may be passed through in a few
centuries.   And he made an especially bad blunder
in the case of the moon, which at the time he assigned for her formation had actually passed
through and beyond the phase of capability for supporting animated existence on her surface, and
become a " died out world."   Of course he was
not to blame for lack of acquaintance with these
facts, since they are included in a kind of knowledge that has been permitted to man only within
the last few years.   Had he known more he would
have written less;—at least in that vein.   But a
similar apology cannot be made for those in our
day who, having studied in the school of physical
science, try to persuade themselves and others that
the Bible account of the creation is worthy of cre-

dence and must be accepted as a direct revelation
from a Being whom they hold to be the essence of
truth. What shall we think then of those among
them who allege that the so-called six days of creation were in reality so many ages, while they persist in regarding it as obligatory to keep the Sabbath Day holy for the reason given in the Fourth
Commandment? That document reads: "For in
six days the Lord made heaven and earth, the sea,
and all that in them is, and rested the seventh day;
wherefore the Lord blessed the Sabbath Day and
hallowed it." The two positions are so inconsistent as to require a faith made of India rubber to
include both, and yet there are thousands of "well
educated" people to-day possessed of the mental
elasticity necessary to the omnivorous feat of swallowing the two.

If we could take the Genesis story of the creation
as literally true, and at the same time admit that
the earth turns on its axis once in twenty-four hours,
we should be obliged to believe that each day's
work was not performed simultaneously. We read
that the evening and the morning were the —th
day, and this must have been equally true for every
place at which the creative fiat was in operation.
It must have held good for America as well as
Africa or Asia. That is, if the reckoning of time
for that epoch were conducted by reference to the
meridional divisions now in use, the creation of
cattle and reptiles on the sixth day in Kamschatka

would have been begun only a few minutes after that of fishes and birds was begun on or near the shores of Alaska; and there would be some points in the Pacific ocean where the two sets of creations were in process side by side. But the "inspired" narrator did not know anything about time differences of longitude, nor did those "Wise men in Israel" who first insisted that the Sabbath day must be observed at the same instant in all places where Jews were to be found. To them the earth's surface was a plane of only a few hundred miles in extent, and its God had at the best but a few millions of human beings to look after, which he could easily do as they were all the time under his Eye. In a physical sense he could every moment survey the whole territory from his vantage place among the clouds, as the devil was subsequently alleged to have done from the top of a high mountain. For aught they knew the sun rose and set at the same instants of time at Babylon and Jerusalem, at Nineveh and Memphis.

Apparently some men of that race are no wiser to-day. They do not know, or do not stop to think, that while they are worshipping in their synagogues at noon Saturday, in Chicago, the Sabbath is ended in Palestine, and that they really assemble while it is the first day of the week in the land of their forefathers, instead of the much respected Seventh Day of the week preceding. Of course it is not to be expected that they should be wise enough to

consider that if they would reckon the Saturday
Sabbath round the earth from Palestine in an east-
erly direction it would coincide in the United States
with the day known here as Friday. Neither is it
to be supposed they have taken into account the
fact that if the Christians had carried Sunday eastward while the Jews carried their Sabbath westward
the two days would have been coincident in the
United States. But if not wise enough for that,
one might suppose it possible for some of them to
think it improbable that the Sabbath count has
been kept up without a slip from the close of
creation; when the date of that event is not agreed
upon, to within several centuries, though their own
Bible be taken as the sole authority in making the
computation. A few grains of reflection in this
line would show them the absurdity of insisting
on the observance of Saturday as their resting time
in the United States while all around them are at
work; and they would thankfully embrace the
opportunity to worship Sunday in their own
synagogues, free from the persecution to which
their race has been subjected in other lands and
past ages.

It will be interesting to compare the Bible
account of creation with the Chaldean legend
quoted by Berosus, who was a priest of Belus in
Babylon, about 300 to 250 B. C. He wrote:

In the beginning all was darkness and water,
and therein were generated monstrous animals of

strange and peculiar forms. There were men with
two wings, and some even with four, and with two
faces. Others had two heads, those of a man and a
woman, on one body. (A.) There were men with
the heads and horns of goats, other men with hoofs
like horses, and some with the upper parts of a man
joined to the lower parts of a horse, like centaurs.
(B.) There were bulls with human heads, dogs
with four bodies and tails of fishes, men and horses
with the heads of dogs, creatures with the heads
and bodies of horses and the tails of fishes, and
other animals combining the forms of various
beasts. (C.) Also there were monstrous fishes
and reptiles and serpents, and divers other creatures, each of which had borrowed something from
the shapes of the rest. The likenesses of all these
are still preserved in the temple of Belus. All of
them were ruled (or contained) by a woman named
Omorka, which in Chaldaic is Thalatth and in Greek
Thalassa (in English "sea"). Then Belus appeared and split the woman in two. Of the one
half of her he made the heavens and of the other
half the earth ; and the beasts that were within her
he caused to perish. Also he split the darkness, and
divided the heaven and the earth asunder, and put
the world in order ; — and the animals which could
not bear the light perished. Upon this Belus, seeing that the earth was desolate yet teeming with
productive power, commanded one of the gods to
cut off his head, to mix with the earth the blood

that flowed from it, and with it to form men and beasts that could bear the light. (D.) So man was made, and was intelligent, being a partaker of the divine wisdom. (E.) Also Belus made the stars, and the sun and moon, and the five planets. (F.)

The two accounts have so much in common that one cannot but suppose them to have sprung from a common source: unless one was taken from the other but changed by a process of mental filtration in being carried in memory a distance of several hundred miles, and probably through some years before being set down formally by the men who had transported the legend from Babylon to Judea. In the story by Berosus we may note (A) that it accords with a classical idea that the first human beings were hermaphrodite; (B) that certain Spaniards on horseback in South America were mistaken for centaurs less than four centuries ago; and is not this centaur referred to in Psalm cxlvii. 10? The verse is " He delighteth not in the strength of the horse: He taketh not pleasure in the legs of a man." (C) Compare the description of these monsters with the visions of Daniel and Ezekiel, both in the land of Mesopotamia. (D) It is not difficult to see in these creatures which "could not bear the light" a recognition of previously existing forms of animated being, the buried remains of which had been found by early explorers. Does not this shame the men of less than four hundred years ago

who contended that like remains were sports of
nature? (E) Compare this with the Bible report of
the dictum by the Elohim, " Let Us make man in
our own image " out of the dust of the ground.
(F) The Berosus story distinctly recognizes the five
planets as sufficiently important to be worthy of
separate mention, which the Mosaic account apparently does not. Though probably the most ancient,
it is the least unphilosophical of the two, the fact
indicating that the writer of the Jewish " history "
was not only a mere copyist, but blundered in the
attempt to reproduce something above his comprehension. There is no room to doubt that the
Berosus picture was the original of a very poor
copy, which but for the claim of inspiration would
be ridiculed as self-evidently absurd.

IX

THE DELIVERER.

" We have seen his star in the East." — Matthew.

Prophecies of a Messiah.—The First was not Jewish, but Astrological;
and Probably Bactrian.—The School at Balkh.—Gjamasp and His
Utterance.—Its Influence on Cyrus and the Jews.—Indian Story of
Crishna.—Fulfillment of the Prophecy.—Matthew's Mistaken Zeal.—
Making History for Christians.—Astronomical Cycles.—"The Star of
Bethlehem."

A great many members of Christian churches are
more than half inclined to concede the claim by
distinguished Bible critics that not one of the books
in the Old Testament, with hardly the possible
exception of Job, was compiled before the time of
Ezra; and that those of them which were written in
his day, including the five ascribed to Mosheh, are
simply collations of traditions then floating in the
minds of the Jewish people, mingled with more or
less historical matter gleaned from the nations
among whom some of the Jews had sojourned during their captivity. Probably a large proportion of
these liberally disposed church members would be
far less inclined to accede to the proposition if they
knew the consequences which such assent involves.
The earliest written of those sentences in the Old
Testament which are supposed to have been pro-

phetic of a coming Messiah were not penned till about 450 years previous to the Christian era, while the astrologers of the Far East were talking of it nearly a hundred years before that time. The Jews obtained their first notions on the subject from the star gazers. The inspiration of their seers came from the observatories from which the wise men of old watched the movements of the heavenly bodies and computed the cyclical periods of the planets.

The shreds of history that have been picked up here and there by the *chiffoniers* of literature are not numerous enough to enable us to make even an intelligent guess at the place where and the time when the prophecy of the Messiah originated. For aught we know it may have been first uttered in Egypt or at Babylon, but we cannot trace it thither. Its earliest known formulation was in far off Bactria, a country situated west of the Hindoo-Koosh and south of the river Oxus. The region is otherwise interesting as having been claimed to be entitled to distinction as the cradle of the race; and it is worthy of note that if this were really the starting area for the prophecy of a Messiah the origin of that prediction was not Shemitic but Aryan. Beginning there the historical web may be traced out somewhat as follows. Many of the threads are wanting, but the attempt here made to describe it has, at least, as much warrant as the efforts of investigators in another field who have undertaken to build up a skeleton and determine the natural history of the animal from the study of a few fragments of bone.

About 2,500 years ago a school or college of astrological students rather than priests flourished at Bactra, or Zariaspé, the modern Balkh. It was the capital of Bactria, and had been the home of Zoroaster or Zarathustra, after whom it was called Zariaspé. Whether founded by him or not is unknown, but it is pretty well established that the school had attained great prominence in the first half of the sixth century before the Christian era, and its principal men had much influence at court, one of them being a brother of the monarch. This man was called Gjamasp, and is said to have been taken into high favor by Cyrus after the latter had invaded the country and subjugated it, which was a few years previous to the capture of Babylon, 538 B. C. This Gjamasp was surnamed Al Hakim (The Wise). He wrote of a beautiful maiden who was to arise in the Sign (constellation), Virgo, holding in her hand two ears of grain and in her arms a child. (The Hebrew word Beth-lehem means the house or place of grain, the latter word being the true equivalent of "corn," as used by the English translators of the Bible in the time of King James I.) According to Al Hakim the maiden was to be called Adrenedefa (the pure or immaculate virgin), she was to bring up her child in Abric (?Hebrew Land), and to call his name Eisi (Yesus). If we compare this with the statement in the first gospel

11

that three wise men came from the East directly
after the birth of the child, and also remember that
Daniel and his companions were astrologers and
soothsayers (Dan. i. 17 and 20), it will not be difficult to understand how the coming of the one afterwards called Christ was first predicted by the astrologers and then appropriated by the captives in
Babylon. There is no escape from this conclusion:
though no fault should be found with any one who
thinks that a happy inspiration was necessary to a
definition of the event. Such an idea is warranted
by Ptolemy, a prince of the science, who tells us
that none but those who are endowed with a divine
prescience are able to predict particulars from a
study of the stars.

[We cannot, however, be sure that this " happy
inspiration " of naming the place was anything
more than a verbal accident. The Shemitic word
Eber means "beyond," which suggests that the
name was given to one of the ancestors of Abram
as a sign of location; and we read in I Chron. i. 19,
that Heber called his son Peleg because in his days
the earth was divided. Similarly his descendant
Abram may have been so designated as coming into
Palestine from beyond the Syrian desert. And for
aught we know that word *Abric*, though perhaps
derived from another language than the one in
which the above quoted vaticination was written,
may have been used simply to mean some country
beyond the horizon,—far away towards the west from

Bactria, in a region where by many peoples in many ages the golden rays of the setting sun have been supposed to shine on an earthly Paradise.]

Possibly the Persian conqueror attached little importance to this prediction when he first heard it. But when he determined on the conquest of Babylon it must have occurred to him with double force: —He might shine in history as the one who made possible a fulfillment of the prediction by restoring the Jewish exiles to their own land, and by announcing himself as their deliverer he could gain their valuable assistance in capturing the city. He surprised the garrison, which could hardly have been done without help from inside, and in return for their aid he not only set them free but returned to them the spoils taken in Judea many years earlier and otherwise assisted them to carry out their darling project of rebuilding the temple and the city of Jerusalem. No doubt the prophecy was told to the Jews before the assault, and it was to them a powerful argument in favor of the proposed alliance with the Persian invader. Joshua, their high priest, was among the first to hear it, and perhaps the one chosen to carry the news to the Israelites in slavery. No wonder if as he told it among those poor serfs it made their hearts burn within them as the words of Moses were supposed to have stirred up their ancestors in Egypt to strong purpose and high resolve. No longer did their harps hang on the willow trees while they refused to sing the songs (chant the

praises) of Yahveh in a strange land. The Messianic
prophecy formed the great incentive to the people
to seek by every means in their power to get back
into the land of a second promise where they naturally supposed a much greater power and glory
awaited their children than had fallen to the lot of
their forefathers; and Joshua was only too well
pleased to be accorded the honor of aiding his people to escape from their modern " house of bondage." Who can suppose that but for this the Jewish slaves would ever have been allowed to return to
their homes in Palestine? They would have been
even more useful as slaves to the new ruler than
their late masters could be, because inured to toil.
The last twenty-seven chapters of Isaiah, " the Messianic Prophet " *par excellence*, are generally considered by the critics to have been written by some
unknown hand during the time of that captivity. It
is more probable they were written soon after the
return; and if so were undoubtedly inspired by the
same thought that most strongly stirred the breasts
of the whole Jewish people on the banks of the Euphrates.

Arrived home, the construction of dwellings, with
an including wall around the city, was not more important than the rebuilding of the temple. The
people wanted to have a place worthy the reception
of their king, when he should come, and probably
the time of his arrival had not then been foretold.
That was a matter for subsequent calculation by the

Magi.   And the new-found sense of superiority
suggested as desirable the writing of the sacred books
from the traditions which had lingered among the
people and been sadly repeated among the captives,
time and time again, while they sat and wept by the
waters of Babylon.   It was only natural that those
traditions, then reduced to writing for the first time,
should be expanded so as to include as many references as possible to the great event of the coming
age.   It would be so easy to look upon the stories
of the past as necessary preparatives for that, and
to accept it as inevitable that the history of a people
now discovered to be chosen of God as the one from
among whom the Messiah should spring must be of
an ante-typal character.   The deduction was all the
more natural as most of the great men who had a
place in the traditions of that people had been de-
liverers from some evil or other, the one important
means used being the temporary agglomeration of
previously scattered elements.   Probably the comparison, instituted about the time of the return
(536 B. C.), was formulated but slowly; the first
migrants doing little if anything to put in shape the
mass of traditionary material at their command.
But those who remained behind in Babylon were
more active.   They ranked equally with the other
residents there, and the more favored among their
youth had access to the treasures of learning which
had been shut up as sealed books from their ancestors who were slaves.   We may well suppose that

as high priest of the Jews Ezra enjoyed all these literary privileges; and that when eighty years after the first party had gone to Palestine he followed them with men and much treasure, he was skilled in all the learning of the Babylonians as Moses had been said to be in that of the Egyptians. Armed with that knowledge he and his band brought into shape if not into existence the literature of the Jews; and gave them a written history, in which the Giver of all Good was alleged to be responsible for their self confessed wickedness. According to it their manifold and heinous crimes had been committed in obedience to a "Thus saith the Lord."

Meanwhile the college at Balkh dwindled into insignificance amid the troublous times which came upon that region. But its work was not ended. There was still a remnant, reserved to witness the fulfillment of the prophecy. If the story told by the writer of Matthew be true, there were at least three of them spared till the appointed time; and when it was near they set out in full confidence on a journey due west to find a place where the shadow of the dial did not mark the time of noon till two hours after the sun had passed the meridian of their home. They found the long expected one, who was not recognized by his own people, and then returned to the East. We need not follow the clue farther.

This prophecy, uttered in mystic language, was transported to India when that country was invaded

by Darius, in the latter part of the sixth century B.
C. and confirmed by the talkers who subsequently
accompanied Alexander the Great thither. The
idea took root all the more readily as the Iranian
(Persian) language of the first invasion belonged to
the same family as the Greek, and was closely allied
to that spoken by the inhabitants of India; though
they have diverged widely since then, and the present language of Persia is more Shemitic than
Aryan. It was more easy to tell the story of a
future Messiah to the Hindoos and Greeks than to
the Chaldeans and Jews, other things being equal.
It was so readily accepted in India that it was there
transformed into a supposed historical narration of
something already happened, instead of applying to
an event of the future. It was a comparatively
easy mistake to make, owing to a common fault of
the prophets, astrological as well as theological, of
talking about things in a different tense to that
which includes the action; or using an indifferent
present which may equally well apply to the past
or the future. In this way was developed the oft
described story about Crishna, whose supposed
memory, virtues and powers, are pretty well ascertained to have been venerated by the people of
India some 250 years before the Christian era. It
will not do to claim, as has been done by some ill-
advised supporters of the religion supposed to be
founded on the teachings of Jesus, that the Crishna
story dates only near the time of Mohammed and

was therefore stolen bodily from the narratives of
the four Evangelists. Many well informed theologians know well that the claim would be just as
good if put the other way, though they are not
willing to admit the fact lest it should sap the foundations of their faith. It is difficult to see why a
reputedly conscientious man in all else should feel
it his duty to wink at a monstrous falsehood for
fear that other people should be spoiled by being
told the truth; and that kind of an individual ought
to heave a sigh of relief on the receipt of an assurance which lets him out of the woods so easily.
But he is not yet released from all necessity for explanations which do not explain to the satisfaction
of the curious. It is unfortunate that the simple
prediction by the astrologer, and the subsequent
prophetic ravings of the half demented ones who
with eyes in fine frenzy rolling traversed Judea
and other lands much as did the friars of more
modern days, were twisted and misappropriated by
the Christian world as well as by the "haythen."
They appear to have been seized upon by the writer
of Matthew's Gospel as so much capital that must
all be employed in the manufacture of a story about
the Messiah, and as sufficient reason for writing all
sorts of improbable and inconsistent stuff "in order
that the Scripture might be fulfilled." But for
that we should never have been asked to believe
the unnecessary account of the miraculous conception (Matt. i. 23), which scientific men in this cen-

tury know could not possibly be true, the story
about the slaughter of the innocents (Matt. ii. 18),
which never occurred, nor the alleged report of the
talk between Jesus and Satan on one of the pinnacles
of the temple (Matt. iv. 6), which needs no denial.
Sensible men may well smile at the description of
the angel at the sepulcher (Matt. xxviii. 3), when
they see it was only introduced to parallel a passage in Daniel (x. 6), and at some other points that
were literally dragged in by the ears to eke out
the narrative. Many of the alleged accounts of
alleged miraculous happenings would have been
omitted by the writers of the gospels but for that
supposed necessity of proving that Christ fulfilled
all the prophecies. And it would have been much
better to leave them out. Intelligent men cannot
believe them to-day any more than they can swallow
the story of St. George and the Dragon, or Aladdin
and his wonderful lamp; and the church is foolish
in asking them to accept such stories for "gospel
truth," seeing that insistence tends to raise doubts
in regard to what would otherwise be believed without question. In this respect the church is its own
worst enemy, by excluding from the fold its most
conscientious members ; and it will have to change
the programme or pay the penalty by losing its
hold upon the hearts and purses of the people of
the next century.

Nor will the Christian churches be able much
longer to ignore the fact that they have borrowed

from the older faiths much to which they have no valid claim; as they enshrouded the history of Jesus of Nazareth with many miraculous incidents told of heathen gods and heroes long before the Christian era. When the early Christians appropriated the Roman temples, and deliberately invented Saints with similar names to whom to dedicate the structures instead of the deities formerly thus honored, they did not commit a more bare-faced robbery than that previously perpetrated by the Gospel writers who seemed to feel charged with a mission to make it out that Jesus in his own person fulfilled all of what they were pleased to regard as "prophecies." For many of those prophetic utterances were purely astronomical in their application, and, therefore, but allegorical in reference to worldly affairs. Others were entirely personal with the prophet or some of his contemporaries, and still others plainly referred only to things that had already passed by into the lap of history. Take for instance the statement put into the mouth of the Messiah by the same Matthew (xii. 40), whom we have already referred to as the great self-constituted harmonizer of all the old with the beginning of the new. "For as Jonah was three days and three nights in the belly of the whale, so shall the Son of Man be three days and three nights in the heart of the earth." Yet that story of Jonah and the whale is purely an astronomical myth, as we shall see in a subsequent chapter; besides which none of the churches credit Jesus with having lain in the sepulcher more than two nights, namely those following Friday and Saturday. Notwithstanding that important failure to verify not only an alleged typical happening but an alleged promise by the Son of God himself, Brother Moody in the present enlightened age often quotes that text as proof positive that the story about Jonah is a narration of actual fact which it is rank heresy to doubt. Ask him to explain the above noted discrepancy in the count, or to name an animal which could swallow a man without breaking all his bones, to say nothing about retaining him alive for half a week, and he cannot do it; but is satisfied the account is perfectly correct " because it is in the Word of God." Ask him how he knows the Gospel of Matthew to be the Word of God, and he replies that the Gospel named is in the Bible, which commends itself to the heart as being every word of it true.

Of material appropriated from other " histories " which antedate that of the Gospels if they are not true, there is so much that to cite it all would be wearisome. Take for instance the story of Buddha, certainly born as much as 543 B. C. He was born of a virgin named Maya, amid great miracles. He left his father's house to become an ascetic previous to assuming the work of a teacher, was tempted of the devil (Mara), had men and women flock to hear him, humbled the pride of the philosophers, taught in parables, and died amid a great convul-

sion of Nature. It is more than merely probable
that many of the stories told about him and Chrishna,
and the acts ascribed to them, first took form as applied to those men at a time long subsequent to that
in which they lived. But it is still more probable
that these statements built up around them in after
years, as votive offerings in the shape of jewels
hung around the necks of idols, were mere aggregations of ideas which had attached at much earlier
periods to several of the gods. These were dragged
in pell mell by the evangelists: who, in their zeal
to make it appear that Jesus in his own person fulfilled all the prophecies, attributed to him all the
virtues and powers said to have been possessed by
the great ones of their own race, and were not over
discriminative in appropriating some of those previously peculiar to the gods and heroes of other
peoples. If we remember that in all this the Jewish Messiah had to be represented as " without sin "
we need find little difficulty in tracing numerous con-
nections previously unthought of, in which Jesus was
made out to be the ante-type of personal history.
Look, for example, at the part played by the hair
of Samson in the interviews between him and
Delilah, and the act by which he killed himself as
well as the enemies of his race. Then compare these
with what was done with the hair of the woman who
washed the feet of Jesus, and his prophecy that the
temple should be destroyed; also his other remark
when " he spake of the temple of his body." Now

let us remember that he was said to have come
with the spirit and power of Elias (Elijah), paral-
leling the raising of the widow's son, the discom-
fiture of the priests of Baal, and the ascension into
heaven, the second of these scenes being repeated
when Jesus drove the merchants out of the temple
with a whip of small cords. The forty days' fast
in the wilderness was a miniature repetition of the
forty years wandering in the desert, and the scene
on the Mount of Transfiguration would hardly have
been described had not something of the kind been
told as happening to Moses. No doubt these pious
frauds were committed "with the best of motives,"
the object of the men who wrote the Gospels being
to convince the Jews that Jesus was really and
truly " He that should come," and that they need
not " look for another." But the Jews had not
witnessed the miracles alleged to have been performed by him, and they did not believe the
story.

Read what the veracious Matthew is reported to
have written of the scenes immediately following
the death on the cross :

" And behold. The vail of the temple was rent
in twain from the top to the bottom; and the earth
did quake, and the rocks rent; and the graves were
opened; and many bodies of the saints which slept
arose, and came into the holy city, and appeared
unto many."

Can any man in his sober senses believe that if
these things had really happened as described the
people of Jerusalem would have remained calm
unbelievers? The writer cannot think so.

The view here presented in regard to the origin
of the Messianic prophecy and its fulfilment is a
consistent one to say the least. It is the only one
that can be accepted without doing violence to the
Christian conscience as well as to known facts of
history. Equally is it necessary to read with the
eye of reason as with the eye of faith the accounts of
alleged miraculous happenings and doings found in
the four Gospels. They cannot much longer be accepted as literally true, except by the same order of
intellect that swallows the story of Jack and the
Beanstalk. And there is no reason, apart from its
strangeness, why the explanation as a whole should
be unpalatable to that part of the Christian world
which aims to be rational, believing in the miraculous only when it seems absolutely unavoidable.
But if the preceding be indeed the history of the
prophecy and coming of the Messiah, the churches
owe a debt of gratitude to the early astrologers
which they certainly cannot repay by reviling those
who are in the present day honest students of the
grand old science that is the great foundation not
only of religion in general but of the faith held
alike by catholics and evangelical protestants.
Surely the thoughts here submitted should suffice to
make them cautious, lest in trying to pluck up the

astrological tares they run the risk of rooting out the wheat of Christian doctrine.

We have not yet, however, seen how completely the expectation of a Messiah was astrological in its origin. It was a favorite theory of the ancients that, inasmuch as the fate and conditions surrounding the individual are determined by the positions of the planets, and as nations are made up of individuals while the world of humanity is composed of nations, a time must come when all will have returned to some original position and the same set of events must happen to a similar set of individuals as at first. In Scipio's dream, as related by Cicero, the phantom of his grandfather is represented as speaking of this entire return of all the heavenly bodies to some position they had once occupied ages before, marking the completion of one universal year; and the spirit adds: "I must tell you that not one twentieth part of that great year has yet been accomplished." A similar idea appears in II Esdras xvi. 11 and 12, "For the world is divided into twelve parts, and the ten parts of it are gone already, and half of a tenth part; and there remaineth that which is after the half of the tenth part." From a consideration of this text Lieut. Totten has rashly concluded that the world will come to an end not far from the close of the current century. But Ptolemy was wiser than they. Some 1750 years ago he wrote, "An entire return of all the heavenly bodies to the exact situation in

which they have once stood with regard to the earth
can never take place, or at least not in any period
determinable by human calculation, whatever vain
attempts may be made to acquire such unattainable
knowledge.'' The illustrious author of the Syntaxis
and the Tetrabiblos may have been all wrong with
his epicycles, but he rightly suspected that the
periods of the planets and stars are incommensur-
able.

This doctrine of cycles is a fundamental one in
the theology of the ancient Aryan inhabitants of
India, the astrological features of which have persisted to the present century with little of the veiling that hides from our view much that was essential
to the early religion of other lands. So far as we
can discover the ten Avatars of Vishnu were supposed to be separated by equal intervals, each equal
to the time required for the completion of one of
these grand years. The prevalent idea in that and
other countries was that each of these years termin-
ated with a grand calamity, followed by a renewal
of desirable conditions; and the Hindoos were far
from being the only people who believed this rejuv-
enation was brought about by a re-appearance on
earth of the god whom they supposed to be their
particular ruler if not the controlling power of
all they knew as constituting the universe. Some
recognized the revolutionizing character of minor
cycles, with variations in the nature of the event
according to the peculiarities of the configura-

tion.   Thus, according to Diodorus Siculus, the
Chaldeans taught that when all the planets are
 in conjunction in Capricorn the earth is destroyed
by flood; and when in Cancer (the opposite constellation), the earth is destroyed by fire.   The
Stoic philosophers of Greece are said to have derived
from the Egyptians their theory that man has several times gradually degenerated from a state of
innocence.   They held that towards the close of
each of these eras the gods became so disgusted with
the wickedness of men that they destroyed the race
by a shock of the elements, after which Astrea re-
visited the earth and renewed the golden age.   It
was believed by the Jews that as the conjunction
of Jupiter and Saturn near the close of 1576 B. C.
preceded the birth of Moses by about three years,
so the birth of the Messiah would follow some other
conjunction of those planets at the same interval.
The configuration came round in the latter part of
7 B. C. in the middle of the constellation Pisces,
and was supposed to be all the more significant as
Mars joined in it.   The sun was then in opposition
to them and not far from the autumnal equinox;
and there seems to have been a pretty general expectation about that time that the long promised
Deliverer would soon come among men.

Probably the precession of the equinoxes was not
known when these cycles were first thought out;
but the allowances of the time made were sufficiently generous to take in not one but many times
12

the period of 25,868 years occupied by the equinoctial diameter of the earth's orbit in making a complete circuit of the heavens. They were generally multiples of a thousand, the 120,000 of Orpheus being only one-third of the period assigned by some for the length of the universal year. The subordinate catastrophes divided this up into shorter periods. The old Egyptian priest who conversed with Solon described the submergence of Atlantis by an earthquake as one of these; and told that many others had occurred, including one that had swept from the earth the fair and noble race of which he asserted the Greeks to be a remnant.

There is, however, no room to doubt that the precession of the equinoxes was a fact well understood by the man who originated the Messianic prophecy, which we have traced to Bactria. And the prophecy was based upon his knowledge of that movement. The star of the first magnitude in the zodiacal constellation Virgo, and called Spica or the Virgin's Spike, is now 22° 20′ of longitude past the autumnal equinox. Its latitude south from the ecliptic is nearly 2° 3′, and its declination south from the celestial equator is 10° 36′. All these quantities are increasing with the time; the longitude at the rate of a degree in a little less than seventy-two years, and the declination one degree in something more than a hundred and eighty years. At the time now generally assumed for the birth of Christ, which is four years earlier than the begin-

ning of the Christian Era as designated by *A. D.*
the star Spica was on the equator and about 4° east
from the equinox. Nearly three centuries later it
arrived at the equinox, its latitude then carrying it
south of the equator.

The tables of star places at present, with accompanying columns showing their annual motions and
the secular changes in the rate of each annual motion, are based on comparisons of ancient observations with those of our own times. These old positions are stated with only approximate correctness,
the observations being crude. Hence the ancient
star places do not all agree with computations from
the modern tables, which are based on averages and
necessarily disregard the small " proper motions "
of individual stars except as they may have been
deduced from observations made with the greater
precision possible within the last three centuries.
Sometimes, if we push the inquiry closely enough,
we meet with wide differences in results. It is so in
the case of Spica. Computing back for the precession in longitude, by means of quantities which
astronomers consider to be probably the most exact,
the star appears to have been at the equinox early
in the year 289 A. D. Using the most approved
tables for precession as affecting declination we get
about 25 A. D. for the time when the star was on
the equator. That difference of 264 years, with
23° 42′ for the computed obliquity, would give
1° 38′ for the latitude south at the earlier date. But

computing back with the formulæ given by Watson we obtain 1° 55' as the latitude about nineteen hundred years ago. Here is a discrepancy, which is not removable by reference to old time observations for latitude. The catalogue by Ptolemy states it as 2°, and the Hindoo tables state it to have been 1° 50' when the star was only 48' past the equinox in longitude.

It is important to remember that if the astronomers or astrologers of the olden time made a prediction by reference to this or any other star the question is not more one about its actual place than of the position they supposed it to occupy at the time;—if there were any difference between the two. The earliest known position stated for Spica is the 170° of longitude given by Copernicus as that corresponding to the time when the first bright star in Aries was at the equinox. The date is not noted, but it was about 427 B. C. which would bring the star to 180° of longitude in 294 A. D. and with latitude 1° 50' it would be on the equator in 4 B. C. Ptolemy's catalogue gives the longitude of Spica as minus 3° 30' in 139 or 140 A. D. He had erroneously deduced it from the longitude given by Hipparchus for 128 B. C. by allowing 100 years to a degree of precession instead of 72 years. Making correction for that error we get the longitude as minus 2° 33', bringing Spica to the equinox in 323 A. D. and with 2° of latitude would place it on the equator in 4 B. C. Copernicus quotes another longitude of minus 3° 10′ for the year 99 A. D., which would bring the star to the equinox in 327 A. D. or only four years later than the last noted deduction, and with a latitude of 2° would place it on the equator in the very year that for many centuries was held by the Christian world to be the one in which Jesus was born;—there being no zero year in changing from B. C. to A. D.

The star Spica was more than three degrees north of the line when the prophet priest of the Bactrian school discovered that it was being slowly carried southward; and reasoned that a Messiah would come when, reaching the limit, the star passed into the southern hemisphere. He did not then know to within many years when the transit would occur. That was a matter for subsequent observation, but his faith was none the less strong; and one can faintly imagine with what intense interest the gradual march of Spica was watched by his successors, and its lessening distance from the line measured again and again with the utmost accuracy attainable by the rude means at their command.

It is easy now to trace the connection, whatever we may think of its value. That lustrous brilliant of the skies was pictured then as in the hand of the Virgin, substantially as it is delineated on the globes and charts of to-day. It represents the handful of grain the maiden has gathered in her character of "The Gleaner." She was the original *Ruth*, and the word *Bethlehem* means "the house (or place) of

grain " (page 161). Her cereal treasure is the gift
which the Virgin of the Zodiac brings each year with
the annual round of the seasons. But it was held
by the Magians of old to mean much more than that.
They believed that when the precession of the equinoxes had carried Spica to the position where it
would be leaving the upper hemisphere and moving
into the lower the passage would be marked by the
descent of a God from heaven to earth,—(and we are
told in the Apostles' creed that "He descended into
hell"). They thought the burden or offspring of
the celestial Virgin would then come down from the
skies;—and if the recital credited to Matthew be
true the priests of that Zoroastrian school calculated
the time correctly, in fact much more closely than
we can compute it to-day.

This, then, is the Star of Bethlehem. It is situated in the Zodiac, close to the ecliptic line; and there
is no need to hunt for it in the constellation Cassiopea, where some have unwisely fancied it shines out
at intervals of a little more than three centuries ever
since the Nativity. One is not obliged to fall back
on the planet Venus, as some others have done in
their anxiety to make the natural square with the
supposedly miraculous. Yes; The Virgin's Spike
was the Star of Bethlehem, rising precisely in the
East at midnight of that first Christmas, and then
wending its way through the arch of heaven till at
the dawn of day it was well up towards the zenith
of "the place where the young child was." It still

shines in our summer skies, setting soon after the sun near the time of our wheat harvest; and telling to those who can read it the story of the great event in the land of Judea nearly nineteen centuries ago as it did to the Bactrian sages six hundred years before the occurrence lapsed into history. But there is one part of the story as it was read by the Aryan prophet which has been lost sight of. It was that what has since been called the millennium would come when Spica reached the equinox. The Apostles understood that to mean the end of the world. They were not wise enough to see that at the date of that equinox passage of Spica their church would rise into State power through the edict of the Emperor Constantine. Nor are the expounders of the faith in our own day sufficiently well informed to be aware that the "reign on earth" was established nearly sixteen hundred years ago, soon after that emperor had noticed the cross of Cygnus blazing in the sky, and fancied it bore the inscription *En touto nika*, "In this conquer." More probably the original was a pun in Latin — "In hoc *cygno* vinces"; the joke being concealed by turning it into Greek as above.

X.

PRIESTCRAFT.

"Thou shalt be to him instead of God."—Exodus.

Priestly Use of Star Lore.—Determining Periods of Sun and Moon.— Eclipses.—Lunar Epochs for Prayer and Sacrifice.—Origin of Terrestrial Fire.—Planetary Dignities.—Passover and Easter.—Other Christian Festivals Fixed by the Priests.—Worship of the Procreative Principle.

Though the priests long refused to accord to the sun and moon an influential dignity, as primary causes of the events which befall mortals, they very early recognized them as essential to priestly power; since the luminaries were to them signs of the seasons, or "times and set times" (festivals), for days and longer cycles. The latter is the true meaning of Gen. i. 14, the word *Shanim*, translated "for years" simply signifying a doubling or repetition of days; and the earlier idea of its meaning was equally indefinite with that now attached to "Alf-Yom," which though literally "a thousand days" is used to mean a time so indefinitely long that it cannot be measured, or what some folks would call an eternity. The probability is that the earliest *Shanim* of the Hebrews were simply moons: the reckoning being substantially the same as that in use by the Indians of this continent since its settlement by white men. The " years" stated in Genesis to have been attained by the antediluvians must have been lunar months. Science does not warrant the belief that less than six thousand years ago human beings lived to a far greater age than do men of the present day.

A savage can reason out as a result of his observation that a complete circuit of the heavens by the sun coincides with the annual round of the seasons. But after emerging from barbarism he would have to observe for perhaps many ages before he could determine the length of the year to within a day or two. The best primitive method for finding when the sun returned to a given point would be to measure the extent of the noon shadow at the solstices, where it is sensibly the same for each of several successive returns to the meridian. We read of the sacrifice of an animal at the solstices about 3,000 B. C. by Fohi, in China, but not of one at the equinox till very long afterwards. The first Paschal lamb is said to have been killed by the Israelites 1491 B. C. In the absence of ability to measure closely the sun's motion the priest had recourse to that other sign maker, the moon; but being unequal to the task of deciding when she is actually between us and the sun, he took as the first day of each month (moon-eth), that on which she was first seen as a slender crescent, setting immediately after him. It was only natural that this should be taken as the beginning of the day,

and hence that every other day should be considered
to so begin; which is well known to be the Jewish
method of reckoning. By and by a few of the
more observant and thoughtful ones discovered
they could assign with reasonable approach to the
truth the times of these successive reappearances,
and do so for several moons ahead of the event.
Here was the beginning of their real power over
the multitude. Being found able to predict the new
moons, which the ignorant man could not, they
were credited with understanding the other secrets
of nature; and when as a result of further watching
they discovered that thirty-seven, (or one more
than three times twelve), were completed in about
three solar years, they were able to fix upon the
first known cycle other than that of the day and
month. This was so important an achievement that
the fact was symbolized by an equilateral triangle,
which afterwards became the mystical sign of the
trinity, and probably first suggested the idea of
a trinity of supreme beings governing the sun in
place of the first four and then five planets which
had previously formed the Elohim syndicate or dory-
phory. Let us add that this triangle, as found on
the seal of Solomon, the wise, was emblematical of
his wisdom, crediting him with a knowledge of that
and other mysteries which were hidden in the
breasts of a few priests. It matters little if the
secret was not discovered by a king named Solomon, or that such a person never existed, as is

most probable. He may have been as mythical a
person as King Arthur in England, or William
Tell in Switzerland; but that did not prevent the
fact from being associated with the name any more
than it was fatal to the telling of the stories about
the knights of the round table and the cap of Gess-
ler. Probably, too, the distinction was accorded
to Solomon ages after the supposed time of his
reign, in recognition of the respect thought to be
due his memory for the building of a magnificent
temple such as the Jews of the restoration said he
had erected. It was a piece of perhaps pardonable
pride on their part to talk of the glories of the first
temple to persons who could not contradict the
story, though it had no more foundation than the
"castles in Spain" about which Claude Melnotte
discoursed to his lady love; but the priests had an
end to serve in helping the distance of time to lend
enchantment to the view of the first structure,
which doubtless was a rude one. Yet poor as it
might be, it was a powerful aid to them in the effort
to fasten the chains of superstition around the
necks of the people. The worshippers would be
far more awe stricken by a walled building full of
mystery than when called on to bow down around
a box hidden inside a tent, more euphoniously
described now as the ark in the tabernacle.

We may infer that from about a thousand years
before the time assigned to Solomon to two or three
centuries after it, the knowledge of the world was

pretty nearly in *statu quo.* There was some poetry
written, and many events occurred which would
have made highly interesting history for us had they
been recorded and the record preserved. For during that period there was active moving about, especially in the western half of Asia, including the
Aryan migration eastward and probably a Shemitic
one westward. But the people do not appear to
have become materially wiser except in regard to
the existence of land areas previously unknown, the
intellectual blank being similar to that which rested
like a pall over Europe for a shorter time during
the dark ages. The discovery of the eclipse cycle
of 223 moons seems to have been made previous to
1700 B. C. by the Chaldean priests, that being a
period of eighteen years plus one-third of a month;
and the recently discovered Sargon library contains
accounts of a good many eclipses that were watched
for from the Belus observatory. But the older
tablets only state that in a named watch of such and
such a day (of the lunar month) an eclipse occurred,
and whether it happened according to calculation or
not. It may be inferred that their "calculations"
were none too precise, since in a report sent to one
of the later kings of Assyria it is stated that a
watch had been kept on the 28th, 29th and 30th of
Sivan (May), for an eclipse of the sun, which did
not take place. The shadow might have fallen outside their ken, but not to know more nearly the
time of the event argues only a rude acquaintance

with the facts of the lunar motion. In these reports of observations mention is made of annular eclipses of the sun. Rawlinson found on one of the Nineveh tablets a record of an eclipse which occurred in that city in 763 B. C. which is inferred to have been nearly total, and this is the earliest for which we have an approximate date. The first eclipse of which we have any account was one of the sun in 2169 B. C. Probably it occurred Oct. 22, B. C. 2137. This is the one that was observed in China without having been predicted by the astronomers, in consequence of which they were put to death. After the blank above noted there was a revival of knowledge among the Greeks, and by about 600 B. C. Thales gained great renown by predicting an eclipse; though it is said he only named the year in which it would happen. The physical sciences could not then have been very far above the zero mark if it be true, as written, that this same Thales taught the Egyptian priests how to compute the heights of the pyramids from measurements of the shadows they cast on the ground.

When the priests had once learned how to predict the occurrence of an eclipse their triumph was complete, albeit they knew not the hour and were not always certain as to the day. That was their master key. Being possessed of that, none might dare to question their claim to knowledge of all things both on earth and in heaven; and then they could utter a "Thus saith The Lord" with a majesty that none might oppose or even doubt. To the comprehension of an ignorant savage the man who could predict an eclipse of the sun might confidently command the luminaries to move at his will, and there was no fear of his power being tested as was that of the mad astronomer told about in Rasselas. It was not open to doubt that the sun would stand still upon Gibeon and the moon over the Valley of Ajalon at his bidding.

The religious festivals of the olden time were mostly regulated by the course of the moon with reference to the sun. Perhaps one of the original reasons for this choice was that the new moon is a revival of strength, as typified by illumination after having been swallowed up in the sunlight; and its reappearance was accepted as a pledge that the whole universe was not going to destruction. Then it was a reproduction on a smaller scale of the annual mounting up of the sun towards the zenith after he had gone down to " Hades " in winter and excited fears that he had disappeared below the horizon forever. Possibly, too, the monthly reappearance of the moon first suggested the question put in the book of Job, " If a man die shall he live again?" as it is pretty certain that the three days and nights passage of the moon among the stars of Cetus (the Whale), every month was allegorized into the story of Jonah and the big fish said to have swallowed him up. But many of the feasts, if not most or all of them, were held at the time of full moon; which had, however, to be determined from the new owing to the difficulty of telling to within several hours when she was most strongly illuminated. There was a practical reason for this in the many ages during which artificial fire and light were unknown, and it may be remarked that at least the tradition of such a time lingered among mortals into the historic era, as is evident from the appointment of vestal virgins charged under penalty of death with the duty of keeping the sacred fires burning; this fact pointing back to a time when fire could not be kindled at will. The first fire may have been obtained from the eruption of a volcano, or from the fall of a still blazing meteoric mass. If the latter supposition be accepted it will be easy to account for the veneration of fire as coming directly from heaven. But whether it came thus or from a lightning stroke it would cause disaster; and the story of the first remembered suffering from this cause was probably crystallized into the myth of Prometheus who was condemned to exquisite torture for the offense of calling down among mortals the fire that had hitherto been the exclusive property of the gods.

In whatever way fire first appeared upon the surface of the earth after it was tenanted by man it must at once have been destructive and regarded as miraculous. This would suggest the idea of placating the wrath of offended heaven by the burning of victims, the smell of whose flesh when offered by Hebel was far more acceptable to the nostrils of the

malignant Yahveh than the flowers and fruits that
had previously been displayed before him by Kayin
his brother.   And is not the miraculous origin of
terrestrial fire brought forcibly before us by the alleged history of Eli-Yah !   In I. Kings xviii, we read
of his contest with the priests of Baal, when fire
came down from heaven " at the time of the evening
sacrifice " (the moment of sunset) and consumed
his offering while theirs remained unchanged on the
altar.   True to his character as a servant of the god
of fire he ended his earthly career, (or they say he
did), by going up in a chariot of flame, or in other
words a blaze of glory; and left the people to be
amused by his successor who made iron to swim
and poisonous porridge wholesome while they
waited for another direct visitation from the skies.
That is, Eli-Yah would have done so but for the fact
that the whole story is a myth, belonging to an age
several centuries farther back along the stream of
time and foolishly injected into the narrative by
some one who did not observe the usual proprieties
of chronology.   The story ought to have been dated
before the flood, in the days when Tuval Kayin
was said to have devoted himself to the sharpening
of "instruments" or tools of brass; to which the
writer of Genesis adds "iron."

To determine when the planets could be most
effectually worshipped was another work of the
priests, which gave them an additional power.   It
was noticed that certain stars in or near the zodiacal

constellations shone with a light which was far from
being of the same color for all; and from this arose
the idea of associating them with the planets, each
of which was supposed to be most powerful, and
therefore more able to act as wanted, when near
stars of like quality. Thus, the principal star in
the Scorpion is a deep red, like Mars, and the star
is known to-day by a Greek name, Antares, which
signifies, one acting for Mars. Hence Mars was
said to rule over the whole constellation, the space
occupied by which was called his House. Some
other reasons, real or fanciful, were called in for
aid in the distribution of the zodiacal groups among
the planets. Each of them had also assigned to
him, or her, a constellation in which it was said to
be exalted, and when in the opposite constellation
the planet was said to be in its fall, where a good
planet was feeble and an evil one more malevolent
in its influence. Thus, Jupiter's houses were Sagittarius and Pisces, his exaltation in Cancer, and his
fall in Capricorn; while the moon had only one
house, Cancer, and her exaltation was placed in
Taurus, that being the sign in which she makes her
first appearance after having been in conjunction
with the sun at the first new moon succeeding the
vernal equinox.

From a consideration of all these facts, or pre-
tending to it, the priests used to arrive at a deter-
mination of the days that should be held sacred by
the people; and they made public announcement,

13

usually at the beginning of each month, that such and such days must be observed. Among the ancient Romans the summoning of the people together for this purpose gave the name to the *kalends,* (from *Calare*—to call out), whence our word "calendar."

To return to the full moon. Its light was the only one available for prolonging festivities into the night time, and equally of great value to the pilgrims in coming to the gathering and returning to it through long distances, in the ages when there were no torches to illumine the darkness of the time. The connection between feasts and the full moon once established, and fastened in the minds of the people by observance through a long flight of centuries, was kept up after the necessity therefor had passed away. It has even been perpetuated to our times; the festival of Easter being always observed on the Sunday next following the first full moon of the spring quarter; though we now know the length of the solar year to less than the hundredth part of a second, and have not only candles and gas to light up the altar during the service of the mass but electric lights by which to see our way to the early morning service or from that in the evening. Nor is this the only one of the features of the olden times which had then some reason for existing, but have been perpetuated into absurd contrast with conditions that mark the advent of a new phase of civilization. Surely no thinking man

can deny that the Christian churches of our day
present abundant room for reform in the matter of
ceremonial observance as well as in doctrine.

The Jewish church has not materially improved
upon the calendar it seems to have adopted about
the time of Ezra. Its year still consists of twelve
lunations, with an extra one interpolated every now
and then to prevent the count from getting too far
out of the way. Hence some years consist of thir-
teen months of twenty-nine and thirty days. But
the calendar is based on the very crude notion that
nineteen solar years contain exactly two hundred
and thirty-five lunations; whereas it has long been
known that the difference in that time amounts to
fully an hour and a half, which has accumulated to
ten days in about three thousand years. Constantine the Great knew enough of the inaccuracy of the
Jewish calendar to find fault with it, and demanded
that for that reason the Christian church should
institute a plan of its own for finding the date of
Easter. He mentioned as one objection that the
Jews sometimes celebrated two Passovers in a single
year. Evidently this undesirable error was in part
due to the lunar reckoning; but the Christian digni-
taries adhered to the full moon as regulator for the
festival while ordering it, as they supposed, so that
Easter should generally fall a week after the Passover. Nevertheless the fixing of the latter has got
so far wrong that in 1891 the Pesach was celebrated
on Friday, April 25, while Easter had been ob-

served March 29, or nearly a month earlier. But
the Jewish reckoning is not more artificial than the
tradition of the event it is supposed to commemo-
rate, and may therefore be said to be fittingly
faulty. The alleged occurrence is not worthy of a
place in the tables of history.

Are not the Catholics and Episcopalians equally
to blame with the Jews in their observance of the
movable feasts? They celebrate Easter according
to the motion of the moon, though well aware that
this cannot happen on the real anniversary of the
resurrection, except by what some people would
call an accident.

It is emphatically a full moon celebration of the
sun's passage across the equinoctial circle in the
heavens, by which he rises out of winter bondage
into the freedom of the summer season, and in
doing this he is for a short time on the *cross* formed
by the ecliptic and the equinoctial circles. And
the Christian observance of the fixed feast of
Christmas is also open to astronomical criticism.
It is well known that in the first three centuries of
the Christian era Christmas was a movable feast,
often confounded with the Epiphany and celebrated
at least by some of the churches in April or May.
The investigation ordered by Pope Julius the First
resulted about the middle of the fourth century in
the fixing on December 25 as the date of the festival. A manuscript by Hippolytus, Bishop of Por-
tus about 220 A. D. has recently been discovered;

and it states that the Nativity occurred on the 25th
of December, in the forty-second year of Augustus.
The value of this statement as testimony may well
be doubted, when we remember that the count by
years would place the event within one year of the
common reckoning, whereas the chronologists are
pretty well agreed that the birth of Jesus must
have happened about four years earlier than the
"vulgar" era or some of the statements found
in the Gospels could not possibly be true. Whether
fixed on for the first time by this illustrious (in his
own day) defender of the church against heresies,
or by some one preceding him, we can hardly
resist the conviction that the date named by Hippolytus was chosen because it is the time of year
when the sun begins to rise from the most southerly
point of his course in the heavens, and not for any
valid historical reason. Indeed, the account by
Luke, that at the time of the birth there were
shepherds abiding in the field, keeping watch over
their flocks by night, is presumptive evidence
against it. Such an accompaniment to the Advent
would be far more likely to occur in April or May
than near the time of mid-winter; the latitude of
Bethlehem being about the same as that of the
middle of Georgia and Alabama.

Evidently the date was not determined for a
uniformity of observance till the time of Pope
Julius; and there are reasons for thinking it highly
probable that none of the festivals, with the excep-

tion of Easter, were obligatory fasts or feasts till
the days of Constantine. During the first three
centuries Easter had been celebrated at the time of
the Jewish Pesach, in obedience to the mandate of
Paul, "Christ our Passover is crucified for us, let us,
therefore, keep the feast." But the observance of
none other was binding till Christianity became the
ruling faith of the empire. And why? Simply
because till then there had been no revenues derivable from such observance. The converts belonged to one of two classes, those who "had all
things in common" and the outsiders, most of the
latter being too poor or too proud to join the mon-
astic community. These contributed as they could,
or chose; but there was no sacrifice of the mass to
be paid for at so much per week by the attendants
on the "service," and the officers of the churches
were either those who preached to the heathen (unbelievers), or those who attended to the distribution of worldly goods, such as food and clothing,
among the members of the close communities. In
fact, the early Christians professed not to believe
in forms and ceremonies other than the formal
assembling of themselves together at probably
stated intervals, which with some may have been
the first day of the week, and with others the first
day of the lunar month. Those assemblies seem to
have been conducted on much the same plan as the
Quaker meetings of later days. One or the other
spoke as the spirit moved him or her — the women

taking part as well as the men till Paul interposed
his authority and forbade the gentler sex to speak
in the churches. We have nowhere any intimation
that during those three first centuries there was any
stated pastor or priest to lead the prayers of the
faithful; and most if not all of the preaching was
done by men who earned their own living at some
other occupation, as the itinerant exhorters of the
Methodist church did in the days of the Wesleys, following the example of Paul himself in this particular, if not in being "the chief of sinners." The
disciples had enough to do to keep body and soul
together without undertaking the responsibility of
maintaining a paid ministry or priesthood.

When the Christians came into power all this
was changed. Their kingdom became of this
world; but they only ruled through the spiritual.
It required ages to grow up to the idea of dictating to
kings and princes what the latter should do, though
doubtless the art of persuasion was pretty well
understood in the time of Constantine, and practiced upon his mother as well as himself. Of
course there had to be separate orders of priests,
and there must be work for all of them to do in
order to earn their pay. They instituted festivals,
many of which were simply the same days that had
been devoted to the worship of the heathen gods,
whose temples they appropriated by wholesale as
Henry the Eighth of England took the property of
the Catholics when he wanted it for his own church.

There was no necessity for keeping up the calculations of the more ancient times, except for the moon; but the priests had now a deeper hold upon the fears of the people, and probably few of them were aware how completely the new theological structure was composed of material that had formed part of the old. They had by this time accumulated a mass of literature as well as property, and were the only ones who could read or explain the first or enjoy the second. From that time they gradually extended their influence, now in spite of the wreck of empires, and then by assisting or even directing their destruction and remodeling; and as the continuous accumulation of spoils invited internal contention the church itself divided, but only to achieve fresh conquests.

It is said that the worship of animals has been traced back to the very earliest times; but there may be some mistake about this. It is most rational to suppose that the figures of certain animals rather than the creatures themselves were adopted as rallying marks or signals for small bodies of fighters, as banners have been used in warfare in much more recent times. These could be respected as symbols of human power without being adored any more than a national flag is to-day; and an act of reverence was not to the object itself but to the ruler of whose right to command it was "the outward and visible sign." Some of these animals may have been worshipped after the original meanings of the emblems were lost sight of amid altered conditions; but it is very easy to err in this particular. There is no satisfactory proof that the Israelites ever worshipped either a living calf or a golden one; and we are not obliged to believe that the ancient Egyptian said his prayers to the ibis or the beetle any more than the Hindoo of our day does to "the sacred cows of Brahma."

The writer has some doubts in regard to the alleged worship of the procreative principle, except as a degeneration from the more primitive association of that with the idea of planetary dominion and influence. But he has no wish to discuss this part of the subject; and leaves it with the remark that reproduction in both the vegetable and animal kingdoms is a phenomenon of the seasons, that the idea of the age of the moon being an element in fertility is "as old as the hills" that Mars and Venus have for nearly as long back been supposed to rule the sexual passion, one in the female and the other in the male, and that all the rest may have been a mere outgrowth from a misreading of earlier astronomical symbols. So, too, the planets, and afterwards the spirits supposed to be associated with them and their celestial offspring, were thought to govern the air, earth and sea; and by the exercise of a vivid imagination these were peopled by a consorting of the aforesaid deities with mortals, producing demi-gods, who in turn were the progenitors of the different races of earth inhabitants. This idea also is Biblical as well as profane. Were not the ante-diluvian giants mentioned in the sixth chapter of Genesis said to be the progeny resulting from a mating of the sons of God with the daughters of men? Nothing can be more natural than that the childish human fancy should people the woods and streams with such semi-supernatural beings when the poetic fancy of a much later age could see a mermaid in the foam crest of the waters, and a writer on natural history gravely describe the growing of the barnacle goose on trees. To the child of to-day it is easy to think that anything strange has dropped from the skies, and in the case of Santa Claus it takes its course straight down the chimney; though the American stove and furnace heating, with the accompaniment of a closed flue, renders it necessary to strain a point in order to make the tale acceptable to the juvenile comprehension.

XI

INCANTATIONS.

" By what power, or by what name, have ye done this?"—Acts.

Magic, as Connected with Astrology and Religion.—Early Conceptions.—
Wonders of Speech.—The Original Logos, and its Tremendous Power.
—Virtue in Names and Letters.—Sorcery in the Bible and out of It.—
Substitution.—Sacrifices.—The Mass.—Special Consecration Insisted
On.—Times Set for Efficacious Intercession.—Man Growing Wiser.

It is not to be wondered at that astrology has been
closely associated with magic all through the ages.
The idea that " Knowledge is Power " may have
been first reduced to a sententious form by Lord
Bacon, but probably is as old as human thought itself. In fact it may be said to be most forcibly entertained at the two extremes of intelligence. The
savage views with awe the person who knows something he does not, especially if that something seems
to have a practical connection with events in which
the gazer is interested. The missionary who " made
a chip talk " was by that act raised to the rank of a
superior being if not a god in the estimation of the
man who carried the chip and brought back an axe;
and the stolidity of the North American Indian
when for the first time he sees the white man avail-
ing himself of modern inventions has recently been
explained as nothing more or less than helpless be-

wilderment, such as is displayed by a sheep in the presence of real danger. The sense of wonder becomes blunted with the progress of the race in intelligence, as it does with the child when it has grown into its teens and finds former mysteries being continually solved. At the other end of the scale the really educated man rises to a true perception of the value of knowledge in giving to the individual power to sway not only persons but things and forces to do his bidding. But between the two there is this radical difference: The latter knows that the desired power is only to be gained by a long and patient study of the great book of nature, page by page and line by line, while the other fancies the result can be achieved at a single bound. Only an uncultivated mind could believe the story said to have been told by the serpent in Paradise, that the knowledge of all things, good and evil, was to be obtained by the eating of an apple. Yet some of the crude conceptions of the far away past furnish a startling illustration of the way in which extremes may meet; and for aught we know that may have been one of the ideas intended to be conveyed by the symbol of the snake with its tail in its mouth. A few score years ago nothing could have been more absurd than the story of Aladdin. It was the height of folly to suppose that the mere rubbing of a ring or a lamp would summon up genii who could perform the works described in that fable. But in our day the mere touching of a button has blown up

Hell Gate, the misplacing of a switch sent hundreds of souls into eternity, the tapping of a key caused to flash across the broad ocean a message big with the fate of nations.

Man must early have discovered that the possession of the faculty of speech by himself constituted a vast difference between him and the brute. Hence language was power. The ability to speak enabled him to tell others what he wanted to have done, and when he found some other man speaking a different language, which evidently gave him a similar control over the actions of his fellows, he must have felt an increasing respect for the gift of speech, almost amounting to reverence:—the historical contempt entertained by many peoples for those who could not speak their language belonging to a later phase, as to that of the growing boy. The ability to speak at all carried with it the power to command those who were inferior in physical strength, and its exercise was perhaps the first effort made towards the domestication of the dog. Hence at a very early period the "Word" was elevated to the dignity of an actor. It exerted an influence which might well be supposed capable of a personal entity, after man's first experience with an echo. It was by a series of fiats that the writer of the first chapter of Genesis thought the world was created, and that same "Word" was afterwards believed to be the entity incarnated in the Messiah. The story of that incarnation is told at full length in the first chapter of the Gospel according to John, though very few in the present day have any idea that the Logos there written of was the self same "Word" said to have been spoken by the Elohim. Yet so it is; and the word specifically referred to is the first recorded utterance, *y'hi-'oor.* "Let there be Light." Compare this with the language used by that monk who wrote the said "Gospel" probably little less than two hundred years after the first Christmas:

"In the beginning was the Word, and the Word was with God, and the Word was God. The same was in the beginning with God. All things were made by Him. . . . In Him was life, and the life was the Light of men. And the light shineth in darkness, and the darkness comprehended it not. . . . That was the true Light, which lighteth every man that cometh into the world. . . . And the Word was made flesh and dwelt among us."

Any lingering doubt as to the accuracy of this deduction ought to be dispelled by the discovery that this primal utterance, *y'hi,* was believed to be the original or root of the name of the Deity, *Yahveh.* Probably the conception arose much later than the first writing of the story of creation, and belongs to a comparatively barbarous order of thought. But it long held its own, and for many centuries it was supposed that the utterance of the name, if correctly pronounced, was a powerful charm, capable of making angels or demons do the will of the speaker. Indeed, one of the beliefs of less than

two thousand years ago is said to have been that
the sacred Tetragrammaton, or four lettered word
which is the Hebrew form of the name called Jehovah in English, was written on parchment and sewed
in the thigh of Jesus, and that this was what conferred on him the ability to work his miracles. The
" Word," uttered by one divinely appointed, was
sufficient to heal diseases, cast out demons, and raise
the dead; but it was thought to be of nearly equal
potency when spoken by any one else, with the radical difference that one not duly commissioned would
use his power only for an evil purpose. That was
the secret Simon Magus wanted the apostle Peter to
sell to him, and refused because the applicant was
still " in the gall of bitterness and in the bond of
iniquity." This fear that the power might be mis-
used was doubtless the reason why the Jewish priests
of the olden time were not allowed to speak the
name in the hearing of the people or in any way to
indicate its pronunciation, and the third commandment was cited in support of the exclusiveness. In
consequence of this the true pronunciation is said to
have been irrecoverably lost fully two thousand
years ago.

Gradually the Magians (wise men), built up other
names supposed to be of only lesser avail in procuring the doing of what the sorcerer might wish
for. Armed with the knowledge of these he could
wield a tremendous power, but thereby incurred a
fearful responsibility; or at least this was told the

common people to keep them from seeking out these hidden mysteries. Scott thus voices the opinion in his Lay of the Last Minstrel:

> And, warrior, I could say to thee
> The words that cleft Eildon hills in three,
>   And bridled the Tweed with a curb of stone.
> But to speak them were a deadly sin:
> And for having but thought them my heart within, .
>   A treble penance must be done.

These additional words were the names of spirits, good or bad. The earlier selections were planetary, the later cabalistic. As the planets and their attendant spirits were denoted by certain symbols those characters drawn on parchment, or graven on the metal supposed to be ruled by the planet in question, were always used in the incantation under the notion that its efficacy was thereby increased. By and by, in the onward roll of the centuries, alphabetical writing was invented, and the symbols of spoken sounds were regarded as equally mysterious in their influence. One of the invocations said to have been recommended by King Solomon, and vouched for by him as capable of reducing to submission the most refractory spirit, either celestial or demoniacal, closes with words equivalent to the following: " And I furthermore abjure thee by those awful and mysterious letters, to-wit, *Aleph, Beth, Gimel, Daleth,*" etc., going through the whole string of the Hebrew alphabet. Not a few of the " fearful names " used were simply cabalistic build-

ings up from the initials of the words composing a
sentence, or the first letters in a series of verses in
the Bible. Thus the name Michael is made up from
the first letters of the Hebrew words which mean
"(One) Who is like unto God." The cabalistic
numbers about which so much trash has been written were simply the numerical equivalents of certain magical or other words, the letters being for a
long time the only symbols used to denote numbers.
Thus 5660 is alleged to be the numerical value of
the letters composing the name *Y-eh-ve-h.* Sub-
tracting from that 3761, which is the Jewish count
from the creation to the Christian era, we have 1899
A. D. as "the year of Jehovah," which for that
reason only an Eastern crank has prophecied will
witness the end of the present order of things. We
have a reminder of these literal values in the Roman
notation still in use, where V stands for five, X for
ten, C for a hundred, etc.

The other fundamental doctrine of magic was the
substitution of one thing for another, a process that
has been carried out by the chemists of the present
century to an extent which would have made the
magians of old turn green with envy had a thous-
andth part of it been done in their day. It is the
basic idea of sacrifice as a propitiation for sin. Some
of the books convey the idea that the smoke ascending from the victim was a pleasant incense in the
nostrils of the offended god; and in Leviticus iv.
31 the priest is expressly commanded to burn his

14

offering upon the altar "for a sweet savor unto the Lord." Also in Exodus xxx we find that Jehovah gave directions for the making of an incense peculiarly grateful to his own sense of smell, and in the last verse commanded that any one who should use the recipe for his own private delectation should be "cut off from his people." Occasionally it is hinted that heathen worshippers believed their deities actually ate the food offered to them. This story is countenanced in the story of Bel and the Dragon, which used to form part of the book of Daniel, and is said to be good doctrine among many of the heathen to-day, including the "Chinee." But if credited then or now it is simply because the statement was made by the priests to begin with, and has been repeated to everybody supposed foolish enough to swallow it. The priests wanted the food for themselves and families, but did not dare to say so: and it is one of the most creditable things told of the Jews that they were honest enough to confess the truth. Their law contains explicit directions as to the portions of meat that should go to the priest, and Lev. x. tells how it is to be eaten by him and his children. Also in I. Samuel ii. 16 we find the sons of Eli taking more than belonged to them, which naturally made the Lord angry at being robbed of his share. The priests of other nations were not so honest, or were less closely watched, and therefore, throve better. The Hebrew *Cohen*, or priest, never ranked as especially sacred among the Jews, and only one of him was allowed to penetrate the mystery behind the veil in the tabernacle or temple. The other priests were shut out from it as rigidly as the commonality, at least for all that the latter knew to the contrary, and only the High Priest was allowed to manipulate the sacred breastplate. On the other side of the picture we see the oracle worked by a comparatively low order of priestly talent in the palmy days of Greece and Rome, and the power of life and death confided to the vestal virgins who used to sit in a row watching the gladiatorial contests in the amphitheater. Much later than that time the priesthood has shown itself more powerful than the emperor; and some of the number are fearfully belied if they have not worked hard for the mastery over thrones within the span of the present generation. In the earlier times the priests had an additional "pull" on the business in the fact that they were the only ones who could repeat the sacred hymns or incantations which had to be uttered (really muttered), over the sacrifices in order to render them acceptable to the gods. Before the art of writing had been invented these could only be handed down by word of mouth from one generation to another, and this knowledge was thus easily kept in the exclusive possession of a caste, such as the Brahmans of India.

Of course all this had to be secular, as well as sacred. The substitutional power was too good a thing to be left forever entirely in the hands of the priests, and so the devil and his servants got hold of it for the accomplishment of mischief. At least this was alleged; and confessed to a good many times, under the insignificant condition that the wickedness was admitted when the poor wretch of a sinner had been racked by torture beyond further endurance. Naturally enough the priests condemned it as a most heinous sin, when not authorized by their consecrating laying on of hands; and the bitterness with which they denounced the ungodly sorcerer was only surpassed by the punishments they visited whenever possible upon those priests who dared to diminish the wealth of the people by offering a part of it on the altar of any other god than the one worshipped by themselves. No wonder the pages of the Old Testament teem with denunciations of witches, sorcerors and priests who served other gods than Jehovah, while it conveys hardly a hint that they were impostors in claiming to do something beyond their power. About the only exception to this is found in the story of Elijah and the priests of Baal in offering sacrifice. The magicians employed by Pharaoh are credited with being able to turn rods into serpents and reproduce the plagues of Egypt. The witch of Endor could raise the ghost of Samuel and obtain from it a true prophecy about Saul: and the wise men of Babylon were in like manner simply beaten at their own game by Daniel, as Aaron had surpassed those of Egypt by putting life into a rod that swallowed up all the other serpents which the magicians had conjured out of inanimate sticks. The whole of this story is contained in the seventh chapter of Exodus; to which the reader is respectfully referred with the question if he can possibly believe it. The Book of Job contains equally incredible narrations of two conversations between God and Satan, where the latter tried what some irreverent people might call a game of bluff with the Great Ruler of the Universe. In that narration the devil is credited with the power to rob the righteous Job of everything but his life, and according to Matthew even the sanctity of the temple did not preserve Jesus from his assaults; while a good many of his accursed brood are said to have subsequently taken possession of the bodies of human beings, and one host actually entered into a whole drove of hogs. This by the by, was a legitimate application of the theory of substitution; and no one can deny that the " poor devils " had to go somewhere, unless annihilated, and for that the hour had not yet come. Let not the reader laugh at this as too much for human credulity. Did not King James of England and Cotton Mather in this country, allow that the human servants and ghostly imps of the aforesaid devil were able to and did work all sorts of diabolical harm to good Christians by their enchantments? History answer " Yes ? "

The wickedness wrought by the wizards and witches of the olden times could not be achieved without cabalistic words, but their great card was substitution. The charm had to be uttered over some object supposed to represent with greater or less fidelity the person or thing over which it was desired to throw an evil influence. It might be an article of clothing or other property, or an image of the person to be injured. If the latter it was stuck full of thorns or skewers, pins being employed at a later time; and sometimes was made of wax, in which case it was exposed before a slow fire so as to be gradually consumed, the obnoxious person being supposed to waste away correspondingly. The same idea is held in this century in less dangerous guise, by those who claim that warts may be removed by burying a substitute in the dunghill.

Naturally enough this theory of necessary substitution has been made one of the corner stones of the Christian temple. Nothing but that persistency of ideas could make intelligent men of our own day hold that a God of infinite mercy is a Being so implacable that He could not consent to forgive the sinner against His own laws on any other terms than by the vicarious sacrifice of a part of His Triune Self upon the cross. Of course this plank in the Christian platform was introduced with malice prepense, for the purpose of perpetuating the power of the priests who otherwise might find their occupation gone and " Ichabod " written on the walls of their temples. It was essential to their influence that the people should think God cannot be approached directly, without the intervention of a

Mediator to soothe His anger; and that this advocate must personally be in high favor with God, either by dint of a special consecration to His service or by the past performance of a surplusage of good deeds called by the Catholics works of supererogation, or above duty. Such an advocate must address the high court of heaven in behalf of the culprit, or the latter must perish. The most important step taken in this direction was the early separation of the laity from the clergy in the communion service, that had previously been a gathering at which all partook of the bread and wine, and the elevation of the ceremony to the rank of a sacrifice in which the body of Christ is supposed to be again offered up for the sins of the world after having been manufactured out of a piece of bread by the utterance of a few words in Latin. Of course this important conversion could be effected only by men specially endowed with power for the work and given permission to perform it, while the faithful were deprived of its saving benefit unless they conformed in all things to the will of the priests, including the payment of such sums as were demanded by these "holy men of God." It was the assumption of this ability to "Crucify the Lord afresh" that gave the church of Rome its despotic power over princes and people, rendered it possible to light the fires of the Inquisition over a large part of Europe, and made the Reformation an absolute necessity to civilization.

The naming of Saints' Days in the Christian calendar was a partial catering to the heathen idea that it was convenient to have the multitude think the court was not always in session. This had been a handy and profitable thing for the priests. To ask an Eastern despot for some favor at the wrong time, when he was thinking of some other case or looking out for a new concubine, was worse than not asking at all; as it prejudiced him against the applicant for his favor. Of course it was not regarded as an insult to the god worshipped to suppose him open to sway by the same motives; and we have already seen that the planetary gods were more powerful at some times than at others, besides being of a more amicable disposition. It is true that the Jews never accused their Jehovah of the sensualities ascribed by the Greek poets to his Hellenistic double, but they did represent him as capable of being in widely different moods;—and no wonder if it was thought dangerous to approach him, even with a peace offering, when in some of them. For, according to the Jewish writers, he would be in a deadly rage, when "real mad." He would kill people by wholesale on such occasions, his own chosen ones among the rest; and the worst of it was he did not always limit his punishment to the actual offenders. He killed off ever so many scores of thousands of the Israelites because David ordered the taking of a census, had many a lot of innocent women and children slain for the satisfactory reason that the husbands and fathers did not do just what he wanted, and at one time drowned out the whole world in order to start the work over again, though in his fury he must have destroyed many " Sons of God " who had married the daughters of men in the absence of any recorded command to the contrary. It was easy for even the children of Israel to fall into the notion that it was not true of their deity as Ralph Nickleby said it would be with himself,— " All times alike." This delusion of God's favoritism of times, places and persons was none the less binding because it was an utter perversion of the original idea that dictated the performance of an act of worship.

That original thought was so apposite to the feebleness of the early human intellect that it may be referred to a little more in detail. The sun was to be propitiated at his rising that his beams might only bless and not scorch to destruction. He was to be worshipped at setting to coax him to rise again. When in the course of what we now know is his annual round (and performed with equal accuracy as when the mad astronomer in Rasselas computed beforehand and assigned every phase of his varying motion), he dipped to the lowest point, he was asked if he had cast the people off forever, and implored to revisit the neighborhood of the zenith with his enlivening beams. On his arrival at the spring equinox he was bowed down to as the harbinger of a coming harvest, and at the summit

of his midsummer career it was fitting to acknowledge his majesty when in the language of Watts:

> His glories shine with beams so bright,
> No mortal can behold the sight.

Similarly the planets were worshipped when in their
exaltations, and some of them prayed to as evil genii
when in their fall (occidental). The important part
taken by the moon in fixing the times has already
been alluded to, and it only needs to add that when
in the plentitude of her mensual brightness she too
was an object of adoration for her own sake as well
as for the reason that she was a monitor of times
and seasons.

To grow out of these delusions was a work of
time. The prophetic chronology was not far from
correct on one point. A day in the lifetime of an
individual corresponds roughly to a year in the history of the race. In ten years the boy of our age in-
creases his knowledge about as much as the race has
done in the last thirty-six centuries. And the most
important part of that progress is in the ability to
distinguish between the true and the false, to see the
early glamour reduced to plain matter of fact, to
find out first that in the language of Betsy Prig,
"there aint no sech person" as Santa Claus, then
that Little Red Riding Hood, Jack the Giant Killer,
and Aladdin are myths, and that miracles are not
performed every day now;—however it may have been
in the long ago. Occasionally a big jump is taken
in a short interval. That was the case with the
writer when a boy. He saw in front of a traveling

show a painting said to represent "William Wallace, the Scottish Giant" and thought him a monster. He paid the admission fee, and found the promise not half verified. The next morning he strolled by the "show" while it was being prepared for removal to another place and saw the "giant" attired in a suit of corduroys piling poles, etc., on a wagon. The said "William Wallace" was then a rather large man, "this and nothing more." The experience of that few hours has risen up in recollection some hundreds of times since then, and found to be far from the only instance in which an early delusion was pretty effectually dispelled on a closer acquaintance with the fact.

So with man in the aggregate. Every now and then a sunburst of intelligence beams out upon the mentality of a nation, and it wonders how a stated thing could have been believed for so long. The average progress of a century is achieved in a decade of years. Yet this accretion of intelligence is apt to strike individuals instead of peoples, and to become disseminated among the latter by a much slower process. It was but the work of a few years for Copernicus to discover that the sun is the center of the solar system and for Kepler to prove to his own satisfaction that the squares of the times are proportional to the cubes of the distances; but it took the scientific world a much longer time to accept these truths as the bases for new investigations of the facts of planetary motion.

XII.

PICTURE READING.

" Wilt thou not show us what thou meanest by these?"—Ezekiel.

Ideography, the Third Step in Theology —Changes from Pictorial Representation to Word Writing.—Numerous Errors Arise in the Translation.—Instances in Babylonian Account of Creation, and Suppositive Shemitic Pictures.—Reconciliation of Alleged History with Fact.—Grecian Myths.—Early Picture Methods in Modern Forms of Speech.

Enough has been said to prove to the satisfaction of the unprejudiced searcher for truth that the most ancient religions originated in astrology and magic; and that those two forms were the twin parents whence sprang the varied brood of ideas around which the ancients grouped themselves in the act of worship. Hence, it "follows, as the night the day," that to those two sources the Christian world is indebted for much of the material that is incorporated in the creeds of the present generation:—they having been formulated by men of like passions with the early thinkers, and being to a vastly greater extent than the world is aware of simply recasts of the very oldest fears and superstitions of the race. If the church members of these modern times were not ignorant of this they would surely hesitate before attempting to kick aside the ladder up which they or their predecessors have climbed to their comprehension of the attitude of the Deity towards erring mortals, and in some measure to their estimates of his character and power. The ladder on which Jacob is said to have seen in his dream the angels of God ascending and descending between earth and heaven is fabled by some of the theologians to have had three "rungs" or steps; and they even went so far as to say the names of those steps were Faith, Hope and Charity. The writer takes the liberty of suggesting a decided improvement on this nomenclature. Two of the steps have already been described. The third is Ideography. It is by the aid of these three that human thought has mounted towards the skies and essayed to pierce the glory supposed to enshroud the throne of the Almighty. Whether or not their success was better than that said to have attended the muscular exertions of the Babel builders need not be discussed here. The writer is unwilling to take the responsibility of asserting that the faith structure is not founded on a rock and composed of good material. His strictures scarcely extend farther than those of the prophet of old who alluded to some men as "daubing up the wall with untempered mortar" in the attempt to hide defects that exist only in their own distorted imaginations.

The earliest attempts at writing were of the picture kind. The first writers were artists, and there are millions of adult human beings alive to-day who have not yet passed that stage, while some have scarcely reached it. The Indians of this continent, who within the memories of white men now living have sketched rude pictures of men and horses on bark or the skins of animals, with simple marks for arrows, etc., as their only means of "writing" an account of a battle or other historical event, do as the people of many ages had to do before the invention of an alphabet. It is fair to presume that the earliest picture writing was strictly literal, as the outline of a lion scratched upon a smooth surface being left in a cave was a sign that the animal had been seen in the vicinity, or perhaps that the person leaving it had gone away on a hunt. This style of writing may have been practiced in the strictly hunting stage of human existence. But we know that it was vastly improved upon and succeeded by the partly ideographic method long before either was driven out by the use of marks each of which represented a sound or a syllable. The writer wanted to convey ideas of qualities and conditions, and therefore employed symbols. For instance, the flight of arrows indicated the fact of a combat, and their direction the side that had gained the victory. The sign for the moon indicated time. Among the more highly cultivated peoples this was gradually developed into comparatively "high art." The picture of a snake signified wisdom, or cunning; when recumbent, craft and secret injury: when coiled, readiness for open hostility; when with the tail in its mouth, an indef-

inite time (as eternity, which is said to be without
beginning or end). The lion was a symbol of no-
bleness and courage, the hawk of rapacity, the tiger
of cruelty and blood thirstiness, the owl of silent
wisdom, etc. The actualization of this class of
thought led to some groupings that to-day would be
called strange. The original Minerva is said to have
had the head of an owl on human shoulders; afterwards she was represented as accompanied by that
bird. Ezekiel in his visions saw a man with the
countenance of a lion, probably intended to be understood as a human being with some leonine quality. The hundred arms of Briareus may have been
intended to mean nothing more than that Mr. B.
could do as much with his two arms as an ordinary
man would be able to accomplish with fifty times
as many; and the story has been parodied in this
century by representing the celebrated pianist,
Thalberg, seated at the instrument, with a host of
fingers on the key-board. Wings appended to the
human form were intended to signify fleetness, and
in this way Mercury was denoted to be the messenger of the gods. The Satyr was a man who lived
among goats, herding them; and the terrible Cy-
clops, pictured with one fierce eye in the middle of
his forehead, was simply a far sighted one. To-day
we have pictures of an old man with an hour glass
and a scythe to represent ''Old Father Time,'' the
astronomical symbol for the planetoid Ceres is the
figure of a reaping hook, and the arrow part of the

mark used by astronomers to denote the planet Mars is a relic of the times when he was universally thought to be the god of war. Other examples of the application of ideography in picture writing might be cited, almost without end.

It took a long time to step from the pictorial method of designating objects and facts up to the representation of sounds by the use of written characters. The change was a gradual one. It is well known that the earliest attempts at an alphabet were made by taking the picture of an object to denote the first sound in the name of that object; and this interesting phase of development has been traced in more than one part of the world. The best preserved evidences of it are found in connection with the Coptic and Shemitic tongues. Thus, in the Hebrew the first three letters are *Aleph* (ox), *Beth* (house), and *Gimel* (camel); and the earliest representations of the sounds *Ah*, *B*, and hard *G* were rude pictures of those things. Of course when (a few among the) people had become used to alphabetic writing it was no longer necessary to employ the full forms. The symbols of the sounds were contracted, and ultimately changed out of all semblance to the objects. These, and the other pictures of a door, the hand, the eye, a fish, flowing water, a hook, etc., became such mere arbitrary marks that very few people now know there was ever any connection between them and alphabetic signs. Another interesting fact in this connection has been developed. The earliest alphabetic writing was not exclusively so. It was mixed with ideographic. The name of a man was written phonetically, while the story in connection with him was told in the older pictorial fashion.

Any one who is interested in pursuing this line of thought will do well to compare the characters of the Hebrew, Arabic, Sanscrit, German and English alphabets as they are written or printed now. Disregarding the few characters in each which represent sounds not common to all, they show widely different forms for substantially the same sounds or letters. Can he doubt that among different peoples using the ideographic form of written expression there should be at least an equal diversity in the values attached to the different symbols? And if he does not doubt that, he can easily see how the ideographic characters employed by one set of people could be misinterpreted in whole or in part by other readers, even in the same age. But now let us suppose that the pictures made by one set of men on the banks of the Euphrates were found several hundred years later by another set hailing from the shores of the Red Sea, that in the interval alphabetic writing had been invented, and that the finders should undertake to translate those picture stories into alphabetic statement. Suppose, if you will, the situation to be reversed, the dwellers on the Euphrates finding such treasures in the valley of the Nile, or in any other to them accessible part of the globe. What would be the result to-day? If some answer

15

can be mentally framed to the last question the chances of misinterpreting must be multiplied many times to find those for a case in which the readers were densely ignorant as compared with the men who have undertaken to decipher Eastern hieroglyphics in this century. Now see to what it might lead. We might say " must " if the deductions in regard to error be understood generally, not specifically.

The Babylonian account of the creation, written in Greek by Berosus in the third century B. C., is given in a preceding chapter. It has been confirmed recently by the reading of certain cuneiform inscriptions of a much earlier period. Doubtless Berosus translated from them; but by whom were they " written?" Not by an eye witness of the event; and we do no violence to the faith of Jew or Christian in saying they were not an inspired production. Were they not, in turn, translations from some earlier record, and that an ideographic one? If " Yes," how easy to suppose that first story was partly misunderstood by the person or persons who read off those pictures into syllables to be represented by the cuneiform characters. How natural the thought that the picture of the woman Thalatth was introduced to convey the idea of generation from or by the sea itself instead of by a gigantic human form. And those pictures of mongrel creatures, aptly described as beings that could not bear the light; may they not have been intended by the artist to chronicle the fact that partly recognized fossil remains (comprising mixtures of the bones of different animals, as we would now read it), had been discovered in the soil, and quickly crumbled to dust when exposed to the air above ground? A few such lenient thoughts as these will enable us to suppose it at least possible that the delineator of the first pictures was a moderately sensible being, for his day; and honestly attempted to tell the truth as it appeared to him, but had the misfortune to be misunderstood by those who essayed to rewrite the story perhaps many centuries after his death.

We cannot hope to recover the first forms in which were told the stories found in the earlier books of the Old Testament. But for the purpose of illustrating the way in which radical blunders might be committed honestly one may think of a few ideographic representations; each of which, owing to pardonable errors in the reading, could differ widely from the story as told in written words. Thus:

1. Picture of a naked woman, with snake erect, both near a tree, and a naked man in the distance. Intention of artist to intimate that the woman is wise, and that being hungry she is going to eat some of the fruit from that tree in spite of the forked lightning in the air above warning her to flee for shelter from a coming storm. She holds an apple towards the man, intimating that he need not be afraid to eat, as the rain will not descend just yet.

Possibly the intention was to show that feminine curiosity first led to the discovery that apples or some other fruit are good to eat. The interpreter translates it to read as in the third chapter of Genesis. In a companion picture the storm has burst, the woman is running away, and the snake is crawling off to get out of the wet. It is translated to mean that God is angry with them for gathering apples when there is nobody else to claim the fruit as his property. In supposing these persons to be the first man and woman, simply because they have no clothes on, the reader of the ideographs is not so absurd as the modern traveler who described the inhabitants of a country from a few seen on the beach getting ready for a swim just as the ship sailed past them. (It may be noted, however, that the Genesis story of the Fall is undoubtedly a phallic one. It reports in symbolical language the initiation of our supposed first parents into what have since been called the Eleusinian mysteries.)

2. Picture of a boat on dry land, this being indicated by sheep and cattle grazing near it. Intention of artist to show that an unusual flood in the river adjoining has raised the water so high that the boat was carried there by a wave and left high and dry. Perhaps also human figures in the water intended to tell that some were drowned or narrowly escaped drowning. Read into the story of a flood "covering the whole earth." Companion picture of men working on a high building, the intention

of the artist being to indicate that the people wanted to have a place to which they could retreat in case of another great overflow. Foolishly translated to read that they wished to get to heaven that way; when the actual aim was to show a desire to avoid going there before dying out of old age.

3. Picture of old man lying on (death) bed, with twelve other men forming a circle around him. Intention of artist to represent the expiring year, with the twelve constellations (corresponding to lunations), during which he has run his course. Tortured into the story of Jacob prophesying the future of his twelve sons and their descendants; though anybody can see in the description of those blessings and forecasts (Genesis xlix), that they correspond to the signs of the Zodiac, and there is no good reason to believe that previous to the time of David the Jews were a homogeneous people or ever assembled under one leadership. Before that they had been nothing more than a number of clans or tribes, owing no common fealty and having no common origin. All before that is shrouded in the thickest veil of uncertainty, through which we have no guide. But we may be pretty sure the stories told in the books of Joshua and Judges are untrue, simply because it is impossible those things could ever have occurred; and it may be added there is lots of stuff in the so called Torah, that is the five books of Mosheh, which is open to the same sweeping exception. They condemn themselves as

the work of superstitious, ignorant men who wrote statements that cannot possibly be true, any more than the claim to have invented perpetual motion sometimes heard now.

We can follow this process of change a little more closely in the Greek, but probably for the sole reason that we have in the classics of that language a larger amount as well as a greater variety of material to draw from. Possibly, too, among the Hellenic thinkers the process of substitution was voluntarily carried out to a rather wide amplitude with little mistake, the change being at first more poetic than supposedly literal, but afterwards accepted as historical by the less well informed. No one need doubt that Zeus (the greatest among the gods), is anything more or less than a poetical incarnation of the planet Jupiter, though we may not be able to trace out distinctly that concept in the minds of the philosophical men who developed the analogy. The wits who tried to hold him up to ridicule belonged to a later generation, but it is hard to read the first few lines of the Phenomena of Aratus without being convinced that the poet regarded him as something far above any mere human form; and Paul's quotation from the fifth line, cited in our seventh chapter, may be thought by some to justify a suspicion that he, too, believed the Latin Jove-h was but another name for the Hebrew Jahveh.

The story of Danæ and the shower of gold may be read as a fable intended to show the power of

riches to corrupt innocence, without intention to
reflect on the character of Zeus any more than Esop
did in his fable of the fox and the grapes; and even
if it be accepted literally it is not much worse than
the tale about David, the " man after God's own
heart" seducing Bathsheba with the glitter of his
kingly tinsel and having her husband killed to get
him out of the way. The story about the father-
god in the shape of a white bull carrying off the
maiden Europa may perhaps be but an idea-graphic
way of telling that when the first migrant passed
over from Asia to Europe there was so little of a
water-way obstruction that a woman could cross it
safely on the back of an ox (Bosporus means the
same as Ox-ford), and some of the latest discoveries
in physical geography point back to a time when
the land surface in that part of the world was higher
than to-day; the two continents joining near the
present Constantinople as they now do north of the
Black Sea. If it be a mere fable without a moral
it is no worse than the one about the Israelites
crossing the Red Sea after having " borrowed"
the jewelry of the Egyptians, with their vessels of
gold and silver, literally despoiling them. Lucian
makes (heavy) fun about Zeus giving birth to
Athena (Minerva) from his head, and Dionysus
(Bacchus) from his thigh. But the idea of wisdom
springing full armed from the brain of Jove is no
more absurd than that of the Logos launched from
the mouths of the Elohim, as told in the first chap-

ter of Genesis, which Logos John says "became flesh and dwelt among us, and we beheld his glory;" though we may be unable to appreciate the fate of poor Semelé which made the femoral parturition a necessity.

We pass by a great mass of this material. With the key to its meaning once in his hand, the reader of the classics will experience little difficulty in tracing out the analogies for himself. It may, however, be permitted to allude to the story of Herakles (Hercules is probably an older as well as a more expressive name), whose mythical twelve labors have been partially identified with the effects produced by the sun in passing through the twelve signs of the Zodiac. We have previously hinted that the twelve sons of Jacob were the constellations themselves, and it may be added that there is some reason to think the Hebrew Shimshon, which the Greek Septuagint made to read " Sampson," is but an imperfect version of the Hellenic demi-god. Also it may interest the reader to note that the Argonautic expedition in search of the ram with the golden fleece is probably a pictorial history of the earliest recorded hunt for gold. The yellow grains of that metal were obtained from auriferous streams by hanging a fleece in the current, and the precious particles became entangled in the wool, from which they were subsequently washed out. When taken from the stream it was literally a gold bearing fleece; but long before it assumed that character in the hands of the gold hunters it had forever parted company with the ram. - Yet it is not impossible that Jason and his companions did not know this till after they had captured the fleece; the mast of their ship not having cared to reveal the secret in advance, though said to have been endowed with the power of prophecy. This very method of catching gold from the stream was heralded to the world as a new thing so late as 1888, being credited to a miner in Montana. Truly did a wise man of old exclaim, "There is nothing new under the sun."

We have noted the identity of Hercules and Samson, and may add that the Dejanira of the one was the Delilah of the other. Perhaps the mythical character of the latter may be inferred from the fact that the name signifies the "weakener," and that according to the story it was conferred upon her before she had earned the title. That is not the way in which nicknames are bestowed upon genuine personages in our day nor in any other. The fate of both heroes menaces the intellectuality of those who accept the old wives' fables of either the Jewish scriptures or the Grecian mythology as veritable narrations of fact. There is no sense in holding to the one and despising the other. The stories of Old Mother Goose are equally entitled to be regarded as literally true, and the Arabian Nights' Entertainments contain fully as good philosophy. But to one who can read between the lines all convey grains of wisdom, apart from their value in helping us to an insight into the mental exhibitions of human nature in the days when there was no science but all the more faith. In the latter respect such things are equally essential to an understanding of present conditions as are the steps in the reasoning to a mastery of a geometrical theorem; and this in spite of the now well ascertained mental law that " The more a man knows the less he believes."

The idea painters of the remote past did not differ so widely from ourselves as many may suppose, except in manner. Our own language is but one of hundreds in which a multitude of terms, having meanings entirely physical, have been adapted to the abstract and made to do it eminent service. For instance, we speak of high aspirations and low motives, moral uprightness, rectitude of character, distorted (twisted) views, and latitude in expression. We use the closed fist as a symbol of avarice, and the lifted eyelids (supercilia), for disdain. We sometimes speak of men as tigers, wolves, foxes, bulls, bears, hogs, and snakes in the grass; and occasionally a woman is spoken of as an angel, or likened to a fawn or a dove, while now and then one of either sex is described as a star. These are familiar examples of substitutions so numerous that if the language were robbed of them it would be reduced to a lamentable poverty, incapable of expressing some of the most common-place facts, to say nothing of the wealth of poetry, which is well nigh all ideographical. Furthermore, many of the differences of opinion that exist to-day about matters of acknowledged fact, arise from the circumstance that two men do not attach the same shades of meaning to expressions which involve comparisons or describe one thing by reference to another. And if this be the case now, among folks who have received a formal training in the use of language as a means of expressing thought, we can hardly wonder that the men of earlier ages made grave mistakes in the effort to translate pictures into words.

The fault lies not so much with them as with ourselves. They did the best they knew how, and this claim may even be made for such men as Eusebius, who there is every reason to believe committed wholesale forgery in the manufacture of "evidence" in support of Christianity. We owe a debt of gratitude to the men who by means of their word pictures left an impress upon the ages to be read long after their bodies had crumbled into dust. No doubt the better class of them would gladly acknowledge their errors if allowed to revisit the the earth and compare their work with what has been discovered of Nature and her methods since their day. It is the foolish ones among ourselves who persist in treating as infallible inspiration that may not be questioned the work of babes in intellect, and mere gropers in the dark, instead of men enjoying the flood of sunlight that now bathes the world in knowledge "as the waters cover the sea." It would be equally philosophical to accept as gospel verity the prattle of children of this generation, and set it up as competent evidence that scientific men do not understand what they are talking about, simply because we give the youngsters credit for acting according to the old maxim that "None but children and fools speak the truth."

The Almighty may have ordained praise out of the mouths of babes and sucklings, but they ought not to be held responsible for the soundness of their views, philosophical or theological. Why then should it be necessary for a man in the present day to say he would willingly give his right arm to be able to state truly that there are no errors in the Bible? It would be fully as rational to deplore the existence of spots on the sun, evil in this world, or "blood on the moon?" What a pity it is that some being equally willing as Dr. Harper to suffer for the common good was not consulted by the Elohim before they undertook the work of Creation.

XIII.

EARLY PHYSIC.

" In his disease he sought not to the Lord but to the physicians."—II. Chronicles.

The First Doctor.—Priests Curing Diseases as well as Caring for Souls. —Prayer the Best Medicine.—Planetary and Stellar Dominion over the Body.—Physicians Among Christians and Pagans.—Demoniac Possession.—Raising the Dead.—Modern Medication.—Ancient Theory of the Constitution of Matter.

As the father of a family was the first priest, so the mother must have been the first doctor; and it seems probable that the older people of both sexes differentiated into these capacities long before a scrap of history had been written or pictured, except what is graven by the hand of Nature upon the rocks. Woman has acted as a nurse for the sick all through the ages, and combined with that function the privilege of prescribing remedies, but usually those of the simplest kind; while the man official mostly took care of souls and revenues—professing to a higher knowledge of the human frame and its needs but using it only in subordinate connection with the more general oversight which he exercised as one standing between the people and the gods. The physician as apart from the priest is a comparatively modern invention, and during nearly the

237

whole course of his history he has been regarded by
the other as an intruder who had no rights that either
the gods or their priestly representatives were
bound to respect. Nor should we find much fault
with the position, though entitled to despise the motive. The surgeon has ever been a benefactor to
mankind, when he has not thought more of a brilliant operation than of aiding the sufferer. The mere
prescriber of remedies to be taken internally has
killed ten where he has cured one, and it may even
be doubted if the enlightened practice of the present
age works more than one cure for fifty patients. The
great majority of those who get well recover in spite
of the medication rather than in consequence of it. A
prominent member of the regular school remarked a
few years ago: "Out of every fifty persons who
fall sick, take medicine and get well, forty-nine
would recover without medicine. The fiftieth is
cured by good old-fashioned medication." It is on
the fact embodied in this statement that the quacks
thrive. They live on the credulity of the public,
and regard the sick as their legitimate prey. Can
much more than that be justly claimed for the average doctor of souls?

Of course the primitive belief that the planets
and their intelligencies were the authors of all that
befell mortals included the idea that bodily disease,
like other forms of suffering, was caused by them
and could only be averted or cured by their agency.
Hence, the one who desired to escape or recover

from physical ailment addressed himself to the gods
directly, or through the mediation of the priests.
We may cite a few examples of this from so-called
scripture history, with the remark that they are
simply exponential of ideas which dominated the
minds of all the peoples of antiquity. The ten
plagues of Egypt were said to have been inflicted by
Yah-veh, through a priest, and even the magicians
were covered with boils because of his anger against
their master. The Israelites are reported to have
been on more than one occasion smitten with the
plague, the ravages of which were stayed when the
anger of the Lord had been averted by suitable intercession. Also II. Chron. xvi. 12 and 13, contains something like a sneer at King Asa, intimating
that he died because "he sought not to the Lord
but to the physicians." Not only the prophets of
the Old Testament but the apostles of the New had
power over life and death as well as disease. The
Acts of the Apostles tell how Peter commanded the
death of Ananias and Sapphira, cured Eneas of the
palsy, and restored Tabitha to life; while Paul healed
a cripple, brought Eutychus back to life, and even
had so much power that (Acts xix. 12), " from his
body were brought unto the sick handkerchiefs or
aprons, and the diseases departed from them, and
the evil spirits went out of them." Certainly no
man who believes this can experience any difficulty
in accepting as true what is told in the Gospels
about the miraculous doings of Jesus. If the apos-

tles could thus subvert the course of Nature at least as great things could be performed by Him who had conferred the power upon them. Nor is it to be wondered at that the same power has been claimed for some of their successors, making the earlier records of the Romish church fairly bristle with miracles. Neither should we be too severe in judgment upon the faith healers of to-day since they have in James v. 14 and 15, the following undisputed apostolic warrant for their belief and practice: "Is any sick among you? Let him call for the elders of the church; and let them pray over him, anointing him with oil in the name of the Lord; and the prayer of faith shall save the sick, and the Lord shall raise him up; and if he have committed sins they shall be forgiven him."

Not much use for doctors in the early church, nor recognition of the value of their services. If the churches of to-day kept the faith as it was once committed to the saints, and believed all that was written by the prophets and apostles, they could not recognize the physician, much less pay him for advice and take his prescriptions. They would have no more use for doctors than John Wesley had for tavern keepers when he issued his pronunciamento against their being allowed to "join the Methodists." They would esteem the doctor as a heretic whose denial of the faith made him "worse than an infidel," since his theory and practice are in direct opposition to the teachings of the Bible and the usages of primitive Christianity.

In very early times the same course of procedure would ensure the gaining of a battle, the finding of treasure, and the removal of disease. The priest was dealt with on the same plan as that adopted in gaining a point with an earthly chief. He had to be bribed with "a present" or offering. If there were no rival claimant, and no previous cause for displeasure, a comparatively small bribe was enough; but in the case of opposition it must be a big one. Hence, for cases of ordinary sickness, where no one else was anxious to get the person out of the way, a little present would do; while when the fate of nations hung in the balance a royal one must be paid, and even then the suitor was not sure the other party did not offer more. But at a rather early stage in the history of the process it was reasoned out that particular powers must be appealed to for help in particular cases, according to the planet or star holding dominion. Man was supposed to have been created under the rule of (and by) the five planets, and they were pictured as shining with a halo of glory around his head when in a state of primeval innocence he held sweet communion with the gods (planetary spirits), during the pastoral age. But his fall placed him under the rule of the Zodiacal constellations, among which his body was parcelled out as it might be cut up by a cook for a cannibal feast. Pictures representing this distribution are still to be met with in the patent medicine almanacs. The key to this change

16

from planets to star groups is furnished by the astrological idea that the power and character of each
planet varies as it moves through the constellations.
It is sometimes good and at others bad, instead of
" all good " as at first; for even Saturn, now the
most malevolent of all, was supposed to cause comfort if not real happiness when well dignified and
in favorable aspect to the significator.

The celestial influences were thought to consist of
varying admixtures of four primary qualities,
namely, heat, moisture, cold and dryness. In this
age we define the latter pair as the absence or negation of the former; but the sensation of being cooled
is pretty much the same whether we consider it as
due to a subtraction of heat or an increment of cold.
The ancients knew nothing of the vast array of
chemical elements now described in the text books.
They recognized the existence of four, the same
being fire, air, earth and water. These were characterized respectively as hot and dry, hot and moist,
cold and dry, and cold and moist. Each of these
was the embodiment of one of the original Elohim,
before Mercury was known to be a planet. Saturn
was earthy, Jupiter airy, Mars fiery and Venus
watery. After Mercury was admitted into the
company he was regarded as always dry, but cold
or hot according to his situation and aspect. The
moon was believed to be always moist but varying
in temperature, and the sun always hot but varying
from moist to dry according to position and aspect—

the luminaries not being regarded as causative till a comparatively recent date. A planet when oriental (rising before the sun), was supposed to operate suddenly, as causing accidents, and when occidental (setting after the sun), to produce disease; the character of the effect in each case being determined by the nature of the planet and of the stars influencing him or her.

The bodily constitution of the individual was believed to be determined by the positions of the stars at his birth. If Saturn dominated, the temperament was what later philosophers called the nervous; if Jupiter, the sanguine; if Mars, the bilious; and if Venus, the lymphatic. The usual result was a mixture of these in different proportions, according to the relative strength of the planets at the time; and the radical constitution was varied during the subsequent life by the movements of the planets over or otherwise with respect to certain significant places in the birth figure. But all other earthly substances were also supposed to be under stellar dominion; and with this fact in mind the reader will have no difficulty in understanding the logic that instigated the treatment of disease when people realized, as we sometimes hear it stated nowadays, that "*something* has got to be done." Occasionally the principle of "contraria contraria curantur" was acted on, as an herb or its root thought to be under the dominion of Jupiter was administered for the cure of a disease believed to be caused by Saturn. But generally the opposite, or homeopathic treatment was resorted to, the idea being that "like cures like." And it was by no means always considered necessary to administer medicine internally. Its exterior exhibition was often enough. We have an instance of this idea (not historical fact), in Numbers xxi. where Moses is said to have made a serpent of brass, a mere look at which was sufficient to cure any one who had been bitten by the fiery serpents in the wilderness. And this is mentioned in one of the Gospels as a sign that the Son of Man should also be lifted up.

The Grecian Æsculapius, probably a fabulous character, though immortalized by connecting him with the constellation Ophiucus, is often spoken of as the father of physicians, and his followers as real practitioners of the healing art. But this is not warranted. The Asclepiadæ were exclusively priests, and confined their consultations to the temples in which they ministered. There was a school of Pythagoreans who visited the sick at their residences, and quack doctors who offered their nostrums in the market places, but nothing is known of the work of either; and it must have been limited by very small boundaries both of practice and patronage. When in the latter part of the fifth century B. C. Hippocrates gathered the scattered medical knowledge of his day he did not find much: but is worthy of admiration through all time for his recognition of the principle of "nature" and laying it down as a rule that the great object of the physician should be to watch the operation of this principle, to aid or restrain it, and rarely to counteract it. The gymnasiarchs had, however, before his time, attained to considerable skill in setting fractures, reducing dislocations and swellings, etc., for those who attended the gymnasium. Aristotle was the son of a physician, and it is thought he practiced the art early in life, as his writings display a good knowledge of comparative anatomy. In the second century A. D. lived Galen and Dioscorides, and then for many centuries medicine was at a stand still. How little of anatomy was understood in his day may be inferred from the advice by Galen to students to visit Alexandria, where they could see a human skeleton. Dissection of the *cadaver* was regarded with horror alike by pagans and Christians, and the prejudice of the latter has not long since yielded to the demands of science for opportunities to study the dead that the living may be benefitted thereby. The opposition of the church appears to have been chiefly based on the theory that the chances of a joyful resurrection were badly impaired by dismemberment. For the same reason it frowned on cremation, and laid great stress upon the necessity for " Christian burial." The body had to be laid away carefully in a sanctified spot, so that the archangel could make no mistake in finding the place on the resurrection morn; and the sign of the cross upon his remains was the priestly certificate that the newly risen one had done his duty by the church and, therefore, belonged to the elect. And be it observed that neither Christian nor Jew is entitled to the honor of first teaching the doctrine of a future life. Human beings carefully buried their dead long before the time claimed for the call of Abraham, and put by the side of the corpse tools, weapons, ornaments and even food, which might be useful when the time came for the awakening. Neolithic man may not have had a sure and certain hope of a blessed immortality, but must have had a glimmering idea that a resurrection of the body was possible, if not probable. Perhaps this idea entered his mind just as soon as he had sufficient mentality to feel flattered by the thought that in this respect he was superior to "the beast that perisheth." And it naturally linked on to the supposed elevation of heroic ancestors to a place among the gods.

Those who accept the doctrine of a final resurrection have no right to find fault with others who have believed that the bodies of the dead have been raised soon after the vital spark had fled. The latter is a small miracle compared with the former, and should be an easy task to one properly endowed with power from on high. The science of these modern days does not permit us to believe in either; though it is far from denying the possibility of a separate spiritual existence, which for aught we know may be eternal. That is a subject with which science does not help us to grapple with a reasonable hope of solving it, except by experience. But the writer ventures to suggest that the persistence of memory does constitute an argument in favor of the belief in a future state of existence, and a far stronger one than any derived from alleged inspiration or an appeal to our vanity.

According to Pliny there was not a physician in Rome for about six centuries. Efforts were made to cure diseases, but they consisted chiefly of superstitious observances. In accordance with the advice given in the Sibylline books pestilence was repeatedly staid by the erection of a temple to Apollo or Esculapius, by celebrating public games, or by the dictator driving a nail into the temple. The first prominent recognition of a physician in Rome was probably that accorded by Julius Cæsar, who decreed that all of them in that city should enjoy the privilege of citizenship.

So far as we are able to discover, the people never took kindly to the idea of medicine till within the last two or three centuries. The priests discouraged it so persistently that physic was hardly ever taken except by stealth, and then only by the strong minded ones who did not believe in the efficacy of sacrifices or incantations. The latter formed for and with the multitude the panacea for human ills, and this has been the case under the Christian dispensation as well as among the pagans. The power to cure lay with the priest by virtue of his consecration to the office of minister for whatever god or gods he might represent; and when the divine right of kings began to be preached in the middle ages the supposed power to heal disease with a touch was one of the penalties of increased greatness. Hence arose the custom of royal touching for scrofula, which for that reason soon became known as the "king's evil," and a lot of other complaints were subsequently added to the list of mortal ills that could be made to vanish with a touch by the finger of "The Lord's Anointed." This obtained among Protestants, while the Catholics took more kindly to the idea of healing by the bones of a dead saint than the flesh of a live king, the latter being after all but a servant of the church.

The Christians are entitled to the honor of establishing the first hospitals and dispensaries. They began that noble work in the fourth century, and under their emperors every Roman town of a certain size had its archieter or chief physician, without an examination by whom no one was allowed to practice medicine in that place. But as against this the Christian church has earned for itself an everlasting shame by standing head and shoulders above all the rest in preaching the doctrine that men and women are sometimes possessed by devils which can only be cast out by one holding a direct commission from God. According to the Old Testament the possessed ones were prophets, divinely inspired; and the only one distinctly stated in that book to have a "familiar spirit '' had power to raise the ghost of Samuel and was consulted by the greatest man in Israel. Among the Greeks the enthusiasts (the word signifies " in a madness "), were at least occasionally made so by being placed on a tripod over an issue of intoxicating gas, and then the words they uttered were oracular. It was reserved to the men who wrote the gospels to discover that numerous devils made a business of entering human beings and abiding in those tabernacles of flesh and blood till cast out by Jesus of Nazareth. They invented these devils for the purpose of finding him work to do worthy of his power, just as after the destruction of Jerusalem had rendered verification impossible they invented for him actions in order that they could point to him as fulfilling the prophecies. The apostles found some of these devils after their master had departed from among them, and the said imps were duly cast out, after which we hear little more of them till nearly modern times. Then both Catholics and Protestants found a plentiful crop of them. It mattered not whether the poor human beings who entertained them were called heretics or witches. The result was much the same. They were burnt at the stake. It may be objected that the heretic was not formally charged with being a subject of demoniacal possession, but none can truly deny that such was substantially the crime imputed to him or her, and it might not even be washed out in the blood of the offender. Compare for a moment the merciless character of the later Christians with the earlier ones who admitted that the possessed man could be restored to his right mind and sit properly clothed at the feet of Jesus. The inquisitors and witch burners had no such charity, but acted as if they themselves were possessed of the devil, if such a thing be possible. Oh Christianity! What hundreds of thousands of foul murders have been committed in thy name!

We may smile contemptuously at the medical follies of the ancients, and pity the fate of the poor patients, whether they paid out their money for priestly incantations, in preparations for receiving the touch of some great one, or for the atrocious compounds which the doctors prescribed for them. But both the contempt and the pity may be spared for those of the last century, and even for some in times which can be remembered by persons still alive. Bleeding to the point of exhaustion of the vital force, and the administration of large doses of virulent poison, constituted the "heroic treatment" which was strictly orthodox till far less than a hundred years ago. Calomel and the lancet were the favorite remedies of the average practitioner, both used on every occasion; though the former was generally mixed with some other drug theoretically intended to "carry it off" ere it got in its deadliest work. During all the years that style of treatment prevailed the doctor was the worst enemy of the sick person, who recovered only in case his constitution was strong enough to come off victorious over the physician as well as the disorder. The medical fraternity is wiser now, giving less medicine and paying more attention to what used to be absurdly called the non-naturals. But the doctor still prescribes too much, often because he knows that the patient expects to be drugged and will call in another physician rather than go without it. Nor was it half so absurd to pay for a prayer in ancient times as it is now to privately dose with quack remedies of the nature of which the user knows nothing except what is told in print by some man who, for aught he kens to the contrary, may be " the biggest liar in Christendom."

If the ancient idea of four qualities determining the constitution and condition of the human frame be not good philosophy to-day it is nearer to harmony with the advanced thought of the age than with the medical theories of half a century ago. The well educated physician now knows that functional derangement is a change of condition which results in diseased tissue if the functional disturbance continues long enough. He does not seek to change the composition of that tissue by pouring in drug material from without. He is aware that the best he can hope to do is to stimulate to increased action or soothe some particular organ, and that interior medication can only accomplish this by a process which would be destructive if the dose be too great or too often administered.

He knows it is the wakening up of the organ or tissue to resist this semi-poisoning and get rid of the material that constitutes the beginning of the change he hopes to effect; and that anything more than that is usually a hindrance to recovery instead of a help towards it. He is wise enough to be aware that good (not pure) air and water are essential to perfect health; but that the amount of moisture in the one and the temperature of the other have much to do with the health of the patient, while variations of temperature and moisture at the surface of the body are among the most important agencies he can employ for the effecting of changes internally. In all this he is acting on lines of thought laid down by the ancient astrologers, and does so more intelligently than they simply because the accumulated experience of the race enables him to be wiser than his predecessors.

Reference has been made to the views entertained by Anaximander, Lucretius, and Horace in regard to the origin of man. It is due to another Grecian philosopher that more extended mention be made of his theory of the constitution of matter. Democritus, whose birth is variously assigned as 494 to 460 B. C. held that the universe is composed of an innumerable number of atoms, too small to be separately visible, which by their union bring objects into being, and by separation cause their destruction. He held that the action of these atoms on each other depends on the manner in which they are brought into contact, and that the unity of an object is only apparent, while all increase of bulk is due to the introduction of other atoms into the structure. He taught that many of the atoms are similar to each other, this similarity forming a basis of union among them; that the heavier atoms gathered at the centre, forming first air, then water, and afterwards the solid earth, and that there are multitudes of such aggregations or worlds, but all necessarily spherical. Also he averred that every body is continually sending forth emanations or images which travel by a process of successive transmission, similar to that by which wave motions travel in the water. It is impossible not to recognize in all this the molecular basic principle of modern chemistry, the well known law that combinations and dissolutions of chemical groupings occur within well defined limits of temperature, the Kant theory of formation of the universe, and the modern law of the propagation of light. Democritus may have erred, or rather disagreed with the Christian philosophers of our day, in supposing that the soul of the universe is only a finer aggregation of atoms than those which constitute grosser matter. But he had risen to a far higher conception of the truths of nature than did the author of " Night Thoughts " in the passage:

> " Has matter innate motion ?   Then each atom,
> Asserting its indisputable right
> To dance, would form a universe of dust."

XIV

DEAD MAN'S DAY.

The waters shall no more become a flood to destroy all flesh."—Genesis.

Festival of the Pleiades.—The Great Pyramid and its Measures.—Its Two
Avenues Pointing to the Stars.—Commemoration of the Dead in the
Valley of the Nile, and Many Other Lands.—Traditions of the Del-
uge.—Babylonian Account of it.—What the Egyptian Priest Told Solon.

There is one notable exception to the previously
stated rule that the religious festivals of the ancient
world were observed when the moon was in certain
positions. It is one which appears to have been
determined strictly with reference to the motion of
the sun among the stars, and the observance was
"world-wide." It prevailed among peoples on
both sides of the equator, and sundered by many
degrees of longitude as well as latitude. The festival was fixed by the position of the Pleiades, that
group of six stars (generally called seven) visible to
the naked eye, which is in the neck or shoulder of
Taurus. It is now nearly one-sixth of the ecliptic
circle past the vernal equinox; the longitude of
Alcyone, its principal star, being at present $58\frac{1}{2}$
degrees. Its latitude is 4 degrees north. About
2200 B. C. this group of stars was at the vernal
equinox, and its declination north was 20 degrees
less than now. In our day the Pleiades culminate

(pass the meridian) at midnight twenty-nine days before the winter solstice, that is about November 23. Two thousand years ago this culmination occurred nearly a month earlier. In 2200 B. C. it fell at the date of the autumnal equinox. Of course the reader is aware that these changes are due to the precession of the equinoxes, which causes the longitudes of the stars to increase at the rate of one degree in nearly seventy-two years, while their latitudes (from the plane of the earth's orbit) vary little in the lapse of many centuries.

In very ancient times the people had no clocks or other appliances for noting the flight of time when the sun was below the level boundary of their vision. Hence they would not be able to tell when the Pleiades culminated at midnight. But if the sky was clear well down towards the horizon they could observe the group rising soon after sunset, and a few mornings later could see it setting shortly before sunrise. During that interval the Pleiades were above the horizon all night, and it would not require a high order of intelligence to infer that about midway between the two dates the group was at its highest in the middle of the nearly twelve hours of darkness. It is not difficult to understand how some people could take so much notice of this annually recurring fact as to fix upon it for the time of a festival dividing the year into two natural halves, one of which was the season of long days and the other of long nights. But it is singular that the observance should be an extremely ancient one in so many lands, in some of which the people seemed to be in the lowest depth of savagery when first visited by Christian missionaries or traders within the last two or three centuries.

The great pyramid of Ghizeh, on the west bank of the Nile, a few miles from Cairo, was evidently built for some other purpose than to serve as the tomb of a king or any number of rulers. Its four sides accurately face the cardinal points of the compass. Portions of the smooth sloping surfaces have been removed to furnish building material at Cairo and other places, but enough remains to show that the original height was 484½ feet and the length of each side of the base 761 feet. Hence a side of the base is very nearly the length of a quadrant of the circle having a radius equal to the height of the pyramid. These and numerous other measures made by Prof. Piazzi Smith, of Scotland, sufficiently prove highly skilled design in the construction. In the interior of the pyramid are two passages strictly in the plane of the meridian but sloping at different angles. These are additional to the one that communicates with a central vault, which may be supposed to be simply the avenue to an interior sepulcher. The passage that slopes south, now called the grand gallery, and leading to the "king's chamber," points exactly in the direction occupied by the Pleiades when they crossed the meridian of the pyramid 2200 B. C. At the same date they were in opposition to the sun at the time of the autumnal equinox; and the northern passage pointed precisely in the direction of the star Alpha Draconis at its transit of the meridian, that being then the pole star, as it was about 3° 45′ from the pole of the earth's rotation. The strangest part of the matter is that the exits of these two passages were closed, so that they might not have been intended for avenues through which to observe the stars named, or any other. And it should be borne in mind that if the pyramids were built some 3000 years B. C. as stated in a previous chapter to be probable, those passages were constructed several centuries previous to the time when the meridian transits of the Pleiades and of the then pole star could have been watched through those avenues had their ends been open. It is hard to resist the conclusion that the design in constructing those passages was to convey information to the people of future ages; and if we accept this we must credit the architect of that far-off time with a knowledge much greater than is indicated by any other circumstances to have been possessed by human beings some five thousand years ago.

In truth the idea is so much at variance with the supposition of an utter blank in regard to all else pertaining to those remote times that some well informed men have asserted their positions must be accidental so far as those stars are concerned. They have objected that the theory of this significance in the construction of the pyramid is not supported by accounts furnished by the ancients nor by Egyptian inscriptions. The pyramids are found in the midst of a necropolis (burying ground), and contain sarcophagi and mummies, while the inscriptions on the tombs of many priests mention it as a special honor that the deceased officiated at the funeral services held at the pyramids. Then the difficulty was sought to be obviated by the supposition that these structures were reared long before the Egyptians made any other records that have been preserved to us, and that there may have been an utter desolation of the country in the mean time. Such a complete change of occupancy seems to have occurred more than once in later times, and why not then? Surely the people who could design and construct such a work as the great pyramid did not need to be told how to measure its altitude, and such knowledge would have been handed down through successive generations of children or pupils. But the ignorance on this point said to have been exhibited by the "wise men" of Egypt who were visited by Thales about 600 B. C., has been claimed to indicate that they were complete strangers to the geometrical knowledge of the builders, and to suggest that they must not only have belonged to an entirely different race but that there had not even been a handing down of tradition from the earlier to the later ones. The very existence of those passages seems to have been unknown through a long course of ages; and when about 800 A. D.

the Caliph Mamoun entered the pyramid in the hope
of despoiling it of contained treasures he caused a
passage way to be broken through the masonry as
his only means of ingress.

Doubtless the face of the country was often swept
by partial revolutions of race as well as by complete
ones of rule before the Christian era. But the ex-
plorations made in the last few years in the valley
of the Nile have brought to light a mass of material
which leaves no room to doubt the continuity of
information and skill among the successive occupants of the country, and we are warranted in
thinking that the story about their being taught by
Thales originated in a mistake. On the contrary we
now know that Egypt dominated Greece at intervals
through many centuries before Thales lived, and
there is some reason to believe that the alphabet was
carried from Egypt to Greece, though it may have
gone by way of Phenecia. And we have one indubitable evidence of continuity from the time of the
pyramid building till several centuries later, in the
fact that as far back as the fragmentary records
permit us to go we find the people inhabiting that
land observed the festival of the Pleiades. This at
once furnishes a reason for the construction, which
could hardly have been undertaken unless with reference to some supposedly highly important event
or position, and confirms the tradition with regard
to observance. Yet we can very well suppose that
the usage may have been derived from one common

source outside the region through which flows the Nile, and this seems probable from the fact that the observance can be traced far and near.

[Six of the nine pyramids in existence at Ghizeh, and the two at Abousseir which are sufficiently well preserved to permit accurate measurement, have passages opening towards the north at angles of 26 to 27 degrees with the plane of the horizon, each of them pointing to the place in the sky crossed by the star Alpha Draconis at its lower culmination about 2200 B. C. It cannot be doubted that they were constructed with reference to that stellar position.]

The Egyptians appear to have derived their scheme of the Zodiac from the Babylonians, and their ideas about the Pleiades from some more barbarous and more general source. But they called the stars of the latter the *Atauria*, a word which possibly gives us the Latin Taurus and the German Thier. Also they called our November Athor or Athyr, and celebrated the feast of the Pleiades on the seventeenth of that month. That was the date on which the Pleiades passed the meridian at midnight, and they regulated their calenders so that they might keep that date unchanged. With the midnight culmination of the Pleiades they began the solemn festival of Isis, which lasted three days. It was emphatically a commemoration of the dead; and in honor of Osiris, whom they regarded as the god of tombs. They connected this with the idea of a deluge. The priest placed an image of Osiris

in an ark and launched it into the waters, watching
it till borne out of sight. The curious may compare this with the story of Moses and the bulrushes,
and then say if it be not in all probability the original of that narration. Still more significant is the
fact that this seventeenth day of Athyr is also
the seventeenth day of the second month of the
Jewish year, when according to Genesis vii.
11, "were all the fountains of the great deep
broken up, and the windows of heaven were
opened." Who can fail to see in all this a wholesale appropriation of Egyptian observances by the
Jewish "historian" as material for his alleged history, or doubt that the Bible story of the deluge,
like that of the creation, had a purely astronomical
foundation? The vernal equinox was with the
Pleiades in right ascension about 2200 B. C., but
they were on the equinox in regard to longitude
more than a century earlier. The most refined
analysis of the celestial motions points to about 20
years antecedent to 2300 B. C. as the time when the
longitude of Alcyone, the brightest star of the
Pleiadic group, was zero. It is probable the people of that day estimated the asterism to be on the
equinox at precisely the date now generally assigned
for the Mosaic deluge.

This paragraph and the next following contain
notes of the observance of the Pleiades festival in other
countries. They were mostly collated by R. G. Hali-
burton, Esq., whose rare work, (a copy of which is in

the British Museum) is quoted from freely in Blake's
Astronomical Myths: "The Arabians called the star
group Atauria, and the Chaldeans and Hebrews gave
it a similar name, though the latter had no sacrifice
for the dead. The Persians formerly called the
month of November *Mordâd*, the angel of death, .
and held a feast for the dead at that time, which
was considered a New Year's festival. In India the
year began in the same month, which was called
Cartiguey, a word that means "the Pleiades."
The Hindoo *Durga*, a festival of the dead, is celebrated on the seventeenth day, and this is said by
Greswell to have been a New Year's commemoration at the earliest time to which the Indian calen-
dars can be carried back. The feast of lanterns
among the Japanese is celebrated about November,
and is thought to be connected with the same day,
as it is certain that nation reckons days by the position of the Pleiades. Hesiod writes that in his
day the Greeks commenced their winter season by
the setting of the Pleiades in the morning, and the
summer season by their rising at that time. Also
he says that the grain is to be cut when the
Pleiades rise, and plowing is to be done when they
set; they are invisible for forty days and then re-
appear at harvest; when they rise the care of the
vine must cease, and when fleeing from Orion they
are lost in the waves, sailing begins to be dangerous.
Indeed, the name by which we now know those
stars is supposed to be derived from the Greek

word *Plein*, to sail, because sailing was safe after they had risen; though others derive it from *Péleiai*, a flight of doves. The Celtic races were certainly partakers in this general observance of the Pleiades midnight culmination as the time of holding a festival for the dead, and this not only points to the origin of their superstitions but enables us to account for some customs that have survived till now. The first of November was with the Druids a night full of mystery, in which they celebrated annually the reconstruction of the world. At this time the Druidess nuns were obliged to pull down and rebuild the roof of their temple as a symbol of the destruction and renovation of the world. If in bringing the materials for the new roof one of them let fall her sacred burden she was lost. Her companions rushed upon her and tore her to pieces, and it is said that scarcely a year passed without one or more of them falling victims to this obligation. On the same night the Druids extinguished the sacred fire, which at all other times was kept continually burning in the hallowed precincts, and at that signal all the other fires in the island were put out one by one, a primitive night reigning throughout the land. Then the phantoms of those who had died during the year passed along to the West and were carried away in boats to the judgment seat where the god of the dead awaited their coming. Although Druidism is now extinct we still have in the calendar November 1, marked as All Saint's Day, and in those before the reformation October 31 was marked " All-Hallow Eve," while November 2 was named " All Souls." This clearly indicates a three days festival for the dead, beginning in the evening and originally regulated by the Pleiades. In former days the relics were more numerous, in the Hallowe'en torches of the Irish, the bonfires of the Scotch, the *Coel-coeth* of the Welsh, and the *tindle* fires of Cornwall, all lighted on Hallowe'en. In France it lingers more than in England, for the Parisians on this day still repair to the cemeteries and lunch at the graves of their ancestors. Turning to this continent, Prescott tells us that the great festival of the Mexican cycle was held in November at the time of the midnight culmination of the Pleiades. It began at sunset; and at midnight, as the constellation approached the zenith, a human victim was offered up to avert the dread calamity which they believed impended over the race. The people had a tradition that the world had once been destroyed at that date, and feared lest it might be repeated. They were not relieved of the dread till the Pleiades were seen to have culminated, showing that they had entered on a new cycle. The great cycle was supposed to be accomplished in fifty-two years.

Passing to the equatorial regions and beyond them we find the very same observance. In Peru, the New Year's festival occurs at the beginning of November, and is called *Ayamarca*, from *Aya* a corpse, and *Marca* carrying in arms, because they celebrated

the festival of the dead with tears, doleful songs
and plaintive music; and it was customary to visit the
tombs of relatives, leaving there meat and drink. The
Society Islanders divided the year into two seasons
of the Pleiades, or *Matarii*. The first was the half
year during which the group was above the horizon
immediately after sunset, and the second was the
other half of the year. In the Tonga Islands the
festival of Inachi is a vernal first fruits celebration
and also a commemoration of the dead, which begins at sunset near the end of October. The Australian savages still hold a New Year's *Corroboree*
in honor of the *Mormodellick* or Pleiades at their
midnight culmination in November, though the
date is now some time after the beginning of spring
with them. The celebration occupies three days,
and includes a worship of the dead. The savages
paint a white stripe over their arms, legs and ribs,
and appear like so many skeletons rejoicing as they
dance round the fires by night. In Ceylon a combined festival of agriculture and of the dead takes
place in November. The Dyaks of Borneo are
guided in their farming operations by the Pleiades,
cutting down the jungle, burning the brush, plant-
ing, and then reaping, by the four principal stations
of these stars; and at the last they celebrate the
feast of first fruits, though they seem to have no
special festival for the dead. There appears to be
no departure from the rule of observing the feast in
November in the southern hemisphere; while among

the better known of the ancients on this side of the
equator, such as the Greeks and Romans, the
anomaly of beginning the year at the autumnal
equinox seems to have induced them to make a
change to the vernal epoch in the year, and with
this change followed the festival of the dead, thoug!
some traces of it were left in November.

The Chaldean legend of the Flood and the building of the Tower of Babel is a close parallel to the
account in Genesis, and in some respects more
rational. God is said to have appeared to Xisuthrus (Noah) in a dream (not face to face), and warned
him that on a certain day mankind would be destroyed by a deluge. He told him to bury in Sippara, the City of the Sun, the extant writings, first
and last; to build a ship and enter therein with his
family and close friends (not exclusively a family
party or limited to eight persons); he was to place
on board winged fowl and four footed beasts of the
earth (not an impossible collection of twos and sev-
ens of all the beasts and other animals, with the
food necessary for them); and when all was ready
to set sail. Xisuthrus asked whither he was to sail,
and was answered, "To the gods, with a prayer
that it might fare well with mankind." Xisuthrus
built the vessel (though of impossible dimensions),
and went on board with his company. The flood
came. When it ceased he sent out birds, which
came back. After some days he sent them out
again, and they returned with mud-covered feet.

The third time they were sent out they did not return. Xisuthrus removed some of the covering of the ark and looked out to find it had grounded on a mountain. Then he went forth, worshipped on the earth, built an altar and offered sacrifice to the gods, after which he disappeared from sight (without getting drunk or cursing his son Ham). Those who had remained in the ark heard only his voice telling them to worship God, return to Babylon, recover the writings buried at Sippara, and make them known among men. He told them that the land in which they then were was Armenia. (Ararat is on the northeastern corner of Armenia, about 500 miles north from Babylon.) The saved ones did as they were told, going on foot to Babylon, which they restored, and built many other cities and temples. The earth was still of one language when the primitive men, who were proud of their strength and stature and despised the gods as their inferiors, erected a tower of vast height, in order that they might mount to heaven (peer into it). And the tower was now near heaven when the gods caused the winds to blow, and overturned the building upon the men and made them speak with divers tongues; wherefore the city was called Babylon.

This account has been severely criticised by Christian writers, and some others who think it cannot be true in those particulars where it disagrees with the Hebrew story. Baron Bunsen has characterized it as having a purely special, local character, "le-

gendary and fabulous, without ideas in every point
which it does not hold in common with the Hebrew."
But it so happens that the account by Berosus has
recently been found to be almost identical with the
one preserved on the cuneiform tablets which appear to have been moulded long before the book of
Genesis was written from these very legends the
recollection of which had been carried away from
Babylon by the few Jews who "returned" from the
captivity. As to the objection that the Babylonian
account is purely local while that in the Bible af-
firms the whole earth was covered, it may be remarked that most certainly the latter is not true for
the time named or any other since man first appeared on the earth, however it may be with the
account furnished from Babylon. There are no
signs of such a flood having occurred as recently as
2349 or 2348 B. C. in the land of Judea, where the
Bible account was written; and the Egyptian records, which undoubtedly go much farther back than
that Jewish date for the catastrophe, contain no
reference to any such event though the priests there
are reported to have told Solon of one that befell
about 11,000 years ago. The Babylonian claim
to a preservation of records which made the Chaldean priests the sole possessors of ante-diluvian history may well be pardoned as a piece of vanity, since
it appears to have been shared with the Chinese, the
Hindoos, and the peoples of some other countries,
much in the same way that each one of a dozen men

will claim to have been the first to interfere to stop a street fight. Another consideration will show that the Bible date cannot possibly be correct, or other statements in Genesis must be untrue. According to that book Abraham was born only about three hundred years after the deluge, yet the whole area from Chaldea to Lower Egypt, both inclusive, was well populated in his day; and a king of Southern Persia, with three allies, invaded the valley of the Jordan. That is, in less than four centuries the descendants of the eight persons who survived the flood had rather thickly peopled what was then thought to be the whole earth. Such a conclusion is hardly admissible even on the theory that there was no fighting in the whole of that time to kill off any of the inhabitants. But it may be noted that the Septuagint translation of the Old Testament allows 1,147 years between the flood and the time of Abraham; which not only obviates the difficulty above mentioned but makes the Bible story harmonize with those of the Babylonians and Chinese nearly enough to satisfy the requirements of chronology for that distant time.

The very widely observed festivals of the dead at the division of the Pleiadic year point to the conclusion that among all the peoples named there was a tradition of some great calamity which had occurred on the completion of some cycle of Pleiadic motion, and that it was sufficiently extensive to kill off all the inhabitants in each case except a small remnant that escaped as by a miracle. Of course such escape was in many instances regarded as a result of especial divine interposition in favor of the saved ones, the Chaldean accounts being in this respect reflections of the rest. And with most if not all of them the catastrophe was supposed to have been a deluge that not only killed off nearly all the inhabitants but forced the survivors to seek a home in some other land. The ancient Egyptians appear to have caught the idea with an intensity that we in these later days can hardly appreciate. When Solon visited their country some 2,500 years ago he talked to the priests about the flood of Deucalion, which was traditional among the Greeks, and tried to account for the generations that had lived since its occurrence. On this an aged priest remarked to him: "Like the rest of mankind the Greek nation has suffered from natural convulsions which occur from time to time according to the positions of the heavenly bodies, when parts of the earth are destroyed by the two great agents, fire and water. At certain periods portions of the human race perish in the waters, and rude survivors too often fail to transmit historical evidence of the event. You Greeks remember one record only. There have been many." Was that priest stating the concentrated essence of reports received from many different lands, as Job heard the stories of disaster that had befallen his flocks, his people, and his family? Or was he speaking simply as one deeply versed in

the lore of the stars, who had full confidence in the
verity of the deductions made by others and himself
from a study of their motions? In either case it
was wonderful; and hardly the less so even if the accompanying talk about the disappearance of "the
lost Atlantis" was not founded on fact. What
would not the searchers after truth to-day give if he
had added a few words about the construction of the
great pyramid, and told whether or not its building
had any direct reference to a deluge in the land
where Napoleon long afterwards told his soldiers
that forty centuries of history looked down upon
them!

The almost world-wide prevalence of the Pleiadic
celebration, connected with the idea of a deluge,
may be understood as indicating a common origin
for the peoples observing it. Does it not mean that
their earlier ancestors were inhabitants of some
island, or perhaps continent, which was engulfed
by the ocean, and that they escaped in one or more
large vessels to lands now occupied by some of their
descendants? If so, the alleged fable of Atlantis
must be a fact of history, though its now submerged
land may not be situated in the region named by
the early geographers.

XV

CROSSING THE LINE.

" *When men inhabited the South.*"—Zechariah.

The Theory of Our Southern Origin.—Not Proven.—Distribution of Land and Water on the Earth.—Alternate Ocean Preponderance on Opposite Sides of the Equator.—Deluges of the Past and Future, and their Astronomical Causes.—Necessary Migrations.—Leaving a Record Behind.

It has been inferred that the traditions spoken of in the last preceding chapter originated in the southern hemisphere, and were brought across the equator by the few who escaped a general calamity that visited the Australian side of our globe at some time in the remote past. The idea finds confirmation in the hints that appear here and there in the traditions and literatures of some countries in the North to the effect that the stars have changed their courses; in other words, that they move in a different direction from that in which they once appeared to journey through the heavens. The persistence of that tradition can be understood without much trouble on the supposition of such a change of habitation from one hemisphere to another; and perhaps in some other way. An observer in this part of the world who faces the sun sees the god of day moving from left to right; and after he has set the moon and stars are seen moving in the same direction. But to a gazer in the south temperate zone the motion is reversed. The sun, moon and stars still rise in the east and set in the west, but to one who faces the sun at noon the east is on his right hand and the west is on his left:—the general motion of the stars is from right to left. But the generalized use of the terms east and west is necessarily a comparatively modern one. In the infancy of observation the movement was remarked as being with reference to the hands of the observer. If situated far on the other side of the equator the sun and stars seemed to move past him from the right towards the left, and if he or his descendants then traveled to the northern side of the tropics the celestial motions would seem to be performed the other way. There would be a complete reversal; and the fact would not fail to impress itself upon the minds of people who had no doubt in regard to the change but were utterly at a loss in trying to understand, much less explain it.

That this is not necessarily the origin of the traditions alluded to will be evident if we consider that the idea of reversal may have arisen not from one but many of such observations of change. A person situated near the equator would see the sun moving from left to right during the time of our midwinter, and from right to left when near its greatest northern declination at the time corresponding to our June and July. Similarly the moon would exhibit this duplicity of motion each month;

18

and when near the time of the full within a few
weeks of the solstice, her movement at night would
be the opposite of that performed by the sun during
the day.   If that person, long accustomed to such
a phenomenon, should move northward, and his descendants continue the migration till they arrived
in the plains of Chaldea or on the banks of the
Lower Nile, the sun, moon and planets would settle down to the one kind of movement, namely,
that from left to right; and naught would remain of
the other phenomenon except the tradition that at
some time in the then dim past the heavenly bodies
had been observed by their forefathers to move in
the other direction. And such a repetition of change
would be far more likely to impress itself upon the
memory of a race than could the fact of a single
reversal experienced only during the slow process
of migration from one clime to another, which may
have been accomplished with little more of celerity
than was that said to have marked the journey of
the Israelites over the short distance between the
northeastern corner of Egypt and the banks of the
Jordan.   We might with equal force argue for an
equatorial transit from the fact that the Shemitic writing is done from right to left, indicating that its direction was determined by that in which the principal heavenly bodies were first observed to move.
But it is pretty certain that the earliest alphabetic
writing among the Shemites was not attempted till
long after such migration was performed, if the said

migration took place at all. And the argument dwindles into insignificance when we remember that while the earliest writing among the Greeks followed the Shemitic or rather the Phenecian order, they soon wrote in both directions. They worked on one line from right to left, on the next from left to right, and so on alternately, from which fact the style was called *Boustrophedon.* The word described the movement of an ox in plowing; going up one furrow and down another. Also, it may be remarked that the cuneiform inscriptions of Mesopotamia are read from left to right, and it is at least possible that these originated with the Chaldean element from which the Jews claim to have sprung. The Bible says that Abram came (westward) from Ur of the Chaldees.

So we may dismiss the idea of a migration across the equator from south to north as having brought to this hemisphere the ancestors of its present inhabitants; though admitting that there may have been some other and more recent widespread catastrophe than the latest glacial visitation, which we have already stated to have been limited by lines considerably exterior to the tropics. Indeed, it is difficult to suppose that the tradition of a general deluge could have survived such a long time as has necessarily elapsed since the last incursion of the polar ice cap extended to the shores of the Mediterranean in the old world and past the great lakes on this continent.

Let us look for a moment at the present distribution of land and water on the earth's surface. Both hemispheres contain wide stretches of ocean, the Pacific and Atlantic dividing the major part of the land into two great continental masses. But on the other side of the equator there is very little land south of the latitude of 35 degrees, while in the northern hemisphere the land masses reach up well towards the pole and within the arctic circle these are separated by comparatively narrow sheets of water. Roughly speaking, there is in our hemisphere a land preponderance fully equal to the combined area of Europe and Asia. That part of Africa which lies north of the equator is larger than the sum of the southern portion and Australia, while the area of North America exceeds that of South America.

Now let us consider what would result from the displacement of a large quantity of water from the southern to the northern hemisphere. Suppose the depth of the water at the south pole to be decreased by only 500 feet, and that at the north pole increased to an equal amount. The double change in depth at intermediate points will be proportional to the *sine* of the latitude. At 45 degrees it will be 707 feet, which is nearly half the estimated mean height of the continental surfaces above the sea level. At 30 degrees it will be 500 feet, or a little less than the elevation of Chicago above the ocean. At 15 degrees the change would be 259 feet, and at the equator nothing at all. Evidently the consequence of such a transfer of water would be the submergence of vast areas of what is now land in the northern hemisphere, and a corresponding uncovering of a large area of sea bottom on the southern side of the equator. And, as the greater the latitude the greater the change in depth, the effect would be most marked in those places where the inequalities are now the widest. The southern part of the south temperate zone would gain enormously, perhaps exhibiting an immense continent in what is now called Polynesia, and those little islands becoming the summits of mighty mountains with broad and fertile valleys between them. There would be big additions to the areas of Australia and Southern Africa, and a broad expanse of land in place of the narrow tract that forms the southern portion of South America. On the other hand a large percentage of Northern Asia, Europe and America would be swallowed up by the relentless waters, the mountain tops becoming islands, and islands themselves disappearing beneath the swelling waves of old ocean. Many millions of Russians would be driven south by the advance of Father Neptune, and the climates of the still habitable portions of the north temperate zone be much modified by the increase of ocean surface in their neighborhood. The great Sahara desert might again become an inland sea, a part of the Arabian expanse of sand be covered by the ocean, and our own Colorado basin fill up with water out of the illimitable supply from which it is now divided by only a narrow bank of sand and mud.

No doubt such a change is possible. Geometrically speaking the earth is a spheroid of rotation, its center of gravity and the direction of its axis being determined by the law that the whole mass must be in equilibrium with respect to them. The surface of its solid portion (crust) is irregular in shape, the depressions being occupied by water, unless where other conditions prevent it. The center of gravity is simply that point in the interior towards which all portions of the mass press with equal force, and any important change in the disposition of the matter on opposite sides of the equator must cause a shifting of that center farther from one polar surface and nearer to the other. The washing down of the land in some places by the ocean waves, and its elevation in others by volcanic agencies, are causes of changes in this respect that are continually in progress; the amount of change being that due to the difference of effective cause in the two hemispheres. But apparently a more potent agency is at work in the neighborhood of the poles. Each of them is at some time, if not always, surrounded by a huge cap of ice that towers far above the natural sea level. Now, if owing to the operation of some cosmic cause the bulk of one of these polar ice caps were continuously reduced through a course of many centuries, while the other was correspondingly gaining in bulk, the result must be such a shifting of the center of gravity as we have described; and this must be accompanied or followed by a flow of water from one hemisphere to the other in order to preserve the equilibrium of the earth as a mass.

That such a change is in progress is indicated not only by what we know of altering conditions on the face of our globe but also by ascertained facts in regard to its motion as a member of the solar system. The major axis of the earth's orbit changes its position at the rate of about 11.4 seconds of arc per year, the movement being in the contrary direction to that of the equinoxes. Hence, the two motions have a synodical period of not far from 21,000 years. About 4000 B. C. the perihelion of the orbit coincided with the equinox, the earth being nearest to the sun in our autumn. Near the middle of the thirteenth century A. D. the point of nearest approach to the sun was occupied by the earth on the longest day in the southern hemisphere, and about 6500 A. D. this nearest approach will be at the date of the vernal equinox. The heating effects of the solar rays upon the earth being inversely proportional to the square of his distance from us it may be thought that from about 6,000 years ago to nearly 5,000 years hence the southern hemisphere receives more heat than the northern, because the sun is in southern declination during that half of the year in which the earth is nearest to him. But this is not the case. Under the operation of Kepler's law that

"Equal areas are described in equal times" the summer segment of the year in the northern hemisphere is now several days longer than the winter segment. About two-thirds of the total heat received from the sun during the twelve months is distributed over a majority of the days, and the other third part over the smaller number of days. The reverse of these conditions of distribution is experienced in the southern hemisphere. Hence between the above-named dates the excess of solar heat above the average tends to a diminution of the ice and snow around the north pole, and for the same reason that in the south polar regions is augmenting. The point in the axis of rotation which is half way between the apices of the two ice caps is thus removed southward from its mean place, while the attraction of the tropical protuberance tends to keep the point stationary. The balance is preserved by a temporary excess of water in the southern hemisphere, which comes from the other side of the equator, part of it being contributed by the melting ice.

We cannot tell just when the epochs of these maxima and minima of effect occur, but know it will not be when the effect of solar action during any one year is least or greatest. We must reason from analogy in the case of the tides, which in the open ocean follow the moon at the distance of nearly half a quadrant, and from the lesser accumulations of heat by days and seasons. Thus, the sun is highest at noon, but the hottest part of the day is usually from two to three hours afterwards, and the coldest part of the twenty-four hours is a long way from midnight towards sunrise. Similarly, the hottest time of the year is generally five or six weeks after midsummer's day, and the coldest at an equal distance of weeks from the winter solstice. The reason why we experience the greater total effect while the cause is diminishing in intensity may be understood by reference to the seasonal change. The heat felt at any time is the sum of all the additions, minus all the losses by radiation, the latter process being less effective than the first while the days are longer than the nights, and *vice versa.*

Hence we may say that while the hemisphere epoch corresponding to the midsummer part of the year was reached between six and seven centuries ago, when the earth was in perihelion at the date of our winter solstice, the maximum of effect will not be attained till more than a thousand years hence During the whole of that time the ice around the south pole will continue to increase in volume, the waters on that side of the globe to augment, the northern ice cap to lessen, and the surface of the northern ocean to sink. But these changes are progressing much less rapidly than a few centuries ago, and may almost be said to have practically ceased now, the differences between present conditions and those of the theoretical maxima being small. So far as this cause is concerned the next two thousand years or so will form a period of comparative repose. Then, under the operation of the same law, the set will be the other way. The ice cap around the north pole will begin to increase, that at the south pole to lessen, the ocean surface commence to sink in that hemisphere and rise in this, and some twelve thousand years hence will witness the maximum of land exposure in the southern half of the globe. Possibly at that remote time Macauley's New Zealander will not survey the ruins of London Bridge; but he may sail over the spot where now that structure stands, and discourse learnedly of the submergence of the British Islands, the position of which will then be indicated by a few hill tops peering up amid the waste of waters.

Such is the programme of earth change deducible from a study of the theory of Adhemar, a statement of which may be found in Croll's "Climate and Time." The theory is not universally accepted among scientific men, and the preceding description of the process might not be endorsed by all those who think his theory is tenable. But the writer believes it to be in the main correct and in harmony with the facts of mundane history so far as understood. In particular we may note that it would place the greatest submergence of the northern hemisphere at about nine thousand years ago, and indicate for some 6000 B. C. the first indubitable signs that the waters were receding, permitting the extension of the pastoral life beyond a few small areas. It may also be thought possible that this phase is referred to in the more remote chronological epochs alluded to on page 69. It appears to be more than possible when we know that Beta Geminorum, the brightest star in the constellation of the Twins, and bearing the proper name of Pollux, was at the vernal equinox about 6150 B. C. It may also interest the reader to know that while the Kali-Yug date of February 18, B. C. 3102, has been objected to as artificial it was in reality one of the most remarkable to which we can look back. True, the planets were not then all in conjunction, but they were within a space of only a few degrees, and Saturn and Jupiter had been in conjunction a few months previously; while although the star Aldebaran was then 20 minutes away from the vernal equinox the Pleiades were exactly on the equator, rising from the southern to the northern hemisphere. Perhaps the significance of this position may be inferred from comparison with the concluding portion of our ninth chapter.

It may be supposed that the hemisphere changes here described must be gradual, and therefore the effects be radically different from the cataclysmal revulsions the memories of which seem to have been embalmed in the traditions noted in the last preceding chapter. But such an inference would not necessarily be a correct one. True, there must be a gradual increase of annual effect through several thousand years, followed by a stationary period and that by a long continued stretch of time during which the annual supply of heat force slowly lessens by successive steps; the process of increasing and decreasing temperature at either pole being something like what we experience on a much smaller scale in the changes of the seasons. But the course of the latter is by no means a uniform one. It is apt to be marked by violent fluctuations of the mercury in both the barometer and thermometer, and corresponding irregular disturbances in the atmosphere divided by periods of calm. And the change from the winter to the summer half of the year is usually accompanied by equinoctial storms, while another set is generally experienced nearly six months later, a little in advance of the autumnal equinox. So in the grand seasonal cycle during which the floating balance of water in the oceans shifts from one side of the equator to the other and back again. Each annual change in the relative volumes of the ice caps around the two poles must be quickly responded to by a change of ocean level. But just as we often have a series of several winters much "harder" than the mean, and then a set of mild ones, with similar deviations from the average of summer temperatures, so the grand cycle of some 21,000 to 26,000 years is probably broken up into a series of minor ones, not uniform in their duration. Of course this is not much more than a matter of inference; but it is easy to fancy such a parallel, and illogical to suppose it does not exist. Hence

the occurrence of wave movements between the two
hemispheres, something like those which often
mark the approach and recess of the tides, must at
least be regarded as most probable; and these ought
by analogy to occur at the time corresponding to
the annual equinoctial disturbance. That is to say,
the last greatest convulsion may be supposed to
have occurred about 4000 B. C., that being the
time when vast areas in the southern hemisphere
were deluged with water, and such inhabitants as
escaped did so by fleeing to other lands nearer the
equator. The disturbances in the two oceans of air
and water may well have been so severe as temporarily to overwhelm lands on the seacoasts in the
middle tropics, but those in the interior of continents and near the equator would be unaffected
except by atmospheric storms which always accompany extensive perturbations of water surface.
Hence the absence of necessity for supposing a
migration of the race or any part of it across the
equator as a consequence of the wide spread catastrophe which overtook dwellers nearer the south
pole.

If there be no mistake in our reading of these
conditions, the southern hemisphere is now near
the phase of greatest submergence; and only a few
centuries will elapse before the great ocean current
begins to set the other way. That epoch will mark
the commencement of the process by which a large
part of the land surface on this side of the equator

will be covered up, and the southern hemisphere permitted to become the theater of widest human activity and perhaps the highest civilization on the face of the globe. When that change is accomplished will the receding ocean have left exposed on the other side of the equator any such monuments as the pyramids now standing in Egypt? Will any such pile of masonry testify to the fact that those areas were once occupied by dense populations of whose very existence we have no present knowledge, but who left behind them works proving their right to be accorded a high rank in the scale of human intelligence? And shall we in the meantime have constructed anything sufficiently durable to last intact through the wild rush of water surging back and forth over our valleys for several thousands of years and after they have subsided testify of us to those who shall repeople the region of the Mississippi? If we do it must be something that has not been done yet. A few excavations have been made on the mountain ranges of the United States which may be too high for submergence; but they might be obliterated by the cankerous tooth of time eating down the rocks to a lower level and burying them in a drift formation before the face of the continent was restored to the sunlight and the lunar beams.

There is little doubt in the mind of the writer that the great pyramid was built with such a purpose, however it may have been with some of the rest. It has not stood the ordeal, but the architect was not to know the trial would be so long deferred. It seems probable that the deluge in the Nile valley was so recent at the time of its construction that the story had been handed down through not very many generations, and the design was to leave a monument that would survive the next great flood, which the architect may have expected to occur on the completion of the great Pleiadic year when that prominent group of stars in the shoulder of the Bull would be in the equinox (2320 B. C.). This is so far from being an unreasonable hypothesis that it seems to be the only one offering a sufficient motive for the undertaking of a work so vast and apparently of no immediate use. And the placing of that pile in what was probably the exact latitude of thirty degrees at the time of construction may be similarly accounted for as intended to furnish to future ages a means of ascertaining if any change in angular distance from the equator would have been caused by such disturbance at the surface.

In view of these possibilities it may be asked if it would not be well for the inhabitants of the United States to take into consideration the advisability of erecting some such structure as the great pyramid for the information of those who shall visit the scene after it will have been uninhabitable by human beings for some thousands of years. If such a monument were decided on, the pyramidal shape would commend itself as the most durable; it should be of sufficient magnitude to leave some portion visible through an accumulation of perhaps two or three hundred feet of solid matter deposited by the waters, and present features of interior construction bearing unmistakable marks of design so as to stimulate curiosity to search for records securely placed out of the reach of damage by flood. The selection of the literary material and of the best means for recording it so that the characters could be deciphered and understood in the far distant future, might well engage the attention of the greatest scientists living. For its location probably the most suggestive place would be precisely in the geographical (not geocentric) latitude of forty-five degrees, and nearly due north from New York City, in the yet to be determined exact longitude of the earth's minor meridian. As nearly as is now known that meridian is seventy-four and a half degrees from Greenwich, and passes near if not through the spot of land first touched by Columbus on his voyage of discovery of the New World. A pyramidal monument on the site indicated would furnish a double means for precision in earth measures, that could not but be highly appreciated if found by a people wise enough to understand its significance, and able to read the full meaning of the story of position.

XVI

STAR GROUPING.

*" Canst thou bind the sweet influences of Pleiades, or loose the bands of Orion?"—*Job.

Origin of the Constellations.—Where and When the Zodiacal Groups were First Named.—Babylonian or Egyptian Origin?—But we Know Them Mostly Through Greek Channels.—They were Picture Stories of Natural Phenomena.—The Bears and the Dragon.—Grecian Facts and Fancies.—Jonah Among the Stars.—The Ancient Chaldeans.

The picture mode of representing quality, attribute, or function must be looked to for the origin of the constellations; that is, those of them which were named by the ancients. The oft quoted remark that the men who parceled out the stars into those groups had no other than fanciful reasons in making the allotment, because there is no traceable similarity of form among the stars to outline of figure, simply proves that he who first uttered it was equally unphilosophical with the Englishman who said the Frenchman's talk was a meaningless gabble as it was impossible to make out a single word. One might think that the very absence of similarity renders it necessary to look for some other explanation. And so it does, unless we are prepared to assert that the early star observers were bigger fools than are the children of our own day.

In regard to the constellations of the Zodiac we have historical hints sufficient to enable us to sketch the general character of the process by which the stars near the ecliptic were parceled out among them. The work was performed by Asiatics occupying a country in not far from thirty degrees of north latitude, or by dwellers in the northwestern corner of Africa. That is to say, the naming was done in Egypt, Arabia, Lower Mesopotamia, or Persia. That the climate was so warm as to be subtropical may be inferred from the presence of the Scorpion, and the Crab on the list points to the conclusion that it was near a considerable body of water. But this may have been either on the southern shore of the Mediterranean, the northern shore of the Persian Gulf, or on one of the contributing rivers. Most probably it was in the Chaldean country on the east bank of the Euphrates, in the southeastern part of ancient Babylonia. In other words, it was in the land of the (Hebrew) *Chasdim*, who are first mentioned in the Scriptures as the owners of the region where dwelt the ancestors of Abraham;—who were also a caste of priests or astrologers, the two words meaning the same thing. It has been suggested that the zodiacal and other star groups were originally named in a country farther north, perhaps in Bactria, because the list transmitted to us does not comprise several prominent stars that rise well above the horizon of thirty degrees north. But that argument does not

count for much when we remember that the earliest
known figures of the constellations, those on the
sphere of Eudoxus, are less than 2,300 years old.

Furthermore, we have very good reason to believe that the zodiacal star groups were named after
phenomena observed, not when the sun was among
the stars of any particular constellation but, when
they were first seen rising in the east before the sun,
being sufficiently out of his beams to be visible.
They could not be discerned when in conjunction
with the sun, and certainly were not named with
reference to the lunar motion. Now, the Beehive
cluster in Cancer, often called the Cradle Nebula,
though it is not a nebula at all but a nest of stars,
is near two gems of the fourth magnitude,
named the Aselli, or the Two Asses. In a clear
sky they can be discerned under the condition
named about a month after being in conjunction
with the sun, and they are now with him about
the close of July. But the zodiacal group of which
the cluster and the Aselli form the most conspicuous part was named Cancer, or the Crab, because
that animal progresses sidewise; folks used to say
"backward." The name appears to have been
suggested by the observed fact that on reaching the
tropic (of Cancer), the sun for a few days passes
sidewise along a parallel of declination, and then
seems to retrace his course toward the south. As
the precession of the equinoxes causes the stars to
seem to advance in longitude at the rate of one

revolution in a little less than 26,000 years, the Aselli were thirty degrees in advance of the sun at his rising when in the solstice some 3000 years B. C., and in the absence of precise information on the subject we may infer the star groups were named about that time, if not earlier, or probably at least 1,500 years before the formation of a Greek mythology. It may be remarked that the Pleiades, which some have supposed were at one time taken to announce by their matutinal appearance the time of the vernal equinox, rose at the required distance before "the sun on the line" not far from the usually accepted date of creation according to the Bible chronology. It is considered probable that the older pyramids of Egypt were built at least 3000 years B. C., and it may be presumed that the naming of the star groups had been previously carried to that country from its Chaldean place of origin, though the observations made from the temple of Jupiter Belus are supposed not to be worthy of dating back farther than 2300 B. C. About that time the stars in the neighborhood of the ecliptic were considered as divided into twenty-eight groups, or rather that number of approximately equidistant stars was observed, and their places were called "Stations of the moon." Undoubtedly the division into twelve signs or constellations was chosen because that most nearly corresponded with the number of lunations in a year, as previously noted. It is impossible to say which of these divisions was made first; possibly the lunar, but the claim that this certainly preceded the other lacks proof.

It may be considered probable that the list of zodiacal constellations (with the possible omission of Libra) was carried into Egypt by the Hyksos, or Shepherd Kings; and it is tolerably certain that the pastoral occupation was a prominent one among the people who gave to the constellations the names that have come down to us. The three first on the zodiacal list prove this. They are the Sheep (Ram), the Bull, and the pair of young goats now known as Gemini, the twin character of the latter being suggested by the pair of bright stars which the Greeks called Castor and Pollux and mark the heads in the present figure. The matutinal appearance of the stars in these three groups marked in succession the most important pastoral phases of the three spring months. Then came Cancer, already described, and those parallels to the rest which have persisted to the present century belong to a more northern latitude than that of the Nile Delta or Babylon. They are as follows: Leo, the Lion, which being an animal belonging to the hotter climates (in what we now call the torrid zone), was thought to be appropriately chosen to indicate the raging heat of the summer, the average temperature being highest about six weeks after the solstice. But that heat matured the grain, and by the time it was ripe the Sickle of Leo was prominent in the morning sky.

The conclusion of the harvest season was marked by the figure of the Virgin, with an ear (handful), of grain in her hand, which she was supposed to have gleaned after the reapers had done their work. Virgo is the sixth on the zodiacal list, and the fact of its finding a place there shows that the astronomers also lived in the neighborhood of cultivated fields in which the people gathered a cereal supply for the wants of the ensuing twelve months. The seventh sign was for a long time vacant, but when later its comparatively unimportant stars were formed into a constellation it was as the Balance (Libra), not because the arrangement of those stars bore any resemblance to a pair of scales, but for the reason that when they rose just before the sun the days and nights were of about equal length, that being the time of the autumnal equinox. The next group, Scorpio, or the Scorpion, is a conspicuous one, and probably was so named because when in position the sickly season was upon the people, partly on account of its being the middle of autumn, and perhaps in part because of the sickness usually following the eating and drinking excesses which too many indulge in on a sudden accession of plenty. In the earlier Zodiacs, the Balance being absent, the claws of the Scorpion extended towards Virgo; perhaps even more significant of the fact that plenty leads to gluttony, and that to sickness. Then follows Sagittarius, the Archer, on horseback, which denotes the season for hunting, though some of the stars in the

group form a tolerably good representation of a bow
and arrow.   And probably this was the earliest offensive weapon invented after the club and the
stone thrown by hand, notwithstanding the Biblical
legend about Tuval Ka-yin (Tubal Cain).   The
Goat, Capricorn, naturally marked the winter solstice, when the sun begins to mount upward in the
heavens after a six months descent towards the
south, the goat being a climbing animal.   Aquaries,
the Water Bearer, noted in the Bible as "He that
shall pour the water out of his buckets," marked
the rainy season; and Pisces, originally two fishes
tied back to back "end the circling year" by marking the fishing season and the time of Lent, during
which all good Catholics and Episcopalians to this
day limit themselves to a fish diet.

Laplace argued, with some plausibility, that the
zodiacal constellations must have been named nearly
15,000 years ago, when the stars of the Crab were in
what is now called the tropic of Capricorn.   The
conclusion is hardly warranted by what we know of
the facts in the case.   It is difficult to think that
any portion of the race was at that time sufficiently
intelligent to leave such an indelible trace while the
first half of the period since then is an utter blank.
Besides: it would seem that if the constellations had
been designated so far back in the history of the
race the scheme must have been confused to complete obliteration by the precessional movement of
the solstitial and equinoctial points through more

than half the circle. Nevertheless, the point is of so much interest that we give in the following paragraph a synopsis of the argument for this greater antiquity, summarizing it from the statement of the case made by Prof. Peck of Edinburgh, Scotland:

Egypt without the Nile would be nothing. Therefore, if the Zodiac were an Egyptian institution many of the constellations of which it is composed must be expected to be more or less directly connected with the rise and fall of that river. This is found to be the case when due allowance is made for the precession of the equinoxes during the last 15,000 years;—the principal events and their duration are then fully explained. The solar year is believed to have begun with the winter solstice, which was the time immediately following the sowing of the seed in the Nile valley. Three months afterwards, when the sun was crossing the vernal equinox, the harvest took place; and this was followed by the valuing of the crop and the payment of the annual tribute. During the two months preceding the summer solstice the most unhealthy season and the greatest climatic disadvantages were experienced. For fifty days the Khamsin (Arabic for fifty), or deadly south wind prevailed, as it does still, bringing with it disease and death. The plague appears during that interval if at all. Near the time of the summer solstice the Nile begins to rise, and continues to do so till the time of overflow, about six weeks later. The inun-

dation was at its highest about the time of the
autumnal equinox, overflowing the whole Delta.
A month later the waters had subsided, and in the
time corresponding to our November the land was
put under culture, being covered with luxuriant
crops three months later. This phase corresponds
to Virgo, while Scorpio and Sagittarius were occupied by the sun during the Khamsin blow. Capricorn (the goat) is certainly a climbing animal, grazing in the rocky heights of the mountains, and
therefore much more likely to have been originally
placed at the summer solstice than at its opposite.
Besides, the fish-formed tail of the animal, which
is a very ancient feature, would mark the sun's
position among the stars when the Nile began to
rise. Aquaries and Pisces corresponded to the
season of flood, and the other fishes near them in
the heavens would also have a reason to be. When
the sun was in Aries the waters had receded so much
that sheep could be sent out to pasture, while in
Taurus the oxen were yoked to the plow; and when
in Gemini it was the lambing season, as also the
time for bringing forth kids among the goats. The
ancient Egyptians were not very familiar with the
crab, but they had the Scarabeus, or Beetle, which
was held sacred by them; and we may well suppose
it was because the animal marked one of the seasons. Now it is remarkable that they held this
beetle to be a representative of the resurrection or
the continuance of life, which would be exceedingly

appropriate if its sign were at the winter solstice.
Leo, the Lion, is not an Egyptian animal, though
probably not unknown to the inhabitants of the
Nile valley, and may have been placed on the list
because of its supposed rarity, which rendered it
sacred.

These namings may also be referred to the later
period by supposing them to have been made for
midnight culmination, as in the previously described
case of the Pleiades.

The Old Testament contains no indubitable references to any of the extra-zodiacal constellations
except Orion and Boötes, the principal star in the
latter being called by its name, Arcturus, in Job.
It is probable that his "Mazzaroth" means the
Zodiac, and the "sons of Arcturus" alluded to by
Job *may* be the principal stars of Ursa Major, preceding Arcturus in the nightly circuit. We get no
aid from the Arabic on this point, because the
Mohammedan astronomers deem it a sin to speak of
any group of stars as presenting or suggesting the
outline of a human form. As about all of the old
constellations except the preceding are known to us
only as we have them from or through the Greek
they are enshrouded with Grecian mythology. Max
Müller thought the seven principal stars in the
Great Bear, forming what is popularly known as
the Dipper, were called *Rikshas*, meaning "the
shining ones," by the early inhabitants of India, and
that the sounds of this word were transposed to

form the Greek word *Arctos*, a bear, from which
and the word *ouros*, a guard, we have Arcturus, the
bear ward or guardian. But the derivation from
Rikshas must be conceded to be far fetched, seeing
it is brought across a large part of the Asiatic
continent, and it is hardly worth while to go so far
for the etymology of a single constellation when
there are no others to keep it company. In the
absence of better information we may suppose
these prominent stars were called the Bear because
it was found they always circled over countries to
the north of the early observers, and they had heard
of bears as inhabiting the far North; though it is
evident from the length of the tail in the constellation that the astronomers had never seen a bear or
listened to a good description of one. Undoubtedly
the Lesser Bear, Ursa Minor, was added later; and
for the reason that the principal stars in that group
form a figure somewhat like that of the Dipper in
the Greater Bear. It could not have been named
because of its proximity to the pole, as we know
that on account of the precession of the equinoxes
the Little Bear was far from the Pole of the early
astronomers, the star now known as Alpha Draconis
being the nearest to the pole some 3000 B. C.
Also the oldest name we know of for the present
polar star is *Alruccabah*, which means "the hinge"
in the Arabic, and it was in no sense a hinge for
the apparent celestial motions till well down
towards the Christian Era.

But for the origin of Draco, the Dragon, we have
a noble conception.　That long, straggling lot of
stars has been said to have no reason but a fanciful
one for its naming; and especially not as the Natural histories of our day do not include the dragon in
their lists of animals.　But look at the arrangement.
The fold near the head encloses (partially) the north
pole of the zodiac, and the last one towards the tail
similarly curves partly around the pole of the earth's
axial rotation.　We have in this what seems to be a
recognition of the double phenomenon of earth motion with reference to two axes; the dragon symbol-
izing the unity of the two systems of diurnal and
annual motion, and furnishing an imperishable record of astronomical research and patriarchal wisdom
in the days when books and paper were unknown.
But previous to about 3000 B. C., when the pole
was midway between the brightest of the stars in
the two bears, that pole was not encircled by the
Dragon; and we may, therefore, suppose the latter
constellation had not been chosen to symbolize the
duality of motion.

There is some little reason to suppose that the
constellation now called Orion was at a very early
date looked upon as the great originator of the Shemitic peoples, and subsequently thought by the Jews
to be the celestial representative of their father
Abraham; while the two branches of Eridanus that
are confluent at his raised foot (in which is the star
Rigel, Arabic for leg), were the Euphrates and Ti-

gris which on the earth enclose Mesopotamia (between the rivers). They are now named as one constellation, Eridanus: (the river Po). The three stars which form the Belt of Orion were called by a name signifying Jacob's Staff, long before there was an English language. Orion was also supposed among the Shemites to be Noah, and then Samson, the Jewish equivalent of Hercules. Orion was formerly called Herakles by the Greeks, the other constellation now named Hercules being with them simply Engonasin, the Rester or Kneeler. Southeast from Orion, and nearly in line with the stars in his belt, is the brightest star in the firmament. It is named Sirius, from a Greek word meaning scorching; but long before that name was given the star had been denominated in Egypt the monitor, because when it was seen rising just before the sun it was to the inhabitants of that country a sign that the annual rising of the Nile was near at hand. Hence the idea of a watch dog, and from that the group of stars of which Sirius is the chief came to be called The Dog, the adjective "greater" being subsequently used when it was determined to apply the term Lesser Dog to a star (Procyon) which forms a nearly equilateral triangle with Sirius and the star in the eastern shoulder of Orion. Hence the constellation Canis Major belongs to the higher order of antiquity. Probably also does Ara, the altar, which lies far south, in right ascension about 17 hours 23 minutes: but some 4000 years B. C, was on the meridian at midnight at the time of the autumnal equinox. Being seen in Shemitic latitudes only for a short time above the horizon, and then almost due south, it may have been so named as marking the time for sacrifice, and possibly also as indicating the commencement of that half of the year in which artificial warmth is necessary to comfort even in that climate.

There is one other extra zodiacal constellation which can be faintly traced far away back towards the beginning of recorded time. It is Cetus, the Whale. Its head is south from Aries, its breast abuts against the stream of Eridanus where that turns sharply to the south after having stretched west from Orion; and the tail of Cetus extends to the stream of Aquaries, after passing below the fishes of the Zodiac. The earliest known picture of the " animal " represents it as a monster with upturned proboscis like an elephant, and a huge tusk rising from the lower jaw, but with pectoral fins and a true fish-form from that region to the tail. There is little doubt that this is an astronomical representation of the Oannes, which " half man and half fish " is fabled to have come out of the Persian Gulf, and speaking with human voice, was perhaps as much the progenitor of the Chaldean people as Noah was of all the men who lived after the flood or Adam of those who lived before the deluge. But considering that the Hebrew letters signifying *J* and *O* are very much alike, differing only in the

length of the stem, it is not difficult to suppose that
the early Oannes became a somewhat later Jonah
(*Yo-nah*), and that this fact may have had something to do with that very extraordinary story about
Jonah and the big fish which is told in the Old
Testament. But the constellation is about forty
degrees in length, and lies along the course of the
ecliptic. It takes Mona (the moon), just about
three days and three nights to pass through that
part of the heavens, which may be poetically described as the "belly of the fish;" and at the end of
that time she literally emerges from the mouth part
of the picture as drawn on some of the celestial
globes to-day. Also she is then increasing her
north declination, or literally "rising" if not
passing upward to dry land. It is hard for the
writer to resist the conclusion that this is the true
explanation of the story of Jonah and the Whale,
which becomes a beautiful astronomical allegory
instead of a narration of something that could not
possibly ever have been a fact in the sense in which
the Christian churches are said to believe it. Did
any member of one of those churches ever stop to
think of the possible significance of the remark attributed to Jesus that the people asked for a "*sign*,"
and that no sign should be given them but that of
the prophet Jonah ?

Furthermore: It takes the sun forty days to
pass through or near to the stars of the Whale in
making his annual journey around the heavens.

He is forty days or six weeks in passing through the fish, a symbol of impoverishment or privation. That is the length of time stated for the fast of Jesus, mentioned in the Gospels. It is also the time of the Lenten fast observed by the Catholic and Episcopalian churches. And singularly enough the time of the Lenten fast, if it be taken as beginning and ending on the average dates for the first and last days of Lent, would exactly coincide with the days the sun used to occupy in passing by the stars in the constellation of the Whale 3000 years ago, or a very few centuries before the story of Jonah and the whale was written; which was also the time when was penned the story of the first fast, that of Moses when he was communing with Yahveh. But at the prophetic rate of a year for a day we have that also assigned as the time the Israelites wandered in the wilderness (fasted away from the flesh pots of Egypt), after Moses had himself spent a like time as an exile from the land of Egypt where he had lived forty years.

It needs not to follow the other "ancient" constellations as to their Grecian titles, which are so manifestly artificial as to suggest that they were simply re-namings, the terms by which they were originally designated being irretrievably lost. No one can suppose that the flight of Perseus, his rescue of Andromeda, and the convenient placing of her parents Cepheus and Cassiopea near her in the sky, were anything more than adaptations of previously

named groupings to the mythological ideas of the
Hellenes. So with Lyra, the harp of Apollo,
Cygnus, the Swan, under the form of which Jupiter
seduced Leda, and Aquila with his Antinous accompaniment. They may be relegated to the domain
of what Wendell Phillips called "the lost arts."
But it may be remarked in passing that the cross of
Cygnus was observed, and probably so named, ages
before the alleged siege of Troy; and that Algol,
the Demon star in Perseus, may have been so termed
because of its marked changes in brightness long
before the fable of Medusa was passed down from
one generation to another. Yet it is singular, if
merely accidental, that the head of the Gorgon
borne by Perseus is placed on the astronomical
globes immediately north of the Whale, while the
naturalist Pliny gravely assures us that the bones
of the monster killed by the sight of that head were
brought to Rome from the town of Joppa on the
coast of Palestine, the supposed scene of the combat. The beautiful connection of this story with
the "big fish" narration in the Bible may be discoverable by one who remembers that this very
port, Joppa, was the place from which Jonah is alleged to have set sail when he tried to go to Tar-
shish. The story of Ophiucus, the Serpent-bearer,
as the original Esculapius, was probably first told
on the eastern side of the Mediterranean Sea, before the siege of Troy, the name Asclepias appearing to be of Phenecian origin.

20

It does not, however, appear that the Chaldeans proper are entitled to the honor of having first divided up the stars into groups. The first now known of them is as a little tribe somewhere around the head of the Persian Gulf, whence they moved northwestward about two hundred miles, and spread themselves over the rich alluvial soil in the valley of the Euphrates, a little below Babylon. But Shemitic names were found in that region 2280 B. C., when what was the land of the Chasdim or Chaldeans was conquered by Cudur Mabig; and it is probable that the naming was done by a semi-pastoral Shemitic tribe antecedent to that invasion, though undoubtedly they were preceded by Turanians. In fact it is not difficult to suppose that the great Shemitic wave which first impressed itself upon the history of the Asiatic continent flowed across its western portion, approximately between the northern end of the Persian Gulf and the southern shore of the Mediterranean, a very few centuries previous to 3000 B. C., that the migration was caused by an unusual flood in the lower valley of the Euphrates, though the commonly accepted Bible chronology places that event 2349 or 2348 B. C.; that the tradition of the flood lingered among the several settlements, perhaps assuming a crystallized form within a thousand years afterwards, and that everything preceding *that* is entirely mythical, the ante-diluvian story being a pure invention of the priests. Also, it is probable that the Baby-

lonian story of the Deluge, not many years since
unearthed from the library of Assurbanipal, was the
one drawn upon by the scribes of the time of Ezra
for their account as ostensibly given in the first
book of Moses. Their writing was done some two
centuries after the 660 B. C. that is assigned as the
date of the Babylonian record, but which in all
probability was compiled from some now lost picture account, or from a writing itself transcribed
from the picture. Indeed, we may conceive it as
possible that the division of the stars into constellations was incited by the closer watch which a lot
of wanderers from their recent home would keep on
the skies as well as on objects surrounding them on
the earth. But would not the same idea prevail
among those of the number who ,after perhaps many
years of wandering, reached the Valley of the Nile?
They found there in the annual overflow of that
river a strong suggestion of a possible catastrophe
at some time in the future; and the recollection of
the deluge on the Euphrates was still fresh and
vivid in the popular memory, having been transmitted through but few mouths, perhaps not more
than a single generation intervening. What more
natural than that as soon as they were numerous
enough and sufficiently settled they should build the
pyramids named after Cheops and Kephrenes, and
that the distorted recollection of that building should
form itself into the story as told by Josephus about
the two " pillars " built by the immediate descend-

ants of Adam and Eve? It may be remembered that the Hebrew historian (?) says those monuments were inscribed with the principles of the science (of astrology), that their knowledge of the stars might not be lost to the world by the deluge which they foresaw to be approaching. Is not this a case of foreseeing after the event, something like that attributed to Daniel? The reference to Ararat as the mountain on which the ark of Noah rested after the flood was more naturally made at Babylon, which is 500 miles due south from it, than at any place in Judea.

It would be no wonder if far back towards the infancy of the race the starry firmament was in imagination peopled with bulls and lions, sheep and wolves, bears and birds. gods and human forms. This would not have been out of harmony with the later thought of the Bactrian Magi, who saw a deliverer in the hand of the Virgin, or the idea of Constantine that the cross of Cygnus was an omen of victory. Nay; almost in our own day we find the Jesuit Padre de Rheita fancying he spied out, through his imperfect telescope, in the constellation Monoceros, the Veronica, or *true image* of the countenance of Jesus, said to have been impressed on a handkerchief used on his face shortly before the crucifixion. We should not ridicule a part of this unless prepared to laugh at all of it.

XVII.

SCIENCE OF LANGUAGE.

" All the peoples, the nations, and the languages."—Daniel.

Language as an Exponent of Thought.—Its Earlier Stages of Growth.—
Syllable Building.—Illustrated by Comparison of Simple Roots in
Latin.—Radical Meanings of Single Sounds in That Tongue.—Word-
making Not a Hap-hazard Process, but a Selective One.—Far Reaching Analogies.

The history of language is the history of human
thought. It is a record of the growth of ideas.
Not a name, but the exponent of one, the word conveys the thought and is the means whereby it is
perpetuated. A word, or an assemblage of words,
may be likened to the shell that surrounds the mol-
lusc, and not only marks its form but retains an
individuality long after what was the interior living mass has mouldered away. It thus not only
forms an embodiment of present vitality but serves
as a record of action and influence, bearing with it
the thought of the past into a far distant future.
There is a world of philosophy as well as of
fact in the remark:—" Words are the only things
that endure forever."

The form and consistency of the shell tell the
story of growth as well as of mere existence. So
with the word. It is often an index to the history

of a people; and if not always so the fault, "Dear
Brutus," probably lies not with the language but
with ourselves in failing to read the underlying
meanings which were earliest traced upon what is the
palimpsest of to-day.   We may not be able to follow the process of word development sufficiently
close to demonstrate it as a fact.   But so far as they
have been traced the analogies warrant the belief
that the gradual development of spoken language
has accurately marked the growth of the mental
vision, from the first dawn of reason to the full man-
hood of intellectual perception which distinguishes
the most civilized people on the face of the globe to-
day.

The first cognition of a quality, an object, or an
action is immediately followed by the introduction
of a new word into the vocabulary.   If that word
be supplied by others who are already possessed of
the knowledge we adopt it; if the void be not filled
from without we supply " the missing link " for
ourselves.

The ancient maxim that man is a microcosm is
beautifully exemplified in the linguistic comparison
of the individual with the tribe or nation.   The infant speaks not, because it thinks not.   A few months
elapse, and the child has a very limited stock of
words at command:—which so far as we are able to
decide is not far from being the exact equivalent to
its stock of ideas.   The objects with which he has
become familiarized are all named, and if the name

in use to signify any noticed object be not supplied
by his attendant the child gives it a name of its own
coinage. In such a case the appellation expresses
the child's conception of the qualities, appearance,
or use of the thing seen. Still further; the juvenile
observer not seldom manifests a wayward preference
for his own nomination; but this only when the orthodox word fails to convey to him the meaning
which is couched in the other. As the observing
faculty takes a wider range the vocabulary is correspondingly increased, and still more rapidly does
it augment as the thinking powers are brought into
play. It is certainly possible in this age of pre-
cocious progress to cram the mouth of a child full
with words; but unless that verbal acquirement be
accompanied by a corresponding substantive educa-
tion those words are only parrot-like enunciations:
—mere sounds without sense. For any intelligent
purpose they are as valueless as would be the ability
to utter a string of Choctaw syllables the mother
tongue equivalents of which were not even attempted to be communicated.

The man exhibits the same traits as does the
child. The verbal range of the uncultivated classes
in a civilized community extends over but a few
hundred words, while that of the well read man em-
braces many thousands, and the investigator is every
now and then obliged to fall back on the treasures
of other tongues for words that will represent newly
discovered objects, fresh qualities, or additional ac-

tivities;—which will express ideas hitherto uncon-
veyed, or indicate shades of meaning with a precision
greater than that previously attained. It is in this
way that our own language has become within the
last few years so much enlarged from the fullness of
the preceding century. We know more, and think
otherwise, than did our forefathers, whose wealth of
language has therefore become too poor to subserve
our needs. The process of enlargement and corresponding change is still going on, and at a rate
which suggests that the English language of 300
years hence might be barely recognized by the average Britisher or American of the present day if he
could be revived long enough to hear it as it will be
then spoken. The prophecy that *that*, or any other,
will become the universal language can be fulfilled
only by virtue of an enormous expansion of its present comprehensiveness, if at all.

This train of thought might be pursued almost
ad infinitum. It is impossible now to see where it
would terminate. The history of the future bids
fair to be much more extensive than that of the past,
unless the progress of the race be arrested by some
cosmic calamity, such as another glacial period or a
visitation like that pictured in the pages of Ragna-
rok. But we propose now only to look backward.
In doing so we are struck by one feature of the individual word-making process which is peculiarly
significant, and furnishes the clue to a wide spread
treasure. It is the fact that the process is marked

by a continuous succession of similarities and contrasts. The faculty of Comparison, which the
Phrenologists have located in the forehead, would
seem to be much the most active in the effort. The
thing, quality, or idea, for which a name is wanted
is always associated with some other that is already
provided for, and in accordance with the degree of
real or supposed similarity does the new word approximate more or less closely to the old one. There
can be no doubt that this held true in the comparative childhood of the race; but with this important
difference between the then and the now:—the child
of the present has the advantage of being surrounded by persons who have learned to use words to
which they attach more or less definite meanings.
But in the infancy of the race there was no spoken
language:—only such sounds as we may suppose to
be uttered by some of the lower animals to-day.
Then the growth of ideas was in advance of the process of word forming. The idea struggled to find
expression; but we might be mistaken in supposing
it was not till after a very long time that anything more than the onomatopoetic utterance was
indulged in or understood. This assumption is not
in harmony with the latest deductions of science.
The idea of attaching certain meanings to a few
sound groupings may be regarded as almost instinctive. But the development of this fundamental
thought into the formation of a vocabulary of more
than a very few words may be conceived of as be-

longing to the history of several generations. It was possibly a much slower process than was the subsequent emerging of an alphabet from the merely symbolical mode of writing, which marked one of the grandest steps ever taken by the human mind in rising above the level of the brute whose knowledge perishes with the termination of his own existence.

The processes of comparison and contrast in the extension of a vocabulary are recognized with regard to compounded words in any language, and have been proved to dominate over a very large area of research into the radical agreements in different languages belonging to the same family. The study of these relations in a really scientific way dates from the labors of Bopp, some sixty years ago. But it has already opened up a vast fund of knowledge in regard to the relations between words in different languages and the way in which they have been derived from others. These researches show how divers people have probably started from the same origin, and under the influence of different situations, surroundings and events have diverged more or less widely. They also give the key to some national peculiarities of thought, expression and character, and are so far of high value to the student of humanity. But the established relations are mostly those between syllables. It is true that the process has furnished some hints of the process of composing syllables, but they are of a meager char-

acter. Investigation in that direction has been
brought to a pause by the discovery that the different languages not only do not agree in this particular but that they exhibit flat contradictions. Thus
the sound of *p* is prominent in the word signifying
"father" and *m* in that signifying "mother" in
very many languages, but there are others in which
the application of these sounds is reversed. For
instance, we have for the masculine and feminine
parent names in the Hebrew *ab* and *am;* in Greek
patér, matér; in Latin, *pater, mater;* in Spanish,
padre, madre; in French, *père, mère;* in German,
fader, mudder; but in Georgian these are *mama*
and *dada.* The exceptions do not, however, prove
the absence of agreement as to plan, but only with
regard to the starting idea and to the subsequent
details of the process. Probably there are very few
exceptions to the rule that the labials (counting *m*
as one of the number), take the prominent place in
naming the parental relation. It is also true of by
far the greater number of languages that the radical
idea is embodied in the consonant, and the modification is obtained by resort to the vowel. The few
exceptions, such as the Latin *i*, which is the root of
the verb meaning "to go," are not numerous
enough to form a stumbling block;—especially as
there is some reason to believe that even those exceptions are found only in languages of comparatively modern origin.

Possibly, however, we have at hand material that will enable us to catch at least an intelligent glimpse of the process of syllable building, and one can hardly imagine a more interesting field of study. The investigation, if possible, will carry us back a long way further than does the history of word forming, not only in point of years but also in the history of human mental development;—tracing out in languages understood at the present day the first dawnings of knowledge, the earlier analyses of thought, and the primal comparisons of quality, function, and potence. Starting far down the mighty vocal stream we may by this means look up to its source, noting the little verbal rill, watching the sinuosities of its flow, the deflections it has sustained, the augmentations it has met with in its progress, and measure with wonderful exactitude some of the gradual or impulsive widenings and deepenings of the stream that at our feet has become a mighty river flowing onward to the ocean of universal language in which all the diversities of nationality will be swallowed up and the distinctions of spoken thought be all ultimately merged.

Nor is it necessary to penetrate the whole length of the dim vista of ages for this purpose. We might study the radicals of the Shemitic tongues, and trace out from a score or so of prominent objects the hieroglyphs that were at first employed for recording purposes. We might track them down to the alphabetic system, and detect thence the growth

of the language into the plenitude of its later power.
But in doing so we should labor under the disad-
vantage of delving among the ruins of a dead tongue
whose grandest details may for aught we know be
reduced to such a complete debris that even their
general outlines are not certainly determinable.
Nay; more than this. In the case of the Hebrew it
would be necessary to disentangle that heap of ruins from a heavy covering of fungus vegetation that
has sprung up over it in the shape of a system of
pointings which has dethroned the three original
vowel elements of the alphabet and dageshed the
consonants into a "begadkepat" entirely unknown
to the men who spoke the language in the times of
the prophets. The same associative result may be
obtained by enquiring nearer home, and of a somewhat more recent era with the character of which
the general reader is more familiar. And we know
enough of the older specimens to be able to verify
in this case the assumption that human nature is
radically the same in all ages and all climes, and its
modes of manifestation subject to the same all per-
vading laws, varied only by the operation of dis-
similar sets of surroundings. The history of the
formation of language has repeated itself "many a
time and oft" since the first names were given,
whether that were in the Garden of Eden or elsewhere; and the more recent examples belong to no
distant epoch.

It is proposed to take a partial view of the Latin
language in those traits which seem to reveal something of its origin.   The Latin is chosen because it
is one with which many readers of English are more
or less familiar, and its radicals are all found in our
own tongue with the same general meanings;—not
because any other non-conglomerate language does
not offer equal facilities for the study. Yet it may be
remarked that the Latin is entitled to rank along-
side of the Sanscrit in point of age, and perhaps
compares well in that respect with the oldest Hebrew manuscript that has been handed down to us;
though in previous chapters facts have been noted
which point to the conclusion that the Shemitic is
an older family than the Indo-European.   We shall
not dip so deeply into the subject as to make the
line of argument a difficult one to follow, and it
should be distinctly understood that the analogies
here presented are only suggestive.   The subject is
involved in too much obscurity to warrant dogmatic
assertions.

It may, however, be accepted as axiomatic that
the first formed words of a language are all monosyllabic.   The exceptions to this rule will be the
intensitive doublings in such words as pa-pa and
ma-ma, and some first forms in those so-called distinct languages which have been gradually evolved
by progressive changes from some other or others.
A single utterance is the expression of a simple
idea.   These unisyllables are the roots of the great

mass of words of which the full language is composed. The cultivated word is made up of two or more radicals when ideas are associated, and is varied by grammatical inflection when only a modification of the original is intended to be conveyed. The most simple words are those consisting of a single vowel. These are, however, so very few in number that they afford but little range of expression. The most simple word, properly so called, is that which contains one vowel and one consonant, and it is with this that we commence the vocal definition of thought. It is in the consonant that the character of the utterance lies couched;—the vowel gives it force, volume, makes it audible, at the same indicating the direction of the original idea. The vowel is not employed for the purpose of designating radical distinctions till after the resources of the consonantal alphabet have been apparently exhausted.

Let us take one family of roots as a sample; the principle that governs the choice of the several members will be apparent on casual inspection. *N* is the principle of negation or contrariety; and with the vowel *e* it makes *ne*, not. The Saxon equivalents are *un* and *no*. The monosyllabic children of this family are numerous, to say nothing of the vast number of words into which it enters as a particle, or of which its offspring form what are generally understood to be primal roots. The meaning is intensified by a guttural consonant; hence we have

nec and *neg*.   A change of vowel gives *ni*, nothing, which we may suppose to have been expanded
into *nihil*, though the latter is possibly a contrac-
tion from *nihilum*, by a process of phonetic decay.
Nec or *nex* is death, or destruction, and cognate with
it is the Greek *nec-ros*, both of which signify that
the individual is not.   Another radical is *nem-o*,
nobody; *m* being a consonant of individuality or
prominence, and generally indicates the positive, as
n represents the negative.

Correlative to the idea of nothingness is that of
indistinctness or indefinability.   Thence we have
neb-ula, a mist or vapor;—something not well defined, uncertain.   The labial, too, embodies the idea
of paternity. as in the Hebrew *ab* (we are told to
call it *ac*); and the Latin *ab*, from, bears with it
the idea of origin.   A change of vowel gives us
nub-ium, a cloud; and by substitution of the perfect
and perfecting labial, *p*, we have *nup-tiae*, a cloud-
ing or veiling; the idea being applied to the marriage rite because of the veiling which used to be an
essential part of the nuptial ceremony.   A change
of vowel gives *nob-ilis*, noble; the word being applied to the better class for one or both of two
reasons;—that they were supposed to have been over-
shadowed by the gods, or that they were looked
upon as having been hedged in, set apart, enclosed,
shut out from the vulgar gaze, *veiled* with dignity
and virtue.   The laborious guttural changes this
form into *nox*, night, or rather evening, the season

of blackness, when the veil of darkness hides all
things from view. *Nig-er*, is black, the quality of
darkness; and returning to the full vowel we have
noc-eo (the *c* is hard), to injure; the work of an enemy being done in secret, and also causing a cloud
or partial death. The idea of hiding is continued
in *nid-us*, a nest, where the young are hidden,
sheltered, screened from observation and danger.
The same radical furnishes *nux*, a nut, the fruit of
which is protected or hidden by the shell, and *nic-
tare*, to wink, or veil the eyes. Also *nix*, snow,
may be considered to have been so called not on account of its whiteness or quality, but because it veils
the earth and covers up all objects from the sight.
We may add that *nim-bus* is translated by the word
"cloud," but it also means a storm, the *m* carrying with it the idea of acting. But the storm is a
cause of concealment, as it drives to shelter man and
beast, leaving the landscape bare of animated existence.

Were the Latin a pure tongue, built up on this
as one of its basic principles, we ought not to expect
that the general idea of negation would attach to
the consonant *n* wherever used. The processes
of derivation may and would lead to different and
even opposite meanings. We need only instance
the root *nit*, which expresses the fact of brilliancy;
shining *like snow*. This develops an idea of prominence out of the original one of concealment. But
the almost opposite meaning of prominence attached

21

to the letter *n* is grafted into the language from another source;—one that is probably much older in point of time than that born of and with the Latin as a branch of the Indo-European family. It belongs, in fact, to one of the earliest of the post-diluvian tongues, and seems to have been adopted through the Greek from the Phenecian. In that ancient mother of thought *n* signifies prominent existence. Hence the radical *On*, the being; a term applied to divinity and forming the nominative terminal to a large class of Greek substantives. It is from this root that we have *ne-os*, new; an object being most prominent when first brought into notice. It is continued in the Latin *na-tus*, born. Hence also *na-o*, to swim, or to be cast up prominently from the water. In the Latin this is *no*, and a secondary derivation gives *nauta*, a sailor, he being one who is kept up above the water in *navis*, a ship. Another radical derivative is *nu-dus*, naked, the person being unhidden by clothing, and *nuto*, to nod, as indicating a gesture whereby we convey information or attract notice. Manifestly of the same origin is the Greek *gno-mon*, a style or index, a prominence of projection; and from this comes *gnome*, a shadow cast by the style, or a spirit. And because the shadow of the gnomon was depended upon to enable the observer to know the time by the sun dial many ages before the clock was invented, the word *gnosco* may have come into use to signify the act of knowing. From this is *nomen*, a name, or that by which a thing is known and by which its qualities or properties were supposed to be expressed; also *nom-os*, a law, an index pointing out what is right or what should not be done. It is not difficult to trace out the Latin *nunc*, now, the present time, that which is pointed at, as a scion of the same stock.

We have already characterized the guttural consonant as "the laborious." It signifies exertion, and has a transitive meaning. We find it first taking vocal shape in *ag-o*, to act, which in the perfect is *ac-tus*, the *t* being added rather as a natural sequence to the *k* sound than as having any real meaning. This *ac-tus*, at first formed the *making* termination in Latin, but probably it was soon found that there was little need for both consonants, and the one requiring the most exertion was dropped out of the great majority of words, leaving *at-us*, as the termination. And this is continued in the English of our own day as *at-ed*. We say "animated" though we retain the *k* sound in fact, manufacture, etc. The process of substitution here noted, where *t* becomes invested with the power of *k*, is often met with; and doubtless occurred at a very early period in the growth of the language. Hence arises another idea which attaches to *t*, but must not be mistaken for the radical meaning. It comes from another source, but within the language. It is simply the result of an impulse to save vocal labor.

We may now see also how the guttural gives meanings to words previously quoted. *Neg* and *nec* mean "*made* nothing," or nothingness which is caused;—death as distinguished from primal non-existence. Also *noc-eo*, to injure (we have no reason to believe that *c* had any other than the *k* sound given to it by the Romans), has in it the element of action the result of which is injurious. Founded on this root are *ag-er*, a field, space enclosed, worked ground; *ag-ger*, a heap (of earth) requiring labor to throw it up; and *ag-ilis*, quick in movement. The Greek *ag-on*, is evidently of similar origin, signifying a combat or action in which every power is strained to the uttermost. With preceding consonants on this radical guttural we have *fac-io*, to make, the act with a result; and its perfect *fic*, made. Also its derivative *fee*, which often signifies the deed done to the uttermost, and sometimes overdone. We may trace the same original in *fig-ura*, a form; that is, matter shaped; also in *vic*, to conquer, to make subject; in *voc-o*, to call, to make a noise; and its perfect *vec*; in *vac-uus*, empty, made empty; and in *vaga*, vague.

The *r* sound carries with it the idea of strength. We do not mean by this the half-hearted *agh.h-h* of some of our Teutonic friends, which makes a sad mess of such a line as:

> Ghound the ghugged ghocks the ghagged ghascal ghan.

And still less the worse emasculated *ah* which to-day passes current as the correct thing in some English and American circles, to say nothing of the colored man's remark about shutting the *doh*. The sound here referred to is the vigorous *r-r-r-r* of Celtic origin, which one sometimes hears from the mouth of a Frenchman or an Irishman. And it may be remarked here that it is the tongue which is generally conceded to be the most effective factor in the production of speech; also that this accords with the recently discovered fact that the ability of man to talk depends upon the muscles which are inserted in the chin tubercles. The existence of these tubercles is considered to be essential to the act of speaking. They do not exist in the non-speaking animals, nor in the oldest known specimens of human skulls; from which it is legitimately inferred that the primeval man was not able to talk, and that the first speaking human beings lived but a few thousand years ago. This may seem to be a digression, but it is introduced here for the purpose of calling attention to the fact that as it is the talk motion of the tongue that originates in these muscles, and as the trilling sound is the very one that brings the tongue most effectively and rapidly into play, therefore the trilling of the *r* belongs to the most highly cultivated form of speech. It is a logical inference that the speech which does not include this sound in its range of vocal utterance is to that extent of an inferior order, and its omission in the speaking of a cultivated tongue is a sign of degeneracy either in the language or the individual speaker.

The employment of *r* in the Latin as indicative of strength gives us *reg-o*, to rule or govern; and *rog-atio*, a duty imposed by the governing power; with their inverse *ger-o*, to carry or bear (a burden). From the same consonant we have *rectus*, right or straight;—that which governs, as might made right in early times and does so too often in the present day. With the outside consonant *l* the root becomes *lig-o*, to bind, to make fast, or literally to make or put a band outside; also *leg-is*, (lex), a law, or that which binds to a certain course of action; and *leg-o*, to read the law either of dictum or precedent;—those being the only things read, as they were the only things officially written. That this is no fanciful idea is easily proven by reference to the subsequently written histories of Latins, Greeks, and Hebrews. The book of Genesis tells of stones being set up as witnesses (Mizpah); but the earliest record claimed by the Jews is that said to have been inscribed by the finger of Jehovah himself on Mount Sinai. The exterior character of *l*, already noted, may be further illustrated by reference to *latus*, a side; *alt-us*, high, or raised out of the general mass; and *lat-eo*, to be hidden or concealed away from that which is before us.

The generic character of *r* as representing force, strength, is displayed in *rob-ur*, an oak; *rum-po*, to burst; *fran-go*, to break, etc. The idea is fully borne out in *ira*, wrath, stormy or strong passion; and *era*,

an epoch, which impresses itself on future time;—
though we need not be unmindful of the fact that the
word E R A is made up from the initials of the sentence *Ab Exordio Regni Augusti;* "From the commencement of the reign of Augustus." *R* is equally
the element of strength in *ara*, an altar, the lever of
power with the gods; *aro*, to plow, or break up the
ground forcibly; *oro*, to flow, the fullness of action; *are-o*, to be dry, having strength to absorb;
ar s, art, the force or power of knowledge; *ard-eo*,
to burn, or destroy violently, and the Greek *aris-
tos*, the best or highest or most powerful. It is
not less distinctive in *aur-um*, gold, the metal
which gives power (though that word appears
to have been toned down from *aus-um*); and *fer-
rum*, iron, the strong metal of which tools were
made and of which we make other things. All
these words are distinctly associated with the trilling
sound as an indication of strength; and the terminal
or-e, one who holds or grasps, is equally potential.

It may be observed in the latter examples that
where no vowel follows the radical consonant the
power is rather passive; where the consonant leads
in the syllable it is more active. The change of
vowel from one side of the consonant to the other
is equally distinctive in the case of the rest, though
not always in the same direction. For instance, *k*
and *g* are most active with a preceding vowel. And
this remark leads us up to a view of the thought
qualities of the vowels themselves. Their general

determinations are as follows: *a*, breadth or height; *u*, depth; *o*, fullness; *i*, smallness; *e*, fineness, exquisiteness. We may observe the shades communicated in *mar-e*, the sea; *a-mar-us*, bitter; *a-mar-e*, to love; *mar-s*, war; *mor-s*, death; *mur-um*, a wall; *mir-a*, a wonder; *mord-eo*, to bite or leave a mark; *mor-es*, manners, that which makes a man; and *mer-it*. All these have the fundamental idea of positiveness and force or strength attaching to *m* and *r;* varied in the shade of meaning or circumstantial applicability by the intermediate vowel, as previously noted. An intensification of force is also expressed by the doubling of an initial syllable, and this is by no means confined to a single language. In the Latin it marks the perfecting of an action, as *momordit* (he did bite or has bitten) from the simple root *mordeo;* and a similar modification is observable in the Greek. In a more familiar tongue the already quoted ma-ma and pa-pa serve as examples of this strengthening by repetition at so early a date in the life of a child that we may almost call it instinctive.

We might carry out these analogies much further. They could be extended to take in most if not all of the consonants, and shown to govern in at least a few of the double consonant groupings; which it may be incidentally remarked signal one of the first steps in modification by contracting or eliminating some of the sounds previously recognized as necessary to embodiment of the thought. But the line of illustra-

tion is already extended sufficiently for the purpose
of showing that the process of syllable building in
the Latin language was by no means the hap-hazard kind of work which some who have discoursed
on the subject would have us believe marked the
first use of spoken sounds. Of course this, if admitted, does not prove that the same is true and to
an equal extent with all other languages. Indeed,
there is good reason to think it is not true in degree though it may be so in kind. In the first place
such a comparison evidently could not be made for
a language of multiplex origin such as the English
of to-day, except for that part of it which is derived from several sources that have admittedly
diverged from a common origin. But if we can
once see good reason to conclude that a single
tongue presents indubitable evidence of intelligent
selection it certainly will not be difficult to concede
it as probable that many others have an equally
rational base; however widely they may differ in the
selection of a simple sound as suggestive of a root
thought, or in the grand results due to subsequent
combination and transformation.

XVIII.

ORIGIN OF SPEECH.

" Who hath made man's mouth?"—Exodus.

Mental Tubercles.—Lingual Development.—Primitive Growth of Language.—"First Families."—Monkey Talk.—Mutations of Speech.—Philological Studies.—Derivations of Words.—Parallels.—Lilith and the Story of the Fall.—Genesis and the Book of Nature.—The Original Curse.

The recent discovery that certain tubercles and muscles are necessary to the production of articulate speech has been alluded to in the last preceding chapter. They are called *mental*, a word derived from the Latin *men-tum*, chin, not from *mens*, mind. The directive power which governs the movements of these muscles seems to reside in the third or lowest convolution in the frontal lobe of the human brain. That convolution is found to be rudimentary in the highest apes of to-day. It is absent in the lower animals, and is said to be entirely wanting in the oldest human skulls that have been unearthed by modern delving among the ruins of a buried past. Not only that convolution but the mental tubercles also were absent in the Neanderthal skull, proving the possessor of that cranium to have lacked the power of articulate speech. These peculiar conformations are found on other

330

crania, the wearers of which lived long ago but later than the Neanderthal man; and he walked the earth since the close of the River Drift period. These facts strongly support the previously stated theory that man as a non-speaking animal may have lived on this earth some hundreds of thousands of years, being during the whole of that time very little removed in intellect from what we now refer to as the "level of the brute." But the first *speaking* human being came into existence hardly more than ten thousand years ago, and possibly less than that. We are not able to say how he acquired the extra convolution and tubercles; but it may have been in some such way as that in which certain members of a family in this age of the world are born with a sixth finger. Possibly it was what some people would call a "fortuitous" addition, which was perpetuated by selection; as some strange varieties of the animal kingdom have been made to persist within the memories of men alive to-day.

But what a change did that addition involve. Only a step upward in the scale, and that perhaps one which might as truly be called accidental as was the assuming of the first skin or any other of the events that men ascribe to chance when they are not wise enough to see the hidden causation which has brought it around in strict sequence to other facts forming a line that stretches away back into the eternity of the past. But it was a step that carried him at once from darkness into the dawning of light.   Previous to taking it man was not much superior in intelligence to the anthropoid apes of which so much has been said in discussing the Darwinian theory of evolution.   We are obliged to believe that the first speaking man was able to think, at least as well as the little child of our own times, and his thinking powers found expression in a way that marked a recognition of the fitness of things. He naturally associated certain sounds with the supposed qualities of the things or ideas they were intended to represent; though we must admit that the same radical ideas were not mentally associated with the same sounds by the different peoples who first belonged to speech families so widely sundered as are those with which the Hebrew and the Latin are affiliated.   In fact there are some that are utterly lacking in more than one of the sounds common to those two.   For instance, Captain Cook, the celebrated voyager, found a people in the Society Islands who were unable to pronounce his name because they had no gutturals in their language.   They called him " Taptain Toot."   Similarly, the Chinese and negroes have no sound common to our *r*, the Australian no *s*, the Greeks were unable to represent the *sh* sound of the Hebrew when the Septuagint translation was made, the Frenchman has no *th*, and we read of some peoples whose battery of sounds includes only seven consonants.   But these facts do not even weaken the force of our argument, much less destroy it; any more than would the comparison of an elephant with a squid disprove the assertion that each of those organisms is built up in obedience to certain laws which govern the formation of tissue in the animal kingdom.

Yet the belief that the earliest spoken languages were formed by starting in with such a selective process by no means carries with it the admission that man as a speaking animal came into existence in some such fashion as did Minerva, springing full armed from the brain of Jove. Nor is it even tantamount to the idea that human language did not originate with a series of wild shriekings or mere attempts to copy the cries of animals and then improve upon them. We can at least in imagination watch the process of development much further back towards the mental infancy of the race (*in-fans*, not speaking), than the selective making of syllables: though that in turn preceded the transformations to which Grimm's law furnishes the master key. We are obliged to admit that many animals communicate with their kind by means of sounds, though it is exceedingly probable this is mostly effected by alternations of tone. In other words, it is music rather than speech. The recent investigations of Prof. R. L. Garner, of Washington, by the aid of the phonograph, prove that the "monkey talk" heard by him is a series of intonations, each of which is an imperfect harmony with *F* sharp. He has proven that these sound series are varied to express the few wants of the animal, and has identified a few of them as corresponding with such simple words as *food* and *milk*. Yet he also claims to have discovered that the monkey has a sound (alphabetic), vocabulary, consisting of three consonants and two vowels. We can readily suppose that the first attempts at what may be distinctively called human speech were not far above this range of expression when we know that within the present century the speech of some wild men has been described as a mere alternation of clicks, and that of an Indian chief in this country as nothing more than a sequence of grunts. Nay; we are by no means sure that the consonantal character of the Hebrew alphabet is not based upon the comparatively modern fact of a mere consonantal clicking among the inhabitants of Asia Minor. True, the theory has been advanced that this peculiarity in the mode of writing arose from the first attempts to translate Egyptian hieroglyphs into phonetic characters; but if true that explanation would not render our supposition untenable. For aught we know the earliest Egyptian vocabulary may have consisted only of consonants. It is equally possible that some of the earliest vocal utterances consisted only of vowel sounds.

Undoubtedly the earliest human companionship must have been that of the mother and her child. Without maternal care the infant would perish, and the fact that it survived proves the existence of a mother's love for her offspring through ages when

the relations between adults of opposite sexes were
no more binding than those between the merest
brutes. The crooning of the mother would be understood by the child, and before the two separated
for life a few sounds would be understood by them
in common. But as between every other mother
and her children there might be a more or less different set of meanings attached to the same articu-
lations, and there was thus room for as many incip-
ient languages as mothers; while the child would
have at least "something to say" in establishing the
character of the verbal communication between itself
and the parent. When able to leave the mother the
youth of early days would hunt for itself, and intimacy between the sexes would not necessarily include much conversation till another mother had an
infant to care for. Efforts at talking between
individuals of different families would be rare. But
when owing to some unusual circumstance, as the
simultaneous pursuit of an animal, two adults had
an inducement to communicate with each other the
experience would be as described by Paul: "Unto
him that speaketh a barbarian, and he that speaketh
a barbarian unto me." Unless one were so strong
as to be able to dictate to the other, the speech between them would have to be a matter of mutual
concession; and if the acquaintance of the pair were
continued it would practically result in a language
sui generis. When they finally separated that particular language would die out: except as a part of

it might perhaps be a contributor to another set of
utterances agreed upon subsequently by one of those
two in common with a third. It would seem probable that in the purely hunting stage man could
hardly rise far above this condition; but that with
the beginning of the pastoral era, and the perhaps
nearly simultaneous recognition of a family tie as
between parents, would commence a perpetuation of
set forms of speech from one generation to another.
Then. from the mingling of families, would arise a
partial community of speech, into which some of the
more important words from each source might be
concentrated. And thus would arise the "poetic
plenitude" of several hundred words for each one
of a few objects, which has been observed in at least
one language spoken to-day. It is evident that the
condition of things leading up to the latter phase
would include as an almost essential feature the existence of as many different modes of speech as there
were families on the face of the globe attempting to
speak at all, and that most of these would be in a
state of perpetual change the rapidity of which has
no modern parallel.

Evidently these earlier attempts at speech would
not improve and widen in scope as rapidly as the language of a child now developes into that of the man.
Ideas and wants were alike few, and man's knowledge of his own capabilities exceedingly limited.
Probably the earliest vocabularies which survived
the parting of the two or three individuals consent-

ing thereto contained not more than a score or two of words, with hardly a dozen different sound elements to express them, after it had been in use for a century. The rest was a matter of gradual growth up to the point at which man became conscious of his power to adapt himself to new conditions, began to feel new wants, and commenced the thinking process that inevitably accompanied that widening out of his mental vision. Even if we should accept the Bible statement that the first man gave names to all the beasts of the field and fowls of the air, it would by no means follow that his list was a hundredth part as long as those printed in our books on Natural History. The uneducated man of this generation who passes his life on a farm, and knows nothing except the objects that he sees around him every day, finds in a list of about a hundred words very nearly all the material required for communicating his ideas and wishes to another. When the world of humanity was made up of beings most of whom were lower in the scale than he is now, and none of them higher, the possibilities for the growth and expansion of speech were bounded in a very small area. It required agriculture, then organized warfare, and that followed by commerce, to call out the mental energies, form word accumulations out of the scattered verbal elements at the command of individuals, and set in motion the enginery of thought which wonderfully increased the number of words employed when means had been invented for recording them.

22

(The discovery that a bony process on the chin is necessary to human speech is a very recent one; but it is at least entitled to be regarded as a curious coincidence that the terms "chinning" and "chin music" were employed long since to designate superfluous talk. The anticipation is almost as happy a one as that by which Dean Swift spoke of the two moons of the planet Mars a hundred and fifty years before they were first seen by the aid of the telescope in the Autumn of 1877.)

Max Müller tells us that the number of roots in the Sanscrit is only about 800, and that every one of those has a general or conceptual meaning, such as striking, pushing, rubbing, cutting, bearing, tearing, binding, measuring, building, moving, going, falling etc. But as it often happens that two or more roots have the same or nearly the same meaning, the fundamental concepts may be reduced to 121. The number of roots in English has dwindled down to 461, while the sum total of words in that language has risen to about 250,000. Some of the 121 concepts, such as to cook, to roast, to measure, to dig, to plant, to milk, betoken an advanced condition of life, and probably would not occur in the dictionary of primeval savages. But Müller suggests that with few exceptions, "the roots express the *repeated acts* of men in a simple state of civilization." He concludes that the primitive roots of Aryan speech may owe their origin to the sounds which naturally accompany many acts performed in common by members of a family, clan, or village. He instances *mar* as expressing the concept of rubbing, and *dar* that of tearing, as supporting the theory of Noiré and others that our roots are the remnants of sounds that accompanied common acts, and which being used not by one man but by men acting in common were, therefore, intelligible to the whole community. Of course this is not given as a well ascertained historical fact; but as explaining all that has to be explained, and having the advantage that it does not run counter to any facts or any well established theories.

Till within a little more than two centuries ago it was generally supposed that the Hebrew language was the one spoken in the Garden of Eden, and that from it have been derived all other tongues, ancient and modern. This was expressly stated by St. Jerome, who translated the Old and New Testaments into Latin, and by other early fathers of the Christian church. It was accepted as axiomatic alike by Jews, Christians and Mohammedans till Leibnitz, the contemporary and friend of Sir Isaac Newton, called it in question. Though believing in one primitive language he wrote that to call Hebrew that primitive tongue was like designating branches of a tree primitive branches. In the latter half of the last century the study of Sanscrit, the ancient language of India, led to the discovery that it is a sister of the Greek and Latin. Since then most of the tongues of Europe have been shown to be derived from them or cognates, and classed as forming an Aryan or Indo-European family of languages, differing fundamentally from the Shemitic to which the Hebrew and Arabic belong. A rather large number of previous identifications of words belonging to individual members of these two families were discarded as not furnishing satisfactory proof of a common origin, and it was laid down as a rule that the true affinities of different tongues must be determined by similarities of grammatical construction instead of words. Recently, however, the subject has been taken up by Dr. Karl Rodosi, who points out a surprising resemblance between a long list of Hebrew roots and the corresponding irregular verbs of the English language. As these are of Saxon origin it is not surprising that their parallels are also found in German. The writer has recently called attention to the close agreement in the order in which words are arranged in Hebrew and English sentences expressing the same thought. The latter fact may justly be urged as proving an affiliation between the two, closer than that linking English to Greek or even Latin, and in marked contrast to the wide diversity found in comparing either with Chinese. This suggests that the old simile of a language tree may be improved upon. In a criticism of Rodosi's work the writer said (July 20, 1891), we may conceive languages to compose a "plant that sends up several stems from a single root, each of those stems sending off shoots that dip down and

take root in the earth, becoming in turn the parents
of other branches. If now we suppose those
branches and their foliage to have mixed and inter-
leaved luxuriantly, and the more recent ones to retain their vitality while the older stems have not
only decayed but the resulting dust mingled with
the soil, we shall have some such parallel as I conceive to exist between the modern and most ancient
languages. It is evident the further this process is
carried the more difficult it will be to distinguish
between the separate origins for the components of
any particular section of this mass of vegetation.
And the direction in which the twigs, runners, or
filaments lie with regard to each other becomes the
fact of greatest prominence in the effort to trace the
now living ones back to their dead primitives."

It is difficult to resist the conclusion that there is
such a parallelism between the Hebrew and that
branch of the Indo-European family to which the
Anglo-Saxon belongs; much closer than of the
former with the other twig bundle of the latter
which includes the Greek and Latin. This may
lend interest to an effort made by the writer several
years ago to show that the Bible legend of the fall
of man harmonizes to a great extent with the previously explained theory of the origin of language.
The story cannot be accepted as literally true, and
yet it may be interpreted into consistency with the
knowledge that has been revealed to man by a
study of the great book of Nature. But in order

to do this we must call in the aid of a Jewish tradition which appears to be as old as the (Jewish) race itself, and is thought by some to have possibly formed at one time a part of the story in Genesis:

Probably many readers of this book have heard of Lilith, though they may not be familiar with the details of the Jewish legend concerning her. She was the first wife of Adam. (In many languages the word for *wife* is synonymous with that for *woman.*) She belonged to another order of beings, and is referred to as "a demon," but that does not forbid the idea that she was of an order inferior to Adam. Her place as a wife was taken by Eve, and as a consequence she owed an eternal grudge against the offspring of the woman who supplanted her in the affections of "the man." Hell hath no fury like a woman scorned; and the idea that afflictions befalling Jewish children, more particularly the first born, are the work of Lilith, still lingers in the minds of that Peculiar People.

Let us then carry ourselves back in imagination some seven thousand years, more or less, to a scene in a mild climate, such as is to be found in the subtropical portion of Asia. A race of anthropoids exists there. Among them is born a male child distinguished by the possession of the brain convolution and mental tubercles requisite to enable him to talk after he has passed the period of what we now call infancy. When he *does* begin to talk, the exhibition of his strange faculty amazes the other

anthropoids, and either they drive him out of their
company or the maternal instinct prompts his mother
to remove him to a place where he will be safe from
the rage which she fears will kill him if he remains.
She flies with him, as Hagar took Ishmael into the
wilderness. She carries with her a yet unborn babe
of the female sex. Finding a secluded spot, where
nuts and fruits abound, they stay there; and life is
easily sustained in a region of perpetual summer.
The other child is born, and proves also to have the
gift of speech. In regard to the first she is literally
" bone of his bone and flesh of his flesh," being at
least his half sister; she is his equal in point of intelligence, which the mother is not, and the latter is
gradually neglected as the two children grow up side
by side, each finding in the other a companion not to
be met with elsewhere in the world. The mother
dies, or perhaps wanders off alone. One or both,
perhaps only the woman, dreams of her, seeing her in
the vision as if standing under a tree and beckoning
them to follow. Then they fancy they hear a voice
like their own in the distance, and think it is possibly their erstwhile companion who has at last gained
the power of speech. That curiosity, which in all
ages has been strongest in the female breast, impels
the pair to set out on an exploring tour; like Rob-
inson Crusoe, who, after having lived in seclusion
for years, went around to the other side of his
island. They come upon a scene that horrifies them.
A number of anthropoids are fighting among them-

selves, and for the first time the two see blood
flowing from a being fashioned as they are. They
know it means death, because they have seen the
lower animals kill and devour. The pair flies in
terror. They rest not till far away from the scene
of their early felicity. They have left Paradise for
ever.

It is not necessary to admit the serpent into this
narrative, though even his alleged presence can be
accounted for. It may be remembered that Dr.
Adam Clark, one of the ripest Oriental scholars of
the Methodist Church, insisted in his commentary
published in 1810, that the Hebrew word *nachash*,
translated by our word " serpent " really means an
" ape." We must admit that the weight of authority is against him, but a great deal may be said in
support of his view. If we accept it we can very
readily credit Lilith with having acted the part of
tempter. She was the most intelligent (subtile) of
all the animals, having become so by long association with, and observation of, her progeny; could
be regarded as condemned to walk on all fours in
the person of the monkeys lower down in the scale,
and may be supposed capable of imprecating by
gesture if not in speech the curse (said to have been)
pronounced upon her ungrateful children who had
learned to love one another while they despised her.
And if not ready to accept Adam Clark's translation we have only to remember that the earliest
methods of writing were symbolical. It is not

difficult to think that both the serpent and the ape were in the original picture, and that in the translation the symbol was mistaken for the object. The riddle is then solved.

The explanation so far is perfectly consistent, while eliminating from the story all that is miraculous. But there remains something much more important, because more conclusive, to those who insist on regarding the whole Genesis story as having a basis of truth. We read in the sixth chapter, verse 2, that "The sons of God saw the daughters of men that they were fair, and took wives of all which they chose." This proves the existence of another and inferior race—if it proves anything. We can read it as saying that the children and grand children of the first pair had the gift of speech, and were surrounded by anthropoids who possessed it not. The latter were not human beings in the first Scripture sense of the word, nor within the limits of our definition; and it is no wonder if the result of such a union would be a hybrid product, contact with which would be loathsome to those who felt that themselves belonged to a superior race. It can readily be understood that if the first part of the story were true there must have been "giants" (monsters), on the earth in those days; and it needs not to do more than simply refer to the outgoing of Cain to the land of Nod, and there building him a city, as calling for some such explanation as is here offered. The narration is clear on the point

that other beings of human form were in existence
besides the progeny of Adam and Eve; and they
must have been of inferior mold, or it is not true
that Eve was so-called for the reason that she was
the mother of all (men) living.

Whether so ordered or not, by the dictum of
God or demon, language has been a curse, as well
as a blessing; while none may dispute the claim that
labor has been more of a blessing than a curse, in
spite of the deplorable fact that untold millions of
human beings have toiled and died under the lash of
slavery. Language has disseminated more of error
than of truth. By its use the orator has perverted
the ends of justice, and the measured feet of the
poet have stimulated to deeds of blood, surrounding
the wholesale murder of one's fellow creatures with
a halo of miscalled glory. The same verse has
lauded the deeds of the libertine; and always at the
service of the oppressor, praising him to the skies
and handing down his name to posterity as if he
were one of earth's noblest creatures. The same
language has been prostituted to the worship of
false gods; and taken the name of the All Merciful
in vain while ordering untold numbers of poor mortals to the rack, the gibbet and the stake for his alleged glory. As a general rule the most talkative
people are the least practical, the flowery orator
a poor statesman, the eloquent lover insincere and
inconstant. The most voluble utterances are apt
to be precisely those deserving the remark, " Vox

et preterea nihil.'' In fact there is a great deal of philosophy in the statement that by the time a man is sufficiently wise to make it worth the while of others to listen to him, he inclines to the opinion that it is hardly worth *his* while to talk at all.

Yet, in spite of all this, language, and the thought of which it is the embodiment, is the crowning characteristic of man. Without it, and by its aid, the race has perpetuated itself through cosmic convulsions and the minor afflictions of war, famine and pestilence. Its persistence through all, while other forms of animal life have come and faded out forever, except as their fossil remains tell the story, proves that it has been a survival of the fittest. How much of progress is yet to be experienced by the race before it, too, succumbs to the inevitable? Who dare say man will not conquer the heavens, as he has already achieved dominion over the forces of the earth, and by the very means fabled to have been used to prevent him from scaling the starry heights, the "confusion of tongues?''

XIX

LET THERE BE LIGHT.

" And the times of this ignorance God winked at."—Acts.

Modification of Old Ideas Caused by Scientific Investigation.—Man's Beliefs Depend Upon His Knowledge.—Effect of Facts on Faith.—Will All this New Knowledge Revealed to Man by Astronomy, Microscopy, Geology, Chemistry and the Spectroscope Promote His Moral and Spiritual Welfare ?

The last fifty years have brought round a greater change in the habits, modes of thought, toils, and enjoyments of civilized man than did any two or three of the centuries preceding. The world had now and then been overrun by conquering hordes or armies, carrying with them new customs, other languages, and generally fresh burdens: with additional modes of torture for those who were not prepared to indorse heartily the latest assertion of might to be right. The migrations of the last half century have been more extensive, but of the peaceful order. They have peopled a continent in the South Seas, though by courtesy to the older ones it is called an island, have opened up millions of square miles to settlement in the New World the discovery of which is credited to Colon (Columbus), and is now illuminating with the electric light of civilization the interior of Africa, where darkness had reigned in undisturbed repose for untold centuries. The period

referred to is also remarkable as forming an era of
applied science. Previous to that the wise men of
the day thought they knew something, but few of
them cared to turn their knowledge to practical account; and those who had such an ambition met with
so much of discouragement that many of them died
broken hearted and all poor. These men were regarded as nuisances instead of benefactors of the
race; and a liberal percentage of their number were
shut up in prison or burned at the stake as heretics,
or persons who had purchased superior wisdom by a
compact with the evil one.

Fifty years and more ago the most deeply thinking part of the world resembled a crowd in a dark
room watching the projection of shadows on a
screen. It saw a succession of phantoms, most of
them mere coinages of the brain, and accepted them
unquestioningly as realities. Many of these pictures
were beautiful, the productions of genius equal in brilliancy to any of our own day; but nearly all of them
resembled the " baseless fabric of a vision," having
no foundation in fact. This was true alike in the departments of theology, philosophy, medicine, and the
bald array of ideas that were scattered over what
is now a broad and rich field of natural science.
The torch bearer comes along and turns up the gas-
jets one by one. At first the light is dim; then the
members of the " audience" can see each other.
Soon the shadows on the screen fade out, and only
a blank expanse of white remains where but a short

time ago shone forth the accumulated wisdom of the ages. But instead of things weird, and by many supposed to be supernatural, the gazers see each other as human beings, recognize friends, discern around them the living components of their world, and realize that all they gazed at in the darkness was of the unsubstantial order, though opinions may vary in regard to the shades that have vanished. The production is reasoned to be the work of an artist, and criticism comes into play to dissect out the natural from the absurd in a scene which but a few moments earlier had been gazed at as partaking of the sublime.

This lighting up process has revolutionized human thought, not only as to its methods, but even in regard to the topics on which it is exercised. The change mentally is equally great as that which physical illumination has brought about in the domain of manual exertion since nearly 2,000 years ago, when it was said to the disciples: "Work while it is called the day, because the night cometh when no man can work." This radical change is especially noticeable in religious belief, and not more so in regard to what should be accepted as articles of faith than as to whether it is necessary to believe at all. It may be noted that a corresponding change has not manifested itself in the devotional feeling:—which seems to be an integral part of the nature of woman, and of many thousands of men to whom the Credo is a vanishing quantity.

The first three hundred years after the death of Christ may fitly be denominated the conversion era. Within that time the cross changed from an emblem that must be concealed by a possessor who would not court the pains of martyrdom to a banner borne defiantly at the head of conquering hosts. In those three centuries the Christian creed was unified out of a number of discordant elements which had arisen from widely different interpretations of the earlier teachings, first among the Apostles themselves and subsequently among the Fathers of the Church or those who hoped to be recognized as such. Some additions have since been made by the Latin and Greek churches, and changes more recently by the different Protestant sects; but through a long course of centuries the disagreements were of the minor class, with only one formidable attempt to destroy the Christian religion as a whole. That was made by the followers of Mohammed, who in the latter half of the seventh century "converted" by fire and sword the whole of Northern Asia and Northern Africa, then invaded Europe in such force as to threaten to substitute the religion of the Koran for that of the Bible all over the continent, till their progress was checked by the victory gained over 400,000 of them in France by Charles Martel, in 732. Their power continued supreme in other parts of the Old World for many centuries, and Europe can scarcely be said to have struck a retaliating blow till within the last hundred years, as the numerous crusades undertaken before the Reformation were mostly failures, and nearly all of them bad ones.

During the whole time of this attack upon it from without the Church was practically a unit on the "essentials." For a long while after, as before, this unity prevailed. Though divisions occurred every now and then in the ranks of the faithful, the church militant fought for one common cause under different commanders. The work of evangelization was carried on with more or less of zeal by missionaries who took to other lands the truth as they understood it to have been "delivered to the saints;" both they and those who staid at home accepting what have recently been called the fundamentals, and differing only on points since called minor, though they were often deemed sufficiently important to be test questions for life or death. For instance, the schism which first rent the church into two nearly equal parts was chiefly caused by differences as to the jurisdictions of the Bishops of Rome and Constantinople. Luther led the Reformation without questioning the Catholic doctrine of transubstantiation; and many Protestants as well as Catholics have maintained that "Bluff King Hal" had no doctrinal motive at the outset in taking the English Church out of the Roman fold, unless it were as to the duty of a Pope to grant a divorce when it was wanted by a king. The many dissenting sects which sprung into existence during the next three centuries may have held widely different views in regard to the rites and ceremonies that were supposed to be obligatory, but they neither entertained nor permitted doubts as to the obligations themselves.

All of them equally held it to be a duty to attend church services on the first day of the week; to accept with no question except as to minute detail all of their teachings, and to be well grounded in creed formulæ; and all agreed that works could not avail for salvation unless the creed were correct. All of them held that it was rank heresy to accept the teaching of Pope:

> For modes of faith let graceless zealots fight;
> He can't be wrong whose life is in the right.

During all this time the teachings of the Bible were believed without question, the laity accepting the statements of their priests in regard to it when not allowed to read the book for themselves. The meanings of certain passages in it might be subjects for controversy, but always with deprecatory references to any who might presume to doubt that the disputed passage itself was binding on the conscience whether understood or not. The idea of subjecting the books of the Jewish Scriptures to historical tests for authorship or to scientific comparisons in regard to weight of authority was too blasphemous to be permitted expression. It is true that about a century ago there was a school of French infidels, which included Tom Paine of this country and a handful of skeptical Englishmen; but

23

they were regarded with holy horror by the rest of
the civilized world, and their criticism of miracles
and mysteries was a failure, probably more for the
opposition it invited from the church than because
it was a denial of the " divine right of Kings.'' It
is only within the last half century that men of in-
quiring and scientific turn of mind have begun to
doubt the literal truth of dogmas and dared to admit the fact.   At first they did so timidly, but
gathered confidence as one jet of scientific light after another was turned on the human understanding, and they saw that other people were constituted pretty much on their own model, mentally as
well as physically.   Previous to that the lighting
up had been but momentary, the flame being extinguished just as it began to reveal the darkness.
Since then the illumination has become brighter
with each succeeding year, and still we can exclaim:
" More light and light it grows.''

The fact cannot be denied; though there is room
for a wide diversity of opinion as to the value of the
change.   To carry out the simile a little further
one may note the following as among the possibilities of the case: That the light is artificial and
passes through colored media; giving false impressions of color and perhaps exaggerations of outline,
with distortions in the features of the objects it re-
veals.   Also that the eye of the gazer being unac-
customed to the glare he is confused by it and
receives impressions that will be much modified if

not rejected after the optic nerve has become habituated to the now novel experience:—as it is well known that the image of an object which is formed on the retina is upside down, and we judge the contrary by an unconscious reversion of the picture as a result of finding out otherwise that the objects stand, rest, or move, the other way. The writer of this article has no desire to plead or argue for or against any claim that may be set up by the theologian that the illumination is false and misleading, no wish to be understood as intimating a conviction that such light is better than the darkness it succeeded. For aught that he knows the average human being might be much happier and better without it; as the mole does its work blindly, cats are said to see best in the dark, and the unreasoning porker has been fancied to be the happiest animal in all creation. The object is simply to call attention to the fact as a phenomenal phase of historical development which marks the present age as none was ever marked before.

The change has been brought about principally by the discoveries made in the field of scientific research. The dissemination of knowledge among the masses rendered it difficult if not impossible for them to assent to some of the statements found in the Jewish writings or the interpretations put upon them by commentators and preachers. During many years the church denounced as heretical the doctrine that the earth is a nearly spherical body, revolving in company with sister planets around the sun. It was held to be directly contrary to the teachings of "The Infallible Book," and its acceptance was feared as sure to upset its authority and that of the church. But, strangely enough, the predicted result did not follow. The average man did not find the Copernican theory a stumbling-block to his religious faith. He could readily suppose, when told so, that the language of the "inspired volume" was poetical in its allusions to natural phenomena, that "pillars" and "quarters" of the earth could be understood as underlying rocks and the directions of what are still called the cardinal points of the compass, and that references to the sun as going around the earth were relative only, as is similar language in use to-day. But the revelations of geology were another matter. The priest and the philosopher had looked at them askance; but for the multitude they were a tabooed subject till the appearance of the (anonymous) work by Robert Chambers, entitled "Vestiges of the Natural History of Creation," some forty odd years ago, placed a small accumulation of scientific knowledge concerning them at the command of the people. As a result of the inquiry then awakened it was soon found that the history of the earth as written on the rocks could not be reconciled with the Genesis story of creation in the Jewish Scriptures; and the gulf between knowledge and belief was immensely widened a few years ago by the finding of relics of human beings who must have lived on the earth thrice as long ago as given in the Bible chronology and perhaps as much as 100,000 years since. Also it became evident that the creative process was a gradual one, still being carried out as truly as ever it was, and therefore not an act accomplished by a sextuple fiat uttered within the space of a single week.

When Hugh Miller, after his researches among " The Old Red Sandstone," committed suicide because he could not harmonize his newly-acquired geological knowledge with what he had been taught as a boy by the clergy, the silent confession made by his act became a voice that was heard all round the world. And " being dead he yet speaketh."

Then the revelations of the telescope began to be understood as telling another part of the same wonderful story. It was seen that our earth is only one out of countless millions of worlds, and so far from being the most important that it may almost be called one of the least so among those seen by the unaided eye. Then the delicate measuring apparatus of the astronomer indicated the fact of periodic displacements of position among those shining bodies which lead up to the conclusion that they are suns, each having its attendant family of dark worlds like ours, every one of them peopled in the past, present, or future, with beings displaying every possible variety of organized existence. Still more recently the spectroscope has given testimony to the fact that our sun and all the other stars that have been subjected to its analyzing scrutiny are composed of the very same materials (chemical elements) as those which make up the great bulk of our planet; revealing a unity of origin, indicating one common life-bearing mission, and pointing to a similar destruction of vitality on all their surfaces irrespective of the conduct of any of the beings who may at any time live there. By the side of these revealments come those of the microscope, opening up to our gaze the other half of the series at the extremes of which lie what are called by Pouchet "the infinitely great and the infinitely little." This instrument has not only shown that size is no measure of perfection in the organic scale, and that the smallest animalcule, a million of which could be placed on the point of a needle, may

> In mortal suffering feel a pang as great
> As when a giant dies,

but has revolutionized our views of the conditions of human existence.

It proves to us that the living body, whether of man, other animal, or plant, is infested with parasites outside, and entozoa within, that millions of microbes are all the time at work engaged in deadly combat with the forces of the greater life, the balance being so evenly preserved that they are innocuous while the system is in full tone but prevail if the vital powers be weakened by dissipation, improper exposure to the elements, or any other cause of depression to the vital forces. In addition to all this the microscope enables us to understand, as was previously suspected, that the living process is essentially a self-destructive one, insuring its own end ultimately if the organism survive the assaults of the deadly microbe. The jelly-like substances which compose the body of the infant are gradually hardened as life progresses. The continuous assimilation of bony matter brings around the strength of the adult frame, but later fills up the muscular tissues to such an extent that the heart is unable to beat, the arteries refuse to perform the contractile movement which sends the blood through them, the bones of the skeleton become so brittle that they fracture with the least shock and have lost their ability to reunite, and the whole system dies for want of power to longer perform the movements which are the evidence of life. The microscope indicates to us that the animal frames of many thousands of years ago, which left their skeletons in positions favorable to preservation down to our times, were subject to the same laws, and had their spans of existence limited as surely as ours are to-day; though the conditions may have permitted some of them to live longer than their kindred species do in the present age. In other words, it is proven to be true all along the stream of time that animated nature bears the seeds of its own dissolution, and that, in the language of the poet,

The moment we begin to live
We all begin to die.

Hence it is impossible to believe the statement that man was created an immortal being, and that death came into the world through sin, but for which the individual human being would "live forever."

Many another page in the volume of nature has been turned by the hand of science, and its contents read as confirming the tale already told. The meteorologist has shown that storms and drought, the tempest and the whirlwind, are natural phenomena; and not the results of miracles wrought by the hand of man or of direct interposition by Deity. The chemist has shown that human life is maintained in much the same way as the vitality of a steam engine, by the combustion of fuel. The physiologist has proven that both the beginning and the end of life are regular processes, that the first is a result of natural causes and the second a disintegration which does not admit of renewal under the old conditions of individual unison of action of all the particles composing the original organization. This interposes a bar to belief in either supernatural genesis or post mortem life of the body.

Furthermore, the testimony of these and all other delvers into the mysteries of nature is to the effect that all changes in material condition, whether in vitalized forms or inanimate masses, are the results of the operation of natural, fixed law; and do not follow as a consequence of a dictum of any being uttering it from his own arbitrary motive or in response to the prayers of his creatures. Hence, the whole body of the miraculous doings alleged to have formed salient points in ancient history are relegated to the domain which may be described by the old Scotch verdict, "Not proven."

Further, the testimony of those who allege the miracles to have been performed is judged open to question in regard to other alleged facts, by the application of the well-known legal maxim, "Falsus in uno, falsus in omnibus."

Of course all this involves a doubt as to the efficacy of prayer (in causing Deity to perform special miracles at mortal's request) and the duty of worship as generally taught by the churches. It does not by any means necessarily conduce to atheism. On the contrary, it permits, if it does not promote, a far higher conception of the Deity than that which makes him out to be "jealous of his own honor" when he has no competitor; angry with men for not doing as he wishes, when he has the sinner under more absolute control than the boy has over the worm he is impaling on the hook; capable of being cajoled and flattered, like some Oriental despot, into granting a favor to a petitioner which would be injustice to all the rest of his subjects; ever and anon interfering in the quarrels of nations or individuals, taking sides in their petty squabbles; having favorites whose interests must be protected at all hazards; deliberately punishing the innocent for the sins of the guilty; and finally insisting on torturing to all eternity countless millions of these miserables whom he made, after having come down to earth and died on the cross that they might be saved. It does not favor the degrading of the Supreme Being by ascribing to him human passions, prejudices and other weaknesses such as the pagans thought characterized Jupiter, Apollo and other of their gods, to whom were imputed actions and motives that it might well make a decent man blush to think of them. The imputation of such attributes to Him, and of such power to His chosen servants as is claimed in some passages of the Old Testament, is suspected to be partial if not complete proof that all the books of that volume are not inspired utterances ; that some are simply collocations of legends which got badly twisted in the transmission from mouth to mouth through several generations before being committed to writing; that some were originally " put down " in symbolic characters and grave mistakes were made in translating them into alphabetic writing after the latter had been developed from the hieroglyphic ; in short, that much of it is only a reproduction of the comparatively infantile thoughts of the race in its crude and illiterate days, and some of the rest garbled; while the idea that any of it was inspired grew out of the fact that books were at one time treasures worth their weight in gold, because of the labor involved in hand copying and the scarcity of clerical ability to perform the work of transcription.

All this is a legitimate outcome of modern scientific thought, the application of logical processes in the domain of the known to subjects which are unknown unless as we may choose to take for granted the statement of some person or persons that such a thing is so and so, when we are unable to gauge his credibility except as we find him stating some things we cannot believe. It is, however, due to the great mass of scientific investigators to say that their attitude in the matter is simply one of quietly withholding assent from dogmas they cannot indorse because the same require them to disbelieve the evidence of their own senses on insufficient proof that those senses cannot be trusted. Few of them have taken a position of active dissent. Till within a very recent period it might have been truly said that they left this to the mere theorists who talked and wrote about the work of others while doing nothing original themselves. Recently, however, even that film of ice is broken. A prominent instance is the article by Huxley giving scientific reasons why the Mosaic account of the flood cannot be accepted as historical truth, as the water would rush off into the lower sea land. Then we have President White's masterly discussion of the story of Adam and Eve, in which he masses much of the accumulated evidence that whatever of a "fall" there may have been must have been of the kind described by Pat as "a tumble up-stairs"—in other words, that the history of the race is one of improvement, not of retrogression. Perhaps this definite attitude of scientific men will be more pronounced in the future, and yet it is open to grave question if that be really desirable.

In regard to all this it might be well to remember a statement said to have been made by Jesus to his disciples : "I have many things to say unto you, but ye cannot bear them now." For aught we can tell it may be equally unwise to shake the confidence of the unlearned masses in the authenticity of the Jewish Scriptures and the wisdom of their clerical expounders as it is to try to make the child of half a dozen years old think there is no truth in the stories of Santa Claus, Little Red Riding Hood and Blue Beard. At least the advocates of the scientific school of thought as applied to religious topics may be commended to a consideration of their own teaching, as embodied in the quotation from Alexander Pope, p. 353. They hold that it is of comparatively little consequence what a man believes in regard to these things, and praise as one of the greatest facts in the civilized advance of the present century the toleration which permits our neighbor to think as he pleases so long as he does his duty as a citizen. It may with truth be said that the scientific mind of to-day is not yet sufficiently advanced in knowledge to warrant it in dogmatic denial, while at the same time it may be considered to have reached the stage where doubt is justified. But as a fact of history the matter is one of great interest, and not the less so as it occurs within a stone's throw of the time when the Protestant part of the Christian world put out its best efforts for the evangelization of the nations, as if for the first time realizing the force of the command, "Go ye into all the world and preach the Gospel to every creature. He that believeth and is baptized shall be saved, and he that believeth not shall be damned":— the latter sentence being now widely held to be an interpolation by the priests. Some people may fancy they see in this a curious coincidence with the case of the tree said to have put forth its greatest show of luxuriant fruitage at the moment it began to die out at the top.

[As stated in the Introduction this chapter originally appeared as an article in the *Tribune*. The reference on the last preceding page to " dogmatic denial " as not warranted should be understood as applying to generals; not to every particular. For instance: the claim of absolute and complete inspiration of the Scriptures as a whole, is not accepted by many scientific thinkers who are willing to admit the possibility of partial inspiration.]

XX

NATURE AND FATE.

The Lore of the Stars.—Proctor Held that the History and Character of any Portion of the Universe May Be Deduced from a Study of the Rest.—"Confessions of an Astrologer," Long Since Retired from the Business.—He Endorsed It as a Veritable Philosophy, but Disapproved the Art—It is the Basis of Physical and Mental Science.

In those far climes it was my lot
To meet the wondrous Michael Scott.
. . . .
Some of his skill he taught to me.
　　　　　　—*Lay of the Last Minstrel.*

Doubtless some who read the preceding sketch of the way in which the ancient religions and much of our modern theology grew out of the lore of the stars, will feel curious to know if anything can be said in favor of that antiquated doctrine which is now generally supposed to be a long since exploded delusion of olden times. They may ask if it be possible that any of the rules of the alleged science which for so many centuries dominated the human mind, are worthy of serious consideration by thinking men and women near the close of the nineteenth century. The writer may not be able to give an authoritative answer to such queries; and, if able, might not be willing to run the risk of being misunderstood. But it is fair to admit that he has had exceptional facilities for gauging the value of the claim that " the stars rule men," having read several books on the subject and tested the abilities of a few of those who posed as experts. A concluding chapter on the topic may be interesting.

The late Richard Antony Proctor cannot justly be accused of willingness to furnish an argument tending to foster the belief in judicial astrology. That great man, whose chief intellectual weakness seemed to be the Voltaire-like ambition to be considered *au fait* on every conceivable subject, placed himself on record as denying the validity of the claim that " *astra regunt homines*," and even ridiculed the notion as one unworthy of an enlightened age. Yet he unwittingly conceded the very strongest of all the purely theoretical pleas that have been advanced in justification of the theory. In his " Other Worlds Than Ours," (1871,) he wrote:

" If a great naturalist like Huxley or Owen can tell, by examining the tooth of a creature belonging to some long extinct race, not only what the characteristics of that race were, but the general nature of the scenery amid which such creatures lived, we see at once that a single grain of sand or drop of water must convey to the Omniscient the history of the whole world of which it forms a part. Nay, why should we pause here? The history of that world is in truth bound up so intimately with the history of the universe that the grain of sand or drop of water conveys not only the history of a world, but with equal completeness the history of the whole universe. . . . In fact, if we consider the matter attentively, we see that there cannot be a single atom throughout space which could have attained its present exact position and state had the history of any part of our universe, however insignificant, been otherwise than it has actually been, in even the minutest degree. . . . Obviously, also, every event, however trifling, must be held to contain in itself the whole history of the universe throughout the infinite past and throughout the infinite future. For every event, let its direct importance be what it may, is indissolubly bound up with events preceding, accompanying, and following it, in endless series of causation, interaction, and effect.'' (Pages 325 to 327.)

Compare this with the following, written many years earlier:

'' The fundamental principles of the science of astro-philosophy are, that the physical and moral affairs of the universe are regulated by certain laws of action originally established by the Creator; and that all the various parts of this grand total are so intimately connected with each other as that no action or motion can take place among any of the particles of matter of which it is composed without producing an effect upon the rest, and operating at least as a secondary cause of changes, in the economy of the whole.''

It was the lot of the writer in his earlier days to be rather intimately acquainted with the man who composed the last quoted paragraph. This man had for several years practiced the calculation of nativities, or what some people call "the casting of horoscopes," and others "fortune telling," but grew tired of it and took up another line of business. About a quarter of a century after this change he was asked to give his candid opinion of the thing. The following is the substance of his reply, made during two or three separate conversations, which are condensed here from memory. That the recollection is a tolerably faithful one may be inferred from the fact that the conversations referred to have formed the subject of much subsequent thought, and possibly had something to do with shaping the arguments presented in previous chapters of this book:

CONFESSIONS OF A REFORMED ASTROLOGER.

"What induced me to begin?" Why, it came along as naturally as falling in love does to a young man. "Any teacher?" None; except the dead: who taught me through the medium of books they had written while in the flesh. "Why did I give it up?" Because I was tired of it. "Not because convinced that the theory is false and, therefore, the practice a humbug?" Not at all, in generals; in some particulars, yes. The theory is correct, but in its application the honest practitioner is continually

24

tempted to overstep the bounds of legitimate deduction, and it affords a wide field for the practice of fraud.

I firmly believe that there is a certain, and to some extent traceable, connection between the positions of the heavenly bodies at the time of birth and the character and "fortune" of the person then born. I do not mean by this that I at any time accepted as truth all that has been claimed for judicial astrology by some of its alleged exponents, or charged against it by those who affect to ridicule it as a thoroughly exploded absurdity. Neither am I prepared to say that I think the connection between the two is one of cause and effect. It seems to me most rational to suppose that the movements of the stars as referred to any particular spot on the face of the earth are of the exponential order, as the hands of a clock show the lapse of time which they neither make nor regulate. But I have no doubt as to the fact of such connection.

"How did I take it up?" I saw a copy of Sibley's Astrology on an old book stall, bought it, read it through and through, and was fascinated. I had previously a fair acquaintance with the mathematics of astronomy, so that a good deal of the other "came easy." I procured more books on the subject, but without any intention to become a professional. Another line of action lay before me, and it was almost involuntarily given up. The fact is I astonished some of my friends by what I did in an amateurish way at their express solicitation, and they told other people about it. I soon had all I wanted to do without a line of advertising or even "sticking out a shingle."

"Did I make mistakes?" Yes; lots of them. So many that I soon entertained serious doubts in regard to its enabling anyone to do more than strike a few coincidences. I "dropped it like a hot potato," and got a comfortable situation, partly through the influence of friends who were not over well pleased at my being an "astrologer." But by and by predictions made earlier began to be verified, some of them coming out with what was even to myself a startling emphasis, and I re-entered the field.

"How did it pay?" Only "so-so." But I could have made heaps of money had I been willing to stoop to certain disreputable practices for which I had plenty of opportunity. I steadily denied the possession of magical power, clairvoyant ability or any other personal quality not common to the ordinary run of mortals, and thus avoided a great deal of a certain class of patronage. Then my persistent refusal to attempt to "give judgment" when the time and place of birth were not known was accepted by some as a confession of inferiority; there being plenty of people willing to take money and predict freely in the absence of such information. (The *time* he alluded to is not simply the year, month and date, but the hour, and to within a few minutes if possible; information which comparatively few people in the United States are able to give.)

"Have I neglected the study since abandoning the practice?" No; on the contrary, for several years past I have quietly occupied my spare moments in watching and comparing planetary positions with mundane facts and events. And my leading motive in doing so was to determine for myself, in a way as free from bias as possible, whether or not I had in my earlier life labored under a delusion. I think I have during that time tried to sift out the truth, with an equal willingness to confess to myself that I had been wrong as to believe that I had been right. Most certainly I have not wanted to make any capital out of it in the eyes of the world, as I have carefully avoided all reference to it, with rare exceptions. In fact I have refused some offers to calculate nativities for pay, and in more than one instance declined the offer of a rather large sum for the service asked.

"Did I study magic in my younger days?" Yes, some. "And followed that up, too, in after years?" No. I read a good deal in magic, and some in alchemy. I was twice within the "magic circle," each time in company with a senior in the work, and the proceedings interested me so much that I think I could now draw pretty correctly from memory the lines and cabalistic characters there employed. But I prefer to say nothing of results except that I resolutely turned my attention from it

as much as possible, and nothing could induce me to
again meddle with it. Yes, I am willing to admit
that I believe in the existence of spirits, and do not
think they hanker after communication with mortals.
Not another word on that subject.

I am well aware that as a matter of history the
belief in the influences of the stars on human life,
health and character appears to rest on a primeval
delusion. To the early observers the planets were
gods. I have examined that part of the subject to
some extent, and am free to say that the evidences
in this particular proved a stumbling block in the
way of my faith which only a positive and convinc-
ing array of facts could remove. Really and truly,
the "coincidences" I have met with in the course of
my observations have been so numerous, and some
of them so utterly outside the domain of mere guess
work, as to render it absolutely necessary for me to
accept the logic of the situation. I know something
of the mathematical *formulæ* in regard to the science
of probabilities, and have applied them to some extent in comparisons with following events. As a
result I am compelled to believe that there is a radical connection between the positions of the stars at
the time (and place) of birth of the individual and
his or her character and career. When not only
the minor events in the life of a person but the time
of death has been computed by me years beforehand, set down quietly without a hint to anyone
then or afterwards, and the event came round to

within the week calculated for, there is no room for
me to doubt.   I do not know how it may be with
others, but presume those who flippantly call the
whole thing nonsense do not know what they are
talking about.   Yet I do not suppose they are to
blame.   This kind of star lore lies at the bottom of
a deep well, and something more than a tin cup
must be used to reach it.

   "Infallible?"   As a science I think " yes."   As
an art " No."   At least I have never found anyone
who could always " hit it right."   I have already
said that many mistakes were made by myself—and
some of them were complete ones.   I did not understand the science any too well while practicing the
art, nor in more recent years.   But the number of
"hits" has been so great in comparison with the
number of "misses" that I am obliged to conclude
the fault of missing lay with me, and not with the
stars.   It is also true that in some of the cases in
which I failed to predict correctly I was subsequently able to see where the mistake arose.   Generally it was due to my inability to adapt ancient
aphorisms to the widely altered circumstances of the
age in which I endeavored to apply them.   Let me
add that I have yet to meet the doctor who never ,
blundered in a diagnosis, or a lawyer who always
advised correctly.

   That last remark leads up to a most important
point.   The human heart may be said to be the
same in all ages, but its expressions in act vary

widely with the changing conditions of the period.
I might amplify on this topic for several hours, but
will only call your attention to one phase of this
speculation. It has been said that the two delusions, astrology and alchemy, were the parents of
astronomy and chemistry. Yes; and the absurd
natural philosophy of the ancients, with their
medical follies, have given place to the ascertained
truths of to-day. But did it ever strike you that
the ideas of the olden time were simply erroneous
in detail, not in fact or principle? It is so. The
chemistry of to-day is full of transformations quite
as wonderful as those by which the philosophers of
the olden time supposed the baser metals could be
turned into gold, and it is not for me to say that in
some cases the old cannot be identified with the new.
The *similia similibus curantur* of the Hahnemannic
school of our generation is but a reproduction of
the ideas of early Bible times; the steam jet of
Hero was the progenitor of the modern steam
engine, and the ancient magicians were ancestors of
the scientists of our own age. In all of those
primeval studies there was a germ of truth, and in
some of them it was a large one. We may say that
astrology, as delivered to us by the men of many
centuries ago, is sheer nonsense. So it is — if you
seek to apply it literally. The letter will kill; but
that does not hinder the spirit of those primeval
rules from being full of life, and capable of giving
it to those who study old expositions of natural

law in the light of modern developments. The gospel parables were none the less valuable because not understood by the multitude.

"Would I advise other people to study it?" Yes. "To practice it?" No. I would not willingly be the means of increasing the number of those who try to live by the "telling of fortunes." The result of my experience is a deep-seated conviction that the attempt to foretell honestly by means of the stars has not done more good than injury, especially as there is a standing temptation to deceive; while the practice of the counterfeits is undoubtedly a detriment to the best interests of society. But there should be no harm, *per se*, in trying to look ahead as well as backward — if the seeker be right minded to begin with. Unfortunately, however, the great mass of the patronage of the professional has hitherto been drawn from the weaker intellects among those who wish to do right, and perhaps also from among those who know no restraint from crime except fear of the law.

"Can it be used for personal gain?" So far as I know, attempts in this direction have resulted no better than did the alleged reaching forth by our first parents for the fruit of the tree of knowledge of good and evil. The narrator says they got the apple, but intimates they would have been better off had they let it alone. I have no doubt this is about true of all the individuals who have consulted wise men or weird women in the past from motives of personal gain. And why not? If there be such a thing as fate we cannot hope to avoid it by knowing of it in advance, the astrological authors to the contrary notwithstanding. One of these (Coley, 1676), occupied about a dozen pages in telling how to choose times for beginning enterprises so as to secure a fortunate issue; but had sufficient sense to close his rules with the remark, "but I dare not affirm they are infallible." I may say also that I have seen little of real comfort enjoyed by any practitioner of the art. Yet it is not for me to say that the "professors" and their clients will be a set of "miserables" in future ages, when the world will be wise enough to understand the lore of the stars and the seeker after truth not sufficiently base to want to use it as a weapon with which to take advantage of his fellow mortals.

As I regard it, a knowledge of the science in its broadest sense, which must include an appreciation of its practical bearing upon the general course of human life, should be worth to the world more than many millions of dollars. This because it is the grand master key to the philosophy of the sciences, both physical and mental, and in the latter department of study forms what the seventeenth article of the Church of England calls "a most wholesome and comfortable doctrine." I am free to say that I believe its patient study has had a great deal to do in enabling me to comprehend a little of the philosophy of existence. I think it has tended to make me more charitable in passing judgment on the mistakes and motives of others, has aided in curbing the disposition to retaliate for real or fancied wrong; and perhaps helped to repress the foolish feelings of pride or vain glory which, I presume, at times obtrude themselves upon everyone who is credited with the possession of a little more knowledge or skill than falls to the lot of his fellows. And I have sometimes thought that perhaps a recognition of the truth in this matter will prove to be the much needed antidote to that injustice which is apt to arise from the consciousness of possessing superior power or information. At present it seems to me that the peace of the world in the near future is more imperatively menaced by a self constituted aristocracy of intellect than by any that can arise in coming years out of the concentrated ownership of merely material wealth.

"What about the weather, and the rule of the stars over different countries?" Nothing. I do not endorse as valid anything in connection with all that has been called astrology, except the doctrine of nativities. That is a judgment from the positions of the stars and principal planets at the time the child enters on a comparatively independent existence by being separated from the body of its mother. Yet the same rule may be claimed to apply to the positions at the real commencement of any undertaking, great or small. Not a few of the persons known by me to profess to give astrological

judgment were unable to state these positions, or
even to read a scheme of the heavens if placed before them.   Of course the fact that a great many
people have claimed to practice astrology without
the ability to do so should be no more of an argument against the validity of the claims made by
others than is the existence of quackery in medicine a proof that there is no such thing as a healing
art.

"Would you advise *me* to study it, and, if so,
how ?"   Not for the purpose of making a business
of it.   I have already stated it to be my conviction
that even the practice of the true astrology, in a
miscellaneous way at so much per head, is not to
be desired by the true friend of humanity.   The
fact is that whatever I may have done as a practitioner, it was often performed under the same
kind of mental protest as that made by Kepler at
the necessity which compelled him to compile
almanacs.   It was to me a catering to the mere
curiosity of many to whom the exhibition was little
better than the casting of pearls before swine.   To
myself the great value of the science is couched in
the fact that it seems to me to lie at the foundation
of the whole philosophy of nature, and in that sense
I can cordially commend it to the attention and research of any one who may wish to "look through
Nature up to Nature's God," and understand something of the harmony that reigns throughout the
whole of the vast domain of created things.   If

you want to study it in this philosophical spirit
you would do well to obtain a copy of the immortal
Tetrabiblos of Ptolemy, or Ashmand's translation
thereof from the original Greek, and then try to
catch its spirit rather than its letter. It contains
the germ of all that is valuable in the art of judging nativities, but can only be used intelligently by
one who will make due allowance for the changes
that have occurred in conditions since Ptolemy
wrote, and can apply his processes and rules to the
greater planets that have been discovered since his
day. And I may add that it is useless to attach any
value to the reasons stated by him to have dictated
the assigning of the named causative powers or properties to the different planets and constellations. Most
of his alleged reasons are simply childish ones, yet
they have been copied faithfully into some recent
books as the embodiment of truth. Their citation
by Ptolemy indicates to me that he was a mere
compiler in writing the Tetrabiblos, which is what
some have alleged to be true of him in the capacity
of "author" of the Almagest. But as a compen-
dium of the astrological wisdom of the ancients the
former is invaluable, and all the more so as most of
the English writers on the matter have done
nothing better than to pad out the work without
improving it, and added another section which
they called "horary astrology," that being an ex-
cuse for taking a fee in the absence of birth data.
The books on the subject that were written by

Lilly, Coley, Gadbury, Sibley and some others are cumbered up with a vast mass of trash which properly belongs to the thought of the dark ages; and even the works of the English astrologers of comparatively recent years contain a great quantity of rubbish. Some have written with none too much knowledge of the subject, and others as if they wished to "split the ears of the groundlings" by mixing the axiomata of Ptolemy with a farrago of nonsense about magic and the "black art."

"Why do I not write a book about it?" Perhaps for two reasons. Other matters have engaged my attention, and I have somewhat distrusted my own ability to produce anything which would not be open to wide objection in a scientific sense. Thus far I have found to hold good the aphorism ascribed to Ptolemy (though probably written by a much later hand), "From thyself as well as from the Science" must come valuable work. I lack the enthusiasm and perhaps the skill; and so I let it alone. But I think it likely the near future will develop in the field of astrological research a modern Sir Isaac Newton, who can formulate the rules of the science to fit the thoughts and facts of the present, and furnish reasons for the theory that will commend it to the good sense of the many who would fain be wise, but are "nothing if not critical."

SUMMARY.

" Let us hear the conclusion of the whole matter."—Ecclesiastes.

The facts and considerations noted in the preceding pages are believed to warrant the following deductions in regard to the origin of man and the earlier phases of his development. The reader should bear in mind that they are not necessarily presented previously in the same order as stated here, and that equally complete proof is not furnished in each case. The array of conclusions may, however, be confidently advanced as forming a theory which is harmonious with it itself and with what we know of the subject. Therefore it is worthy of dispassionate examination, though far from finished;—much less bomb proof.

Man is the highest in the scale of organized being on the surface of this planet. As such he is the result of a chain of developments beginning with the Eozoön and proceeding through very many stages, the highest type preceding him being the ape.

Man rose from the ape level as a result of climatic vicissitude, and most of the subsequent steps in his intellectual progress would appear to have been originated by a like stimulus, that causing a

382

desire in the individual to adapt himself to changing
conditions. The assumption of the skin of an animal was the first progressive act; and it was taken
as a guard from the effects of increasing cold.

Great alternations of temperature, within the
limits of human endurance, have most directly favored physical and mental progress. The cold regions of the far north and the warm ones of the
torrid zone alike tend to physical sloth and mental
torpor. The temperate zones are those in which the
greatest activity of mind and body are not only permitted but rendered necessary to comfort if not
continued vitality. In the battle of humanity with
at least annually recurring alternations of climatic
condition lies the great spur to the series of other
struggles through which man has risen to the highest pitch of culture and power yet attained.

It is most probable that man differentiated from
the ape in times that were inter-glacial. The depression in temperature, and the consequent change
in food conditions experienced during the advance
of the ice sheet to middle latitudes, caused the first
wearing of skins and resort to the use of the rudest
weapons.

That change occurred not less than eighty thousand years ago; and the adaptation once effected
there would be little spur to further improvement
through a long course of centuries. The ameliora-
tion of climate due to a recession of the ice cap
would rather tend to check progress; and the River

Drift man persisted as a low type, probably following the edge of the ice sheet, though not closely.

Succeeding that glacial epoch, due to great eccentricity of the earth's orbit, was a series of smaller changes of water back and forth between the two hemispheres, according to the Adhemar theory as explained in our fifteenth chapter. The last great submergence of large areas of what is now dry land north of the equator occurred less than ten thousand years ago. This drowned and buried many of the River Drift men, and the duration of that flood accounts for the big gap of time between them and the Neolithic age in the north temperate zone. During that stretch of centuries the southern hemisphere was tenanted by human beings, and some of them may have made considerable progress towards the grade of intelligence exhibited further north four or five thousand years since.

The Neolithic men of our hemisphere probably came in from the neighborhood of the equator, as the surplus waters gradually moved southward. Doubtless the greater number came in from tropical Africa, and probably from some now submerged land in the Indian Ocean. We have no means of judging whether the new arrivals were all of them hunters or if some had developed into the pastoral phase; but it is easy to infer the latter as at least possible. The pastoral mode of life was readily adopted as the southern half of Asia became slowly peopled; and more tardily they would spread over the whole of the Asiatic and European continents except the most northern portions. We may suppose it possible that those of African origin who had found their way into the plains of Chaldea referred to subsequent arrivals from the Indian Ocean in describing the strange creatures led by Oannes. The latter may have been so "strange" as to be driven away by those coming from the southwest. In that case some of them would go to Syria, where originated the Khitas; and others slowly wended their way to China, whence a colony penetrated to Japan.

The use of dates for food was succeeded by the cultivation of the cereals in Lower Mesopotamia. Following that began the aggregation of people into cities and the formation of armies. This commingling laid the foundation of the Shemitic tribes, some of whom gradually spread over Western Asia as far north as the Caucasus, including all Asiatic Turkey. Others of them carried a knowledge of the arts of agriculture into the valley of the Nile, there mingling with people who had descended direct from "first families" migrated from the regions about Abyssinia.

Those who had settled, (in the earlier sense of the term,) in the region west of the Ural Mountains and north of the Caucasus became too numerous, and were obliged to "swarm." Parties left that country at sundry times and went in different directions, each seeking a convenient spot on which to

25

exist. Some of them went southwest and spread over the southern half of Europe, mingling there with peoples whose ancestors had reached the area many centuries earlier. Others went east, and the greater number would appear to have gone round the upper end of the Caspian, then between that body of water and the Sea of Aral and turned south along the bank of the Oxus, the lower valley of which was probably a less dreary waste than in our time. On the upper portion of that stream they rested for many years, sufficiently long to lay the foundations for the language to which the Aryan family of tongues owe their origin. Then some of them spread southwestward into Persia, and others took up the longer march into and through India; finally becoming strong enough to establish themselves as a dominant caste over the earlier inhabitants of that country. The movement of the Aryans who swarmed into Asia was thus over a patch of territory lying northeast from that occupied by the Shemites and extending further south, while it was west of the country settled by what we have considered as the Mongolian stream that had set into China much earlier from about the head of the Persian Gulf.

The possible modes of settling the American continent, noted in the second chapter, may have given for what has in recent centuries been called the New World a more nearly continuous human occupancy than in the case of either the European or the Asiatic continent. But if we suppose an independent beginning here for the River Drift man the origin would be as likely to occur south of the equator as north of it, the migration being northward after the latest Adhemar flood. And this migration is probable even in the supposable case of origin near the north pole.

Human speech is a function of anatomical structure not found in the lower animals, and apparently absent from the oldest known human skulls. As the exponent of thought its range was at first necessarily limited to a very few words, and there was room for the formation of as many different languages as separate associations of individuals. First war and then commerce have caused a fusion of more or less distinct elements, with expansion of the results; and the tendency of commerce is now to reduce the number of distinct languages, though probably to amplify each of the survivors in at least an equal (inverse) proportion. Yet there is no more reason to think the world will settle down to one universal form of speech than to a complete absence of strife.

The earliest writing was pictorial. From that grew the ideographic mode of representing facts and thoughts; and later came the alphabetic, the earliest form of the latter being perhaps not more than 4,000 years old. With these came the inscribing of law to be observed, and then of history intended to justify the formulation of that law. The oldest written history, so-called, contains traditions which had been carried with more or less fidelity through perhaps many preceding generations; and none of it is entitled to be termed sacred except in the sense of its being hallowed by the lapse of time. The miraculous element which abounds in all the more ancient "history" is not worthy of greater credence than that deserved by the tales which children tell to each other.

The "stars" were the first objects of worship, the planets being reverenced as the real gods; the *Elohim* of the Hebrew scriptures, and Jupiter as their chief. He was the Hebrew Yah-veh. The moon and sun were afterwards regarded as planets and ranked as gods, while fire was venerated as the earthly representative of the etherial flames. The days of the week were named after the planets, and according to the account in the first chapter of Genesis the work of creation was performed by them. The seventh day, or Sabbath, was named after Saturn, the resting planet; and was originally a Babylonish festival, regulated by the course of the moon. With the Chaldeans the seventh day of each lunar month was the first Sabbath in that lunation, so that the last week of each lunation consisted of more than seven days. The Sabbath is not proven to have been observed by the Jews before the return from the captivity which was a consequence of the fall of Babylon (538 B. C.), and the Jews had no history as a people previous to the time of David.

Their accounts of the Creation and the Deluge were taken from Chaldean writings, and the only Solomon's temple that ever existed was the one built at Sippara.

The ability of the priests to tell the people what their planetary gods were going to do was the foundation of their power over the multitudes. By fixing beforehand the times of new and full moon, and afterwards other solar and planetary cycles, they led up to the notion that the gods were best propitiated at set times; and then the idea of substitution of an animal for a human being to be sacrificed riveted the chain. The principal festival other than lunar was the one regulated by the apparent motion of the Pleiades, and this seems to have been observed by all nations as far back as we can trace the shreds of history or tradition. It was the festival of the dead.

The belief that the movements of the stars governed the affairs of men was well nigh universal, and soon led up to the priestly knowledge and use of planetary cycles; whence the theory that after a stated number of years, when the planets or stars got round to certain positions, there was a grand catastrophe, followed by a recovery through the appearance of some great one as a Deliverer. The prediction of the coming of a Messiah was purely astronomical;— or astrological, for during many centuries the two words meant one and the same thing. The prediction was made for each of several different nations. The vaticination that a Messiah would visit the Jews seems to have originated in Bactria; being not Shemitic, but Aryan.

The Jewish Messiah was expected to appear when the principal brilliant in the constellation of the Virgin should be carried across the celestial equator by the precession of the equinoxes; this movement being preceded by a conjunction of the planets Saturn, Jupiter, and Mars. That gem in the hand of Virgo was "The Star of Bethlehem." Jesus was a historical character, though his history was confused with that of many of the gods of other lands than Judea. He came on earth at the time computed by the Bactrian Magi, but the gospels as we now have them were written many years after his death, and by men who invented stories of miracles for the purpose of making it out that "He fulfilled all the prophecies" and in order to build up the power of the church. A great deal may be said in justification of the old fashioned idea of stellar and planetary rule over the affairs of men; and when they laugh at it the churches of this generation ridicule that which constitutes a most important part of the foundation of their faith.

The theory of an alternate shifting of water from one hemisphere to the other at intervals of ten to eleven thousand years is so much in harmony with known facts and reasonable inference as to justify us in expecting that a few score centuries hence the northern hemisphere will be partially submerged and vast southern land areas uncovered, the latter being the scene of the greatest activity and highest civilization. It would be well for us to consider the propriety of erecting some durable monument in the United States to bear witness of us then. The great pyramid of Egypt, and possibly some of the others, may have been constructed with some such intent soon after the lower valley of the Nile emerged from beneath the ocean surface.

It may be permitted to add a conclusion legitimately deducible from this cursory review of humanity in its earlier phases of development and a comparison of that with later expansion. It is that motion is essential to life, and competition to progress. It is the apposition of different elements that results in action in the world of chemistry. From that bottom plane in the scale of Nature up to the highest occupied by man in his efforts to develop a new thought or to turn an old one to more practical use, all real advance is the result of competition. The desire to possess what is owned by others leads to struggles in which the sharpness of contending muscle or brain oft determines who shall be the victor; and the world sets out afresh from a higher plane of activity because of what is perhaps called a base passion.

When a man, a community, or a nation ceases to struggle it not only ceases to rise in the scale but begins to sink. This is equally true of competition in business, emulation in study, reach of invention, and even of contests for national superiority.   The stagnation of air or water breeds disease, and in the vegetable and animal organism decay sets in close to the time when the growing period terminates. It is so with communities, peoples, races, worlds, universes.   Hence peace is an idle dream unless as it is a rest between exertions or a retiring from the conflict.   It is not to be attained otherwise than temporarily, except at the cost of deterioration or the ceasing of the existence which it is desired to perpetuate,—whether that be of the individual or the mass.   Activity, motion, is life.   Peace, rest, is decay.   How it may be with another life we know not; but for this—and it is a necessity of the constitution of material organisms— there is no standing still.   As eternal vigilance is the price of liberty, so humanity can avoid falling back into the primeval mud only by virtue of continuous exertion.   So far from being a curse, labor is a blessing in disguise.

INDEX.

THE OPEN COURT

PUBLISHED EVERY THURSDAY BY

THE OPEN COURT PUBLISHING CO.

EDWARD C. HEGELER, Pres.   Dr. PAUL CARUS, Editor

P. O. DRAWER F.   169-175 La Salle Street.

CHICAGO, ILLINOIS.

The reader will find in *The Open Court* an earnest and, as we believe, a successful effort to conciliate Religion with Science. The work is done with due reverence for the past and with full confidence in a higher future.

The Open Court unites the deliberation and prudence of conservatism with the radicalism of undaunted progress. While the merits of the old creeds are fully appreciated, their errors are not overlooked. The ultimate consequences of the most radical thought are accepted, but care is taken to avoid the faults of a one sided view.

The Quintessence of Religion is shown to be a truth. It is a scientific truth which has been and will remain the basis of ethics. The Quintessence of Religion contains all that is good and true, elevating and comforting, in the old religions. Superstitious notions are recognised as mere accidental features, of which Religion can be purified without harm, to the properly religious spirit.

This idea is fearlessly and without reservation of any kind, presented in its various scientific aspects and in its deep significance to intellectual and emotional life. If fully grasped, it will be found to satisfy the yearnings of the heart as well as the requirements of the intellect.

Facts which seem to bear unfavorably on this solution of the religious problem are not shunned, but openly faced. Criticisms have been welcome, and will always receive due attention. The severest criticism, we trust, will serve only to elucidate the truth of the main idea propounded in *The Open Court*.

   * * *

What is Science but "searching for the truth." What is Religion but "living the truth." Our knowledge of the truth, however, is relative and ad mits of a constant progress. As all life is evolution, so also Science and Religion are developing. With an enlarged experience of the human race they are growing more comprehensive, purer, and truer. Scientific truths become religious truths as soon as they become factors that regulate conduct.

The progress of Science during the last century, especially in the field of psychology, has produced the impression as if there were a conflict between Science and Religion, but there is no conflict and there cannot be any conflict between Science and Religion. There may be conflicts between erroneous views of Science as well as of Religion. But wherever such conflicts appear we may rest assured that there are errors somewhere, for Religion and Science are inseparable. Science is searching for truth and Religion is living the truth.

*   *   *

The Open Court pays special attention to psychology. Great progress has been made of late in a more accurate and scientific investigation of the human soul. While the new conception of the soul will materially alter some of the dogmatic views, it will not affect the properly religious spirit of religion, it will not alter the ethical truths of religion but will confirm them and place them upon a scientific foundation.

Since we have gained a scientific insight into the nature of the human soul, the situation is as thoroughly altered as our conception of the universe was in the times when the geocentric standpoint had to be abandoned. The new psychology which may briefly be called the abandonment of the ego-centric standpoint of the soul will influence the religious development of humanity in no less a degree than the new astronomy has done. At first sight the new truths seem appalling. However, a closer acquaintance with the modern solution of the problems of soul-life and especially the problem of immortality shows that, instead of destroying, it will purify religion.

The religion of *The Open Court* is neither exclusive nor sectarian, but liberal; it seeks to aid the efforts of all scientific and progressive people in the churches and out of them, toward greater knowledge of the world in which we live, and the moral and practical duties it requires.

ESPECIAL ATTENTION DEVOTED TO QUESTIONS OF ETHICS, ECONOMICS, AND SOCIOLOGY. The work of *The Open Court* has been very successful in this department. Discussion has been evoked on almost every topic treated of. Wheelbarrow's contributions to practical economics, Prof. E. D. Cope's and Moncure D. Conway's treatment of current sociological questions, Dr. G. M. Gould's, Mrs. Susan Channing's, and A. H. Heinemann's examination of criminal conditions and domestic relations, Gen. M. M. Trumbull's trenchant criticisms of certain ethical phases of our political life. The discussion between Wm. M. Salter, Professor Jodl, and the Editor on THE ETHICAL PROBLEM, and many other contributions of note by Dr. S. V. Clevenger, Chas

K. Whipple, J. C. F. Grumbine, George Julian Harney, John Burroughs, Wm. Schuyler, F. M. Holland, Ednah D. Cheney, E. P. Powell, Dr. Felix L. Oswald, Prof. Joseph Le Conte and others have been received with marked favor.

Authorised translations are made from the currant periodical literature of Continental Europe, and original contributions obtained from the most eminent investigators of England, France, and Germany.

In the philosophy of language may be mentioned the recent contributions of Max Müller on THE SCIENCE OF LANGUAGE, the translations from Noiré's works on THE ORIGIN OF LANGUAGE, and the essays of Mr. T. Bailey Saunders on THE ORIGIN OF REASON.

Articles on vital problems of PSYCHOLOGY and BIOLOGY, appeared from the pens of Th. Ribot, Alfred Binet, Ernst Haeckel, Prof. Ewald Hering, Prof. A. Weismann Prof. E. D. Cope, and others.

TERMS OF SUBSCRIPTION :

For One Year } Throughout the Postal Union........................ { $2.00
For Six Months } .... { 1.00
Australia, New Zealand, and Tasmania, One Year................. ...... 2.50
Single Copies...... ....5 Cents
Volume   I......... ....Bound, $4.00; Unbound, $3.25
Volume II ....   "   4.00 ;   "   3.25
Volume III.......................................   "   3.00 ;   "   2.25
Volume IV...... ....   "   3.00 ;   "   2.25

Express charges, or postage, extra on back numbers.

THE OPEN COURT PUBLISHING CO.,

169-175 La Salle Street.   Post Office Drawer, F.

CHICAGO, ILLINOIS.

THE MONIST.

A QUARTERLY MAGAZINE

PUBLISHED BY

THE OPEN COURT PUBLISHING CO.

Editor : Dr. Paul Carus.   *Associates :* { E. C. Hegeler.
 { Mary Carus.

Price, 50 Cents. $2.00 per Year.

THE MONIST is a magazine which counts among its contributors the most prominent thinkers of all civilised nations. There are American thinkers such as Joseph Le Conte, Charles S. Peirce, E. D. Cope, Moncure D. Conway (the latter a native Englishman, but a resident citizen of the United States). There are English savants such as George J. Romanes, James Sully, B. Bosanquet, and the famous Oxford Professor, F. Max Müller. There are Germans such as Justice Albert Post, the founder of ethnological jurisprudence. Professors Ernst Mach and Friedrich Jodl, French and Belgian authors such as Dr. A. Binet and Professor Delbœuf. The Italians are represented by the great criminologist Cesare Lombroso and the Danes by their most prominent thinker Prof. Harald Höffding. Each number contains one or two letters on bibliographical and literary topics from French, German, or Italian scholars.

The international character of the magazine appears also in a rich review of English and foreign publications. Each number contains a synopsis of the most important books and periodicals, American as well as European, in the philosophical, ethical, psychological, and physiological fields.

The Monist represents that philosophical conception which is at present known by the name of " Monism." Monism, as it is represented in The Monist, is in a certain sense *not* a new philosophy, it does *not* come to revolutionise the world and overthrow the old foundations of science. On the contrary, it is the outcome and result of science in its maturest shape.

The term " Monism" is often used in the sense of one-substance-theory that either mind alone or matter alone exists. Such theories are better called Henism.

Monism is not "that doctrine" (as Webster has it) " which refers all phenomena to a single ultimate constituent or agent." Of such an " ultimate constituent or agent " we know nothing, and it will be difficult to state whether there is any sense in the meaning of the phrase " a single ultimate constituent or agent."

Monism is much simpler and less indefinite. Monism means that the whole of Reality, i. e. everything that is, constitutes one inseparable and indivisible entirety. Monism accordingly is a unitary conception of the world. It always bears in mind that our words are abstracts representing parts or features of the One and All, and not separate existences. Not only are matter and mind, soul and body abstracts, but also such scientific terms as atoms and molecules, and also religious terms such as God and world.

Our abstracts, if they are true, represent realities, i. e. parts, or features, or relations of the world, that are real, but they never represent things in themselves, absolute existences, for indeed there are no such things as absolute entities. The All being one interconnected whole, everything in it, every feature of it, every relation among its parts has sense and meaning and reality only if considered with reference to the whole. In this sense we say that monism is a view of the world as a unity.

The principle of Monism is the unification or systematisation of knowledge, i. e of a description of facts. In other words : There is but one truth, two or several truths may represent different and even complementary, aspects of the one and sole truth, but they can never come into contradiction. Wherever a contradiction between two statements appears, both of which are regarded as true, it is sure that there must be a mistake somewhere. The ideal of science remains a methodical and systematic unification of statements of facts, which shall be exhaustive, concise, and free from contradictions—in a word the ideal of science is MONISM.

Monism, as represented by THE MONIST, is a statement of facts, and in so far as it is a statement of facts, this Monism is to be called POSITIVISM. This Positivism however is different from Comtean Positivism, which latter would better be called agnosticism (see *The Monist*, Vol. ii, No. 1, p. 133-137). There is a mythology of science which is no less indispensable in the realm of investigation than it is in the province of religion, but we must not forget that it is a means only to an end, the ideal of scientific inquiry and of the monistic philosophy being and remaining a simple statement of facts.

Although the editorial management of THE MONIST takes a decided and well defined position with respect to the most important philosophical questions of the day, its pages are nevertheless not restricted to the presentation of any one special view or philosophy. On the contrary, they are open to contributors of divergent opinions and the most hostile world-conceptions, dualistic or otherwise, are not excluded.

PRESS NOTICES ON "THE MONIST."

"The establishment of a new philosophical quarterly which may prove a focus for all the agitation of thought that struggles to-day to illuminate the deepest problems with light from modern science, is an event worthy of particular notice."—*The Nation,* New York.

"The articles are of the highest grade."—*The Inter Ocean,* Chicago.

"No one who wishes to keep abreast of the most widely extended and boldly pushed forward line of philosophically considered science, can do better than attempt to master the profound yet lucid studies set forth in *The Monist.*"—Ellis Thurtell, in *Agnostic Journal.*

"*The Monist* will compete most dangerously with the leading magazines of our own country. . . . *The Monist* is decidedly the morning star of religious liberalism and philosophical culture."—Amos Waters in *Watts's Literary Guide,* London.

". . . .demands and will repay the attention of philosophical inquirers and thinkers."—*Home Journal,* New York.

"It will take rank among the best publications of its class. We hope that it will receive the support to which its merits certainly entitle it."—*Evening Journal,* Chicago.

"It is both a solid and a handsome quarterly."—*Brooklyn Eagle.*

"The periodical is one of the best of the solid publications of the kind now before the public. The articles are substantial, clever, and catching in subject."—*Brighton Guardian.*

"It is a high-class peri dical."—*Philadelphia Press.*

"One of the most solid serials of the times. All will be inclined to give a cordial welcome to this addition to scientific and philosophical literature."—*Manchester Examiner.*

"The articles are admirable."—*Glasgow Herald.*

"The subjects are treated with marked ability."—*Ulster Gazette,* Armaugh.

"A desideratum in the department of philosophical literature."—*Boston Transcript.*

"We welcome it to our homes and firesides."—*San Francisco Call*

"Its merit is so exceptional that it is likely to gain a national, even a European recognition, before it has gained a local one. It deserves to be widely known."—*The Dial,* Chicago.

"We very heartily welcome this quarterly as a great help in the investigation of psychological questions."—*Boston Herald.*

"*The Open Court* and *The Monist* are unusually worthy of perusal by thinkers in the various departments of knowledge and research "—*Dubuque Trade Journal.*

"It is filled from cover to cover with choice reading matter by some of the most noted home and foreign metaphysical psychological thinkers and writers of the age."—*Medical Free Press*, Indianapolis.

"Every reader and investigator will find *The Monist* a most valuable and attractive periodical." *Milling World*, Buffalo.

"The reader will, by an attentive perusal of this most promising magazine, easily bring himself *au courant* with the best modern work on psychological and biological questions. The magazine deserves to take that established and authoritative position which we very cordially wish on its behalf."—*Literary World*, London.

"This magazine will be received with eagerness in the closet of many a student." *Hampshire Chronicle*, Winchester.

"*The Monist* is first-class, and numbers amongst its contributors the most eminent students of science and philosophy in England and America. There is no better journal of philosophy in England."—*Echo*, London.

"Those with a taste for "solid" reading will find their desire gratified here."—*Leicester Chronicle.*

"The October number of *The Monist* covers a wide area, and if it had no other claim upon popular favor than that of variety that in itself ought to be a sufficient guarantee to ensure it success. But it possesses the additional recommendation of being ably and brightly written."—*Morning News*, Belfast.

"The journal numbers amongst its contributors the most eminent students of science and philosophy in England and America."—*Sussex Advertiser.*

"In this number *The Monist* has sustained the high reputation of the three preceding issues. Two things are necessary to constitute a good quarterly, able contributors, and a live editor *The Monist* has both. The articles are all on living questions, practical as well as theoretical. If *The Monist* sustains the position already reached, it will be indispensable to every student who wishes to keep pace with current thought."—*The Canadian Methodist Quarterly.*

www.ingramcontent.com/pod-product-compliance
Lightning Source LLC
Chambersburg PA
CBHW032311280326
41932CB00009B/779